DEATH BY
ASTONISHMENT

DEATH BY ASTONISHMENT

CONFRONTING THE MYSTERY OF THE WORLD'S STRANGEST DRUG

ANDREW R. GALLIMORE

FOREWORD BY
GRAHAM HANCOCK

ST. MARTIN'S PRESS
NEW YORK

First published in the United States by St. Martin's Press, an imprint of St. Martin's Publishing Group

DEATH BY ASTONISHMENT. Copyright © 2025 by Andrew R. Gallimore. Foreword © 2025 by Graham Hancock. All rights reserved. Printed in the United States of America. For information, address St. Martin's Publishing Group, 120 Broadway, New York, NY 10271.

www.stmartins.com

Endpapers: (front) *Neuro-Web* by Harry Pack; (back) *Spectrum Sprites* by INCEDIGRIS

The Library of Congress Cataloging-in-Publication Data is available upon request.

ISBN 978-1-250-35775-5 (hardcover)
ISBN 978-1-250-35776-2 (ebook)

Our books may be purchased in bulk for promotional, educational, or business use. Please contact your local bookseller or the Macmillan Corporate and Premium Sales Department at 1-800-221-7945, extension 5442, or by email at MacmillanSpecialMarkets@macmillan.com.

First Edition: 2025

10 9 8 7 6 5 4 3 2 1

For Mum and Dad

CONTENTS

CONTENTS

FOREWORD

When scientists come up with bold ideas and make even bolder proposals on the basis of them, they're well-advised to do their groundwork extremely thoroughly first.

In the case of neuroscientist Andrew Gallimore, the bold idea is that for countless millennia our species has participated, largely unwittingly, in a dance of interaction with a vast alien intelligence—an intelligence not only not of this earth, but also not of this solar system, not of this galaxy, and perhaps not even of this universe. An intelligence completely *other* from otherwhere and otherwhen.

Gallimore's even bolder proposal is that the most efficient means to explore, investigate, strengthen our interactions with, and ultimately understand that alien intelligence is through ingesting, by various routes, a simple molecule, widely available in nature, known to science as dimethyltryptamine—DMT for short!

It sounds crazy, doesn't it? But as you read Gallimore's masterful *Death by Astonishment*, you'll discover that he has indeed done his groundwork extremely thoroughly. And this is as it should be because his big idea and the proposal arising from it have the potential to turn what science believes to be true about the nature of consciousness and the nature of reality itself upside down and inside out.

Although simple in structure, dimethyltryptamine is a powerful psychedelic—arguably the most powerful known to science. I first ingested it in the Peruvian Amazon in 2003 during research for my book *Supernatural: Meetings with the Ancient Teachers of Mankind.*[1] The DMT from the leaves of the Amazonian shrub *Psychotria viridis* had been rendered orally active by being mingled in a brew with the bark of *Banisteriopsis caapi*, an Amazonian vine.

The brew, of course, was ayahuasca—the "Vine of Souls" or the "Vine of the Dead"—and this was to be the beginning of my own long engagement with the mystery of DMT. Since then I have undertaken more than seventy ayahuasca sessions and around twenty more with smoked and vaped DMT in its pure form.

The effects of inhaled DMT and of DMT absorbed via the gut by means of the ayahuasca brew, although in some ways broadly similar, have many differences.

Of note is the breathtaking speed of onset of the extraordinary experiences unleashed by inhaled DMT—a matter of seconds—compared to the thirty to sixty minutes that can sometimes pass before the full effects of ayahuasca begin to manifest. And inhaled DMT is short-lived, its peak visionary effects typically lasting no more than a few minutes, whereas ayahuasca can hold you in her grip for hours.

I say "hold you in *her* grip" deliberately because for me—I make no claim beyond my own experience—ayahuasca has a distinct personality that manifests in female form, rarely as a woman, more often as a great serpent, sometimes as a powerful jungle cat, and sometimes as a hybrid of human and animal. The personality that shows through beneath all these shifting shapes remains the same: a teacher of immense intelligence, power, and love, which is sometimes tough love that requires me to confront my own dark side and make the necessary changes to allow in more light.

Inhaled DMT also takes me to a realm that radiates immense intelligence. What's strikingly different, however, is that this realm lacks the distinctive single, caring personality and structured teachings of "Mother Ayahuasca," manifesting instead in fractal neon geometries and an overwhelming rush of small insectile or machinelike entities that sometimes radiate indifference, sometimes amusement, sometimes curiosity, sometimes impatience, and that may or may not choose to communicate.

In short, with inhaled DMT I get the feeling that I am a subject in an experiment run by sentient, not necessarily pleasant, but mostly unfeeling nonhuman others. The rapid onset of the drug and its very short duration combine to make it quite difficult to remember what exactly happened while I was under the influence, although I'm often left with a haunting sense that something of the greatest importance has been downloaded that my conscious mind is unable to decrypt.

With ayahuasca, the experience is the experiment, and the being ruling over the visions it manifests—Mother Ayahuasca—seems (to me, anyway) to be fundamentally motivated by love and concern for humanity to whom she delivers moral teachings that can sometimes bring about a completely new outlook on life. The extended duration of the ayahuasca journey, though accompanied by distractions such as diarrhea and vomiting that are not present with inhaled DMT, allows sufficient time to immerse fully in the visions, to interact with the sentient shape-shifting entities that sometimes emerge, and to integrate the revelations that unfold.

To mix metaphors, if inhaled DMT is a rocket ship, then ayahuasca is more of a slow boat, but both ultimately take us to the other side of reality and back.

I will not elaborate further here on the phenomenology of the DMT experience, whether inhaled or mediated by the ayahuasca brew. Andrew Gallimore does so at great length in the pages that follow. The case that he ends up making most persuasively, and that gels with my own experience, is that DMT, although related to LSD and psilocybin, is fundamentally different in its effects from all other members of the tryptamine family.

It is, he suggests, better understood as a molecular technology that, if used correctly, opens a channel of communication with "discarnate intelligences of unimaginable wisdom and power."

I can already envisage the rolling of skeptical eyes and hear the clucking of skeptical tongues at this affront to the paradigm of materialist reductionism that rules in science today. According to that paradigm, only matter is truly real, all mental processes arise from physical states, and consciousness is an accidental by-product—an "epiphenomenon" —of brain activity. Viewed from the materialist-reductionist perspective, therefore, the notion of "discarnate intelligences of unimaginable wisdom and power" seems absurd and fantastical, not because it has in any way been disproved but simply because unexamined preconceptions about the nature of reality have been in place for so long that they've wrongly acquired the status of empirically confirmed facts.

Science does not know that discarnate intelligences do not exist. Most scientists may believe that to be the case, but it is not a fact.

Meanwhile, poking their feelers out from the other side of reality, performing a fairy dance of hyperspace geometry, and holding up glowing tablets with messages inscribed upon them in indecipherable neon cuneiform, the DMT entities continue to proclaim, very clearly and definitely, that they do exist, that their existence is a fact, and that they'll always be just a glass pipe or an ayahuasca cup away from us.

"You don't believe in the possibility of advanced discarnate intelligences outside of normal awareness?" suggests Andrew. "Here's a glass pipe. See you in ten minutes. And I'd wipe that smirk off your face if I were you."

Skeptics may reject the challenge out of hand, of course, but if they wish to mount an authentic critique of *Death by Astonishment*, it would be in the spirit of good science, in my opinion, if they were not only to accept that glass pipe but also consider joining the volunteers in the extended DMT trials now underway at Imperial College in London, at the University of California, San Diego, and most likely at multiple other locations in the years ahead.

Indeed, if Andrew and his colleagues haven't set this in motion already, I take the liberty here of suggesting that it could prove fruitful to enroll a dozen willing volunteers selected for their extreme skepticism toward all things "paranormal," "woo-woo," and "New Age," give each of them a dozen sessions of DMT by intravenous injection, and document their reactions.

Better still, as Andrew will explain in the pages ahead, scientific innovations now make it possible to deliver DMT to volunteers by programmed intravenous infusion and to keep them in the peak visionary state not for a mere ten minutes but potentially for hours. What better way to begin testing the hypothesis that DMT is a technology that gates access to a realm populated by sentient, nonphysical entities than to include hardened skeptics among the "test pilots" on such extended "flights"?

SENTIENT OTHERS

Although officially abandoned by NASA, the Search for Extraterrestrial Intelligence (SETI) continues under the auspices of the SETI Institute,[2] which is headquartered in Silicon Valley and boasts a team of around one hundred scientists.[3] Its endeavors, though worthy, appear to be entirely materialist-reductionist, giving no consideration to the possibility that discarnate intelligences might exist that are truly "extraterrestrial" in every sense of the word but that will never be found with radio telescopes or radio interferometers.

I am not suggesting that traditional SETI technologies or the traditional SETI mission should be discontinued. What I am suggesting, on the basis of the compelling evidence Andrew Gallimore presents in *Death by Astonishment*, is that a separate, parallel institute should be established with a mission to search for extraterrestrial intelligence not in outer space by means of conventional technology but in inner space by means of the molecular technology of DMT.

The appetite to finance such a venture is already there in philanthropic circles—one need look no further than the privately funded DMT research programs at Imperial College in London and at the University of California, San Diego to confirm that.

The next step would be a more sustained and coordinated approach, a much larger budget, and a reasonable certainty that funding will continue. How about $30 million a year, guaranteed for ten years and renewable for a further ten years subject to the agreement of both the institute and the donors? I haven't just plucked the figure of $30 million out of a hat, by the way. It's at the upper end of SETI's annual operating budget[4] and seems to me an appropriate commitment to kick-start a serious, multidisciplinary investigation into DMT realms and DMT entities.

It would also be by no means an impossible commitment for a group of donors or perhaps even a single, very wealthy donor to make. And while it might prove as fruitless as SETI has up to now, the fact remains that the entities encountered under the influence of DMT give every appearance of being not just intelligent but ferociously intelligent.

Wouldn't it be worth spending $300 million over ten years to find out more about them?

And perhaps, as shamans have done down the ages, to learn from them and even negotiate with them?

I know! It still sounds crazy.

But here's a glass pipe. . . .

—Graham Hancock

DEATH BY ASTONISHMENT

INTRODUCTION

Sometimes people ask me if DMT is dangerous, and the honest answer is: only if you fear death by astonishment.

—Terence McKenna

DMT is big news.

Or, at least, it ought to be.

I first read about DMT as a teenager, in an article about a cheeky-looking bearded American of Irish heritage called Terence McKenna, who had apparently achieved cult status among a small countercultural community with a penchant for mind-altering drugs. Toward the end of a strange but fascinating interview that meandered from the origins of shamanism to the limits of the human imagination, McKenna was asked about his "favorite drug." It was a relatively obscure psychedelic from the same chemical family as the active component of magic mushrooms.

I had no idea what DMT was, but McKenna's portrayal of its effects made it sound almost magical: a short-acting psychedelic drug that would almost instantaneously catapult you from the mundane world of normal waking life into one that seemed straight out of the most speculative of 1970s science-fiction novels—hypertechnological cities populated by superintelligent insectoid aliens, fearsome reptilian demiurges from another dimension, and most intriguing of all, multitudinous giggling "machine elves" dancing in endless merriment, jabbering in an indecipherable visible language and singing impossible objects into existence. I'm not sure how much of it I really believed, but I was smitten, and spent every spare moment in the following weeks glued to the screen of my school's sole computer hooked up to the nascent World Wide Web, seeking and absorbing as much information as I could about this seemingly miraculous molecule.

It wasn't until almost a decade later, fresh out of graduate school and worrying about my future, that I finally got the chance to experience this drug for myself. Of course, I'd read all the books that I could get my hands on, listened to as many Terence McKenna lectures as I could find, and spent countless hours lost in the endlessly bifurcating threads of the underground internet drug forums. And, not least, I was by that point a fully credentialed chemical pharmacologist. I was ready. Or, at least, I thought I was.

But within just a few seconds of my first lungful of DMT vapor, alone one night in my bedroom, I was hurtled into something that I had neither suspected existed nor had any way of predicting *could* exist. Its immensity, immediacy, and absolute undeniability shocked and horrified me. The indescribable geometry, the infinitely dynamic complexity, and the intelligence. Oh, the intelligence. Although McKenna's elves were nowhere to be seen and the insectoids remained out of sight, in those first astonishing moments of my first DMT trip it was perfectly obvious that this was no science-fiction novel and undeniably apparent to me that I had somehow found myself in a world constructed by the hand of an immense and timeless alien intelligence.

What seemed like an eternity later, as my neural architecture finally began to reconstruct my humanity piece by piece and I remembered who and where I was, I lay breathless on my bed, shaking to my very bones, having just discovered—for myself, at least—a new world entire. And not just any old new world, but the strangest world I couldn't possibly have imagined, even with the best part of a decade of Terence McKenna lectures under my belt. His famous warning of the risk of "death by astonishment" no longer seemed like hyperbole.

What had just happened to me?

Despite my newly minted Ph.D. and years of studying the chemistry and pharmacology of psychoactive molecules, I had to admit to myself that I had absolutely no idea. I was both intellectually and spiritually at sea. I was utterly lost. I was confounded. It just didn't seem possible.

Anyone who hasn't journeyed to these realms or been confronted by the strange beings resident within them could be forgiven for casually dismissing my experience as mere hallucination: a trick of the mind. A fantasy. A symptom of a brain nudged toward chaos by a molecule that simply shouldn't be there. More considered thinkers might wield more sophisticated tools to explain it away: A DMT trip is simply an unusual type of dream state, or perhaps comparable to the visual hallucinations of florid psychotic episodes, or might even represent long-buried archetypes scuttling up from the darkest corners of our collective psyche, not so much alien but parts of our deepest self from which we have somehow become alienated. But as we shall see, even with these tools, the bizarre, hypercomplex, abundantly populated alien worlds to which DMT gates access with such facility aren't so easy to dismiss. Among those of a more mystical persuasion, the discarnate entities so often encountered during DMT trips have been variously explained as spirits, gods, or even nonphysical alien intelligences residing in an orthogonal dimension of reality; one which, for reasons yet to be uncovered, DMT grants temporary access with ferocious efficiency. But could these beings really be fully autonomous conscious intelligences from some normally hidden realm? If you'd asked me that question twenty-five years ago, prior to my first DMT trip, I'd likely have laughed in your face. These experiences are drug-induced hallucinations—so what? But now I'm not so sure. Of course, for many, to even entertain such an idea is simply unthinkable. But DMT is like that—it forces you to think about the unthinkable.

The British mathematical biologist JBS Haldane wrote the oft-quoted line: "The Universe is not only queerer than we suppose, but queerer than we can suppose." He continued: "I suspect that there are more things in heaven and earth than are dreamed of, or can be dreamed of, in any philosophy."[1] DMT forces us to confront such things—whether from Earth or heaven or somewhere else entirely—that we can neither dream of nor imagine. DMT forces us to confront the impossible, to face how little we really know about the true nature of reality and of our place within it. DMT isn't magic, but remains, in many ways, indistinguishable from it. After dozens of mind-shattering experiences with this molecule, McKenna was compelled to spend his life spreading the news "I intend to keep talking about it until somebody snuffs me or we get some action, because I have taken a complete inventory of world civilization, and DMT is definitely the most interesting thing on this planet."

I couldn't agree more, and almost two decades since I was first left aghast by the bewildering power of this molecule, I've come to consider DMT to be not only the most interesting thing on this planet, but perhaps also the most important. And yet, despite promising what Terence McKenna maintained is the most intense, beautiful, bizarre state of consciousness a human can experience "this side of the yawning grave," DMT remains curiously obscure. Although you'd struggle to find someone who didn't have at least a passing familiarity with the more famous psychedelics—LSD, magic mushrooms, and perhaps the peyote cactus—outside of the small (but admittedly rapidly growing) psychedelic enthusiast community, a mention of DMT will often be met by a puzzled look and the reflexive response, "What's that?" But this isn't because DMT is a particularly rare or new drug. On the contrary, as we will see, DMT is actually—by some margin—the most common psychedelic drug on Earth—and one that also just happens to be the most efficient and reliable reality channel switch, instantaneously transporting the user to a hypercomplex populated alien reality that bears no relationship whatsoever to the normal waking world. How do we make sense of this? Why should such a simple unassuming molecule so reliably induce such thoroughly alien entity encounters? With the techniques of modern twenty-first century biochemistry, pharmacology, and neuroscience, we now know far more about how DMT—and drugs like it—interface with the human brain than we could have imagined just a couple of decades ago. And, yet, the DMT experience remains, for the most part, thoroughly mysterious.

Although Terence McKenna can certainly be credited with popularizing DMT within the drug-infused counterculture of the 1990s, the drug was first studied in Communist Hungary just a few years after Swiss chemist Albert Hofmann created the peerlessly potent ergot derivative, LSD, in 1943, during a period in which a flurry of these mind-altering drugs were either discovered or invented. And after finding its way into the hands of some of the most influential icons of the first psychedelic revolution of the 1960s, including renegade beat writer and drug fiend William S. Burroughs and the undisputed psychedelic high priest of the 1960s, Dr. Timothy Leary, DMT began to develop its reputation as neurological dynamite. Although these prominent countercultural figures would play key roles in transforming DMT from what was then considered to be a novel Hungarian psychotomimetic to one enjoying some clandestine status at the experiential apex of the psychedelic drug family, they were left just as shocked, baffled, and bewildered as I and many others would be in the decades that followed. If we really want to make sense of DMT, the entities that populate its strange realms, and to understand how and why this molecule occasions such encounters, we need to begin our story much further back than the 1960s. DMT's relationship to humanity reaches back millennia, and its appearance in the West and the subsequent scientific struggle to make sense of its remarkable effects sits at the tail end of a long story involving botanists, chemists, anthropologists, and explorers who knew nothing of this molecule, but whose interest was piqued in the middle of the nineteenth century by reports of mysterious potions, powders, and elixirs that, when consumed by the Indigenous peoples of South America, would render visible a menagerie of discarnate creatures of the forest—neither human nor animal, beings that can most succinctly be described as the Other.

THE OTHER

The xapiri are not like animals or humans. They are other.

—Davi Kopenawa, Yanomami shaman

In the summer of 2015, I received an invitation to speak at a small private symposium at a grand stately home in the British countryside. Although I had recently taken up a research fellowship in neuroscience in Okinawa, Japan, and wasn't particularly keen on doubling back to the UK so soon, this wasn't an invitation to turn down. The theme of the intimate three-day event was "Plant sentience and the role of DMT as a possible conduit between spirit and matter," promising a multidisciplinary speaker and guest list of the world's leading thinkers on the subject. I landed at Heathrow on a not unseasonably miserable early autumn afternoon, still dressed for the subtropical climes I'd left behind, and was whisked by taxi into deepest rural Buckinghamshire and to the magnificent residence of our host, property tycoon-turned-consciousness explorer Anton Bilton. After being greeted by Anton, the butler showed me to a lounge, seated me by a roaring fire, and passed me a glass of red wine. "The others are outside looking around the temple," he informed me with impeccable diction.

Having never been to a house with its own temple, suddenly feeling distinctly underdressed, and as yet unaware of exactly who "the others" were, I nervously sipped and waited for them to return from their pilgrimage. Just a few minutes later, I heard a familiar high-spirited guffaw from the hallway, and in strolled my good friend, psychologist Dr. David Luke, together with author Graham Hancock and his wife, Santha, veteran theoretical biologist and parapsychologist Rupert Sheldrake, and one of my personal heroes, ethnobotanist Dr. Dennis McKenna (Terence's brother). For the next three days, we'd be living together under this most opulent of roofs, listening to lectures and watching presentations by the invited speakers; wandering the magnificent gardens discussing shamanistic ritual practices and plant-based medicines; and sharing stories and ideas around the dinner table before gathering around the fireplace to drink red wine, inhale a South American tobacco-based snuff called rapé and, of course, discuss psychedelic drugs. The rest I'll leave to your imagination. One of the last of the luminaries to arrive was Stanford-educated anthropologist Jeremy Narby, who carried out his Ph.D. research living among the Asháninka people of the Peruvian rain forests, and on the second morning, as at least half the congregation was nursing hangovers from the seemingly bottomless glasses of wine served the night before, it was Narby's turn to speak.

Narby arrived in the Peruvian Amazon in 1984 to study and document the Asháninka's use of psychoactive plants and to develop a deeper understanding of their unique spiritual worldview. After speaking briefly about their use of highly concentrated jam-like extracts of ritual tobacco—"hallucinogenic doses of nicotine"—Narby turned to his main thesis: Not the Asháninka people themselves, but the discarnate beings with whom they share the forest.

It isn't known for how long the Indigenous peoples of South America have been communicating with beings invisible to the rest of us, but estimates are in the tens of thousands of years. And the Asháninka are certainly no exception, living among innumerable but normally unseen beings they call the *maninkari*. Although it certainly wasn't a surprise to hear of Indigenous Amazonians believing in what anthropologists tend to call "spirits," what Narby said next startled me: "They also call these entities Asháninka, which is their word for themselves. They say, 'These maninkari, they are members of our tribe.'"[1]

As a Westerner who's used to talking and reading about the gods and spirits and other discarnate entities that populate our folklore and religious traditions, I'd never considered that perspective: what it must be like to not only talk about, make offerings to, or simply believe in such beings, but to live among them as we live among each other—a vast and densely populated cosmology lying parallel, hidden within, and as real as the visible world the reality of which we take for granted. Not mere credos passed down in leather-bound volumes or promulgated from elder to children with a promised face-to-face audience upon death, but living interactive intelligences, invisible but ever-present, as real and communicable as any other member of the tribe. An intelligent Other that is not only spoken about but spoken to—spoken with.

In the Asháninka language, Narby told us, *maninkari* means "those who are hidden."[2] And the Asháninka people, like many other groups living across South America and beyond, have discovered and developed tools for making the hidden visible. But while many of these Indigenous groups have been using these tools for communicating with the unseen Other for thousands of years, until the middle of the nineteenth century, when British botanist Richard Spruce arrived at the mouth of the Amazon,[3] they were little more than legends. Although reports of powerful and strange mind-altering potions, powders, and pellets were to be found scattered across the anthropological literature as far back as the 1400s, it was simple to summarily dismiss them along with the other so-called magical beliefs held by the uncivilized. But Spruce wasn't on a quest to uncover the secrets of these mysterious jungle preparations. His mission was purely botanical—to explore the Amazon basin, to identify and collect new plant species to ship back to collectors in England. But in 1852, while living and working among the Tukano people by the Vaupes River in Colombia, he made a discovery that would seed a scientific struggle that continues to this day. A struggle between the irrational magical beliefs of the "savage" and "uncivilized" and the rational, logical, scientifically grounded convictions of the post-Enlightened.

In November of that year, having ingratiated himself with one of the most senior members of the Tukano, Spruce received an invitation to attend a special feast,[4] held periodically throughout the year, known as a dabocuri.[5] Having attended a similar gathering on the Rio Negro just a few months prior, Spruce was quite aware that, despite their religious overtones, these feasts were primarily an opportunity for different families to meet, dance, sing and, not least, consume considerable quantities of intoxicants.[6] In the three years since he arrived in South America, Spruce had become deeply fascinated by the psychoactive plants and other drugs used by the natives across Amazonia. He'd observed the Mawé people mixing the bitter stimulant drink guaraná on the lower Amazon and the Baré people on the Rio Negro stuffing their cheeks to bursting with powdered coca leaf.[7] He'd also become familiar with the seemingly unquenchable thirst for foamy cassava beers and powerful jungle liquors among most of the natives he'd encountered along the rivers. As such, he was always keen to observe and record the preparation and use of such drugs in a traditional setting and had little doubt that this feast would be another ideal opportunity to witness an entire gamut of intoxicants being consumed under one roof.

Soon after Spruce arrived at his host's residence for the feast, where a great crowd of around three hundred people were already gathered, he noticed a man on his knees pounding furiously with a pestle and mortar, thick woody roots with some much more slender ones being added at intervals, together with splashes of water to keep the mixture lubricated. As the sweat was beading heavily on the man's painted forehead, the roots slowly began to capitulate to form a thick fibrous sludge. All at once, it was done, and the contents of the mortar were passed through a sieve into a bowl. More water was then added—apparently to make it drinkable—the final product a thoroughly unappetizing brownish-green soup, not entirely dissimilar to the waters of the Rio Negro he'd left behind earlier in the year. Perhaps it would taste better than it looked. Or perhaps they weren't going to drink it for the flavor.

But before he could query his hosts on this strange decoction, the women hurried from their dark smoky corner of the house ferrying bloated pitchers of cassava beer to the thirsty guests and the festivities could really begin. Spruce's hosts were keen for him to sample as many of the liquid wares as possible, and he soon found himself being presented with cupful after cupful of the apparently bottomless gourds of beer and wine that were continually being passed about the house. But despite his growing intoxication, Spruce couldn't help but notice the highly un-usual behavior of the men. Each, at intervals, would peel away from the dancing crowd and be presented with a cup filled to overflowing with the as yet unidentified brown-green soup he'd watched being prepared earlier. After draining the cup, barely two minutes would pass before the man—no women or children were involved—suddenly and quite no-ticeably paled and began trembling, his eyes widening and face twisting into a frightful grimace. But this was just the first act. As if possessed, the man would then grasp the nearest available weapon—a cutlass, lance, or bow—rush to the doorway and, in a fit of unfettered rage, begin to attack either the doorposts or the earth, all the while howling. This bi-zarre behavior would continue for several minutes, until the man fell down exhausted. Barely ten minutes after this strikingly animated dis-play had begun, the man would then stand and, after a quick shake of his limbs, return to the dance. Throughout the night, barely a moment passed when there weren't at least half a dozen men engaged in some stage of this performance. Although from his reports it doesn't seem that Spruce ever quizzed any of the men on their experiences, it was clear that their rage was directed at someone—or something. An invisible adver-sary seen only by them.

Several hours into the proceedings, it was Spruce's turn, and as he sat observing the melee, a young man, naked from the waist up, body painted brightly, was running briskly, knees bent, directly toward him. In each hand a small cup was held carefully so as not to spill the liquid within. As he reached Spruce, he held out one of the cups and Spruce took it. It was a foul, nauseatingly bitter liquid and he struggled, fight-ing the urge to vomit, to choke it down. He returned the cup, and the other hand, bearing the second cup, was immediately stretched out toward him. But by this point, Spruce was already ready to vomit and he raised his hand in polite refusal as a wave of intense nausea began to overwhelm him. Fearing he might spray his host in the most indecorous manner, he dashed to his hammock, hoping a quick lie down might set-tle his stomach.

"What did I just drink?" Spruce asked as his friend passed him a welcome cup of freshly prepared coffee.

"That was *caapi*."

Spruce had heard that word before. While working in Manaus on the Lower Amazon the previous year, a Brazilian friend had told him about a magical brew by the same name—a potion—that, when drunk, would reveal a fantastical new world filled with creatures beyond his imagination: "All the marvels I read in the *Arabian Nights* passed rapidly before my eyes."[8]

Unlike the drugs he had regularly encountered during his travels in the Amazon Basin, this caapi drink didn't appear to be a stimulant or appetite suppressant or even an intoxicant as the term might commonly have been understood. No, this was something else entirely.

Although a few obscure texts by missionaries and lone travelers had referred to this enigmatic and diabolical brew that rendered the "savages" wildly drunk, it had remained little more than a legend. So, despite only managing to choke down about half a full dose of the bitter decoction and failing to experience any such magnificent visions himself, Spruce knew this could be an opportunity to make a major botanical discovery. The following morning, he was informed that the plant used to make the caapi brew was being cultivated just a few hours downriver. So, after recovering fully from the festivities, the excited botanist set off in his canoe to find some. When he arrived at the small forest clearing by the river, he was delighted to find that his informants were true to their word and located about a dozen fully grown caapi plants twining up to the treetops in full bloom. The genus, *Banisteria* (now *Banisteriopsis*), he recognized, but the species was entirely new. He named it on the spot: *Banisteria caapi* (now *Banisteriopsis caapi*).[9]

In his fifteen years in South America, Spruce encountered caapi several more times. While exploring the Orinoco plains in Venezuela, he came upon an encampment of nomadic Guahibo people who also used the caapi brew as well as chewing the dried bark of the vine, and three years later, while collecting in the Peruvian Andes, yet again came across the vine being cultivated, albeit by a different name: *ayahuasca*—vine of the soul (this is another of at least forty-two names for the caapi brew.[10] We'll mainly use ayahuasca).[11]

During his travels, Spruce never passed up the opportunity to harvest tales from both natives and itinerant traders he encountered along the riverbanks who had experienced the effects of a full dose of the brew. Barring minor personal variations, they all described the same experience: A feeling of rising high into the air and floating; visions passing before the eyes, of beautiful lakes and cities, of gorgeous and magnificent new worlds filled with creatures both beautiful and terrifying—"birds of brilliant plumage" and "savage beasts preparing to seize them." The Ecuadorian botanist and geographer Manuel Villavicencio provided a particularly vivid description of his own experience with this remarkable visionary potion: "When I have partaken of aya-huasca, my head has immediately begun to swim; then I have seemed to enter on an aerial voyage, wherein I thought I saw the most charming landscapes, great cities, lofty towers, beautiful parks, and other delightful things. Then all at once I found myself deserted in a forest and attacked by beasts of prey, against which I tried to defend myself."[12]

Although to Spruce, his discovery was mainly of botanical significance, he had chanced upon one of the most powerful of the legendary visionary tools for communicating with the Hidden Ones. But most significantly, by identifying the plant used to make the brew, he had taken an artifact of profound spiritual significance and placed it into the hands of science. This mind-altering potion wasn't manufactured from spells and incantations. It was a decoction—an infusion—of plant material and now the key vegetal component had been identified. Ayahuasca wasn't magic, it was chemistry. Of course, the actual chemistry behind this climbing vine's ability to elicit such remarkable effects on consciousness was still a mystery. But, crucially, it was now a mystery that had been pinned to a single unassuming rain forest liana.

Spruce's accounts wouldn't be published for more than a decade after his death, but the groundwork for understanding how and why this bitter decoction was able to transport the drinker to entirely new worlds filled with strange discarnate entities had actually been laid more than three decades before Spruce arrived in the Amazon by a German pharmacist, Friedrich Sertürner, who began to take an interest in an entirely different psychoactive drug: the deliciously soporific preparations of arguably the world's most famous medicinal plant, *Papaver somniferum*, more commonly known as the opium poppy.[13]

Although the medical use of the opium poppy can be traced back to Sumerian times over 4,000 years ago, with its black tarry exudate earning an exceedingly infamous reputation in more recent centuries, like the caapi vine, the source of the poppy's unrivaled powers to melt away the aches and pains of the world and usher in soft and delightful dreams remained, until Sertürner arrived, a complete mystery. But in 1804, by soaking the dried poppy heads in a mixture of alcohol and water, Sertürner found that he was able to separate a sleep-inducing principle from the plant material, which he tested by feeding to a few stray dogs he found wandering on the streets. They at first became drowsy, but then began to vomit and convulse, before one "gentle little dog" died. He named his crude extract morphine—after Morpheus, the Greek god of sleep. In 1817, he discovered that, by adding a solution of strong ammonia to a hot water extraction of dried poppies, the morphine would fall out of solution and he was able to obtain colorless crystals of pure morphine.[14]

After an ethically dubious—to put it mildly—experiment, in which he administered what turned out to be a near lethal overdose to three teenage boys he found wandering in the streets, Sertürner published a discovery, the significance of which cannot be overstated.[15] Although pharmaceutical practice had certainly progressed far beyond medieval alchemy prior to Sertürner's arrival, the macerations, distillations, and powdered blends of the early nineteenth-century pharmacist were more of a practical chemistry to be learned than understood. The majority of drugs in the pre-Sertürner pharmacopeia were, like the opium poppy, either plants or products of plants. Often the plant material—leaves, roots, seeds, or bark—was simply dried and perhaps ground to a powder, but rudimentary techniques for separating the active principles from the fibrous plant material, such as infusions in water—not dissimilar to the ayahuasca decoction—or tinctures prepared by soaking the plant material in alcohol, were also commonplace.[16] Unfortunately, while simple to manufacture, these early plant preparations were of variable quality and extremely unreliable. Medicinal and psychoactive plants often contain complex mixtures of bioactive molecules that can vary dramatically depending on which part of the plant is used, the stage of its life cycle, and even the locality and weather conditions at harvest. The effect of a particular medicinal plant will depend on the particular mixture of these bioactive molecules, some of which might have the desired effect, with others being highly toxic. But all too often these plant preparations produced no effects at all beyond perhaps placebo, either because the plant hadn't been prepared or stored properly or simply because a particular plant specimen was devoid of the desired bioactive molecules.

Sertürner's isolation of a single molecular principle responsible for the medicinal properties of a plant was revolutionary, transforming pharmacy from an artisan craft to a modern science. In the post-Sertürner era, whenever scientists discovered a new plant with medicinal properties, they could be reasonably certain that one or more molecular components of the plant were responsible for its pharmacological effects. Plants containing mixtures of bioactive molecules could be deconstructed, with each isolated molecule tested for its own, potentially unique, effects, and any inactive or toxic molecules discarded. And rather than relying on little more than guesswork, once these components had been identified and isolated, it became possible not only to test and optimize the dosage in a systematic manner, but also the mode of administration. Is the drug active orally or would an injection directly into the bloodstream be more effective? These are now basic principles of pharmaceutical science but were made possible by the work of Sertürner in the early nineteenth century and would later prove to be of immense importance both in understanding how the ayahuasca decoction achieved its visionary effects, and, ultimately, in transforming it into something far more powerful and stranger than anything anybody could have expected or anticipated.

The morphine molecule isolated by Sertürner belongs to a class of naturally occurring molecules—produced by plants and fungi—known as the alkaloids, originally named so because of their slightly alkaline properties in solution.[17] In general, alkaloids are insoluble in alkaline solution (such as ammonia), poorly soluble in water, and soluble in acids. This makes them quite easy to isolate from plant material and is why Sertürner was able to yield morphine from poppies using a simple ammonia solution. As such, in the decades following Sertürner's discovery, a flurry of biologically active alkaloids were isolated from a range of medicinal, toxic, and psychoactive plants: caffeine from coffee beans; nicotine from the tobacco plant; atropine from deadly nightshade; and just three years after Spruce first witnessed the powdered stimulant being prepared from its dried leaves on the banks of the Rio Negro, cocaine from the coca plant.[18] Whenever a medicinal plant was chemically analyzed, more often than not, an alkaloid was found to be responsible for its effects. It made sense then that, like the opium poppy, the caapi potion's power to gate access to an alternate world could also be accounted for by such a molecule. So, when Colombian naturalist and chemist Dr. Rafael Zerda-Bayón trekked into the rain forests to study the caapi vine first identified and named by Spruce more than half a century earlier, he wasn't hoping to coax a forest sprite from its root system or even to isolate an essential oil. He was looking for an alkaloid.

Between 1905 and 1906, Zerda-Bayón began working around the Caquetá and Putumayo Rivers—not far from where Spruce first discovered the caapi vine—with the intention of studying the chemistry of the visionary potion that seemed to have been neglected by science for more than half a century.[19] His hope was that, by extracting an alkaloid from the caapi vine, he would be able to replicate the effects of the ayahuasca decoction reported by Spruce and prove that the source of the vine's supposed visionary powers wasn't magic but simple chemistry. As a Colombian native with extensive experience exploring the rain forests of Colombia and armed with a portable chemistry kit, it didn't take him long to locate and harvest enough caapi vine to isolate the alkaloids, following the general method pioneered by Sertürner. With just a handful of simple chemical steps, that calabash of nauseating brown-green soup choked down by Richard Spruce in 1852 had been transformed into little more than a thimbleful of a colorless, almost tasteless liquid magic. Obviously familiar with the then widespread belief that ayahuasca imbues you with telepathic powers,[20] he tentatively named the alkaloid telepathine.

Like Sertürner a century before, Zerda-Bayón now needed some human volunteers on which to test his isolated alkaloid solution in the hope of replicating the visionary effects of the brew. But unlike Sertürner, he didn't have ready access to a clutch of suggestible teenagers loitering around the rain forests. He did, however, have access to the chief commander of the Caicedo Military Station on the Bacha River, Colonel Custodio Morales, who had previously expressed an interest in experiencing the effects of ayahuasca. Zerda-Bayón said he could go one better, and early one evening, gave the colonel precisely fifteen drops of his alkaloid concentrate. Although it's impossible to know exactly the dosage contained in those drops, it's reasonable to assume that it was extremely low. The colonel experienced almost no effects whatsoever.

Satisfied that his alkaloid concentrate wasn't lethal—in middle-aged colonels, at least—Zerda-Bayón ventured to experiment next on himself. Mindful of the disappointing lack of effects on Colonel Morales, he upped the dosage quite considerably and swallowed two tablespoons of the solution and waited. An hour or so later, unlike the colonel, Zerda-Bayón did experience some effects. Unfortunately, however, they were not the effects he was expecting based on the reports of those who had consumed ayahuasca. His heart began to race, and sometime later he felt somewhat more energized and mentally stimulated. But there were no visions, no alternate worlds, no discarnate beings. So, while Zerda-Bayón was the first person to successfully isolate the constituent alkaloids of the caapi vine, his inability to replicate the visionary effects of the potion suggested something was deeply amiss. Was telepathine the sole active alkaloid? Had he failed to extract another crucial psychoactive component of the vine?

Antonio María Barriga Villalba, a Colombian chemist and professor of organic and mineral chemistry at the Faculty of Medicine of the National University of Colombia, became interested in this "peculiar drink"[21] used by the inhabitants of the Putumayo and Caqueta Rivers and especially by the grand claims made of its effects: "Visions of the future, of things lost, visions at distances and illusory visions." However, whereas Zerda-Bayón isolated a single alkaloid from the vine, Villalba was able to purify and crystallize two distinct molecules. The major alkaloid, which he named *yageine* (after *yagé*, the name given to the caapi

brew by some Indigenous groups), he was able to isolate using a variation of the Sertürner method. After boiling the vine in slightly acidified
water, which extracted the alkaloids into solution, he added an alkali—
quicklime—to precipitate them, just as Sertürner had done with morphine. He then dissolved the alkaloids in hot alcohol and as it cooled, the
yageine spontaneously formed "brilliant needle-shaped" crystals. However, Villalba found that if he evaporated the alcohol that was left behind,
he was able to recover a much smaller quantity of a second alkaloid,
which he named *yagenine*. Unfortunately, when he gave either alkaloid
to human volunteers, there weren't any surprises: They reported a great
feeling of well-being followed by a deep sleep. In the end, he concluded,
no doubt with some disappointment, that "the effects of this liquid have
been grossly exaggerated by white people who say they have drunk it."[22]
It would've been hard to argue with him. Comparing these experiences
with the otherworldly reports heard by Spruce and written about by
Villavicencio and others, something clearly seemed to be missing.

All hope that the caapi alkaloids would replicate the remarkable effects
of the ayahuasca potion ended abruptly in 1927, when Karl Beringer, a
psychiatrist working at the Psychiatric and Neurological Clinic in Hei-
delberg, Germany, began working on the alkaloids in the hope that they
might be useful in the treatment of Parkinson's disease. Prior experiments
in patients with partial paralysis had shown some quite promising, albeit
short-lived, positive improvements in their gait—an effect that would
later be highly significant in explaining the psychoactive properties of
ayahuasca. Although, at the time, they appeared to be completely unrelated. Based on their animal studies, pharmaceutical company Merck,
from whom Beringer acquired the caapi vine, suggested a dose of around
200mg by subcutaneous (under the skin) injection, which they considered to be on the low side—better safe than sorry. However, almost as
soon as the needle had been withdrawn, Beringer's first volunteer—one
of his laboratory assistants—became deathly pale and began vomiting
and shaking uncontrollably as his pulse plummeted to below forty beats
per minute. Although he remained conscious throughout the hour-long
ordeal, he struggled to walk and complained of a constant ringing in his
ears. But despite receiving what was undoubtedly the largest dose of the

isolated caapi alkaloids yet given to a human, what he didn't complain of was being accosted by strange creatures from another world.[23]

The chemists seemed to have hit a dead end: Whatever world-altering principle was contained in the ayahuasca brew was missing from the isolated alkaloids. The reason for this became all too clear when pharmaceutical giant Hoffmann-La Roche began taking an interest in the caapi vine, presumably in the hope that it might contain at least two—possibly more—brand-new medicinal alkaloids for their ever-expanding drug catalogues. The first intimation that this was unlikely to be the case came when George Barger, a professor of chemistry at Edinburgh University and expert on plant alkaloids, visited the Hoffmann-La Roche laboratories in Basel. During his visit, Barger remarked that the yellow material they had isolated from the vine looked strikingly similar to one he was very familiar with: harmaline. Far from being a novel molecule, harmaline and its close cousin harmine had been known for decades as the principal alkaloids of the Syrian rue plant, *Peganum harmala*, from which the alkaloids received their names. The Hoffmann-La Roche team immediately sent its samples to one of the world's leading experts on plant alkaloids, Professor Robert Robinson of Manchester University in the UK, who also happened to be the chemist who elucidated the molecular structure of morphine and would later receive the Nobel Prize in Chemistry for his work in the field. As Barger had suspected, Robinson's analyses confirmed that Hoffmann-La Roche's colorless crystals—Zerda-Bayón's "telepathine" and Villalba's "yageine"—were simply harmine. His yellow extract—Villalba's "yagenine"—seemed to be the brightly colored but entirely familiar alkaloid harmaline.[24] Far from being a novel and rare new medicinal alkaloid with the potential to revolutionize the study of the human mind and perhaps become a treatment for all manner of medical conditions yet to be studied, they had all been chasing a pair of molecules that were not only perfectly well-known, but available in practically limitless quantities from a common and easily cultivated medicinal herb. Fearing—or, frankly, hoping—that the scientists working on the caapi vine had made some basic error in the identification of the plant material, for the next decade several other groups worked to repeat the work with carefully identified specimens of the vine. But the results were always the same. After decades of careful research by some of the brightest minds in chemical and pharmacological science,[25] the enigmatic ayahuasca potion—that supposed magical gateway to a fantastical new world filled with creatures both beautiful and horrifying—appeared to be nothing more than a foul-tasting watery soup of harmala alkaloids, none of which, in their purified forms, had been shown to produce any effects beyond a general drunkenness, convulsions, and colorful but fairly unremarkable dreams.

Nothing about this seemed to make any sense. Were the reports of strange new worlds populated by discarnate entities heard by Spruce and others, as Villalba had come to believe, mere exaggerations? Or was the ayahuasca potion more than just chemistry? Perhaps there really was some kind of supernatural or spiritual force at work in giving this jungle drink its powers. Something was most certainly missing, but nobody had any idea what. As the midpoint of the twentieth century arrived, and as the magic of ayahuasca remained a mystery, just as it had been when Spruce first encountered it on the banks of the Vaupes River a century prior, it became clear that what the ayahuasca brew needed was a completely fresh pair of eyes—a professional.

2

THE FINAL FIX

A paranoid is someone who knows a little of what's going on. A psychotic is a guy who's just found out what's going on.

—William S. Burroughs

Having just shot his wife in the head and narrowly escaping a decades-long stretch in the Mexican penal system, iconic beat writer and drug aficionado William S. Burroughs was looking for a final fix. Killing time flicking through a "he-man" *True* magazine in Grand Central Station sometime in 1951, an article about the "world's most power-ful psychoactive drug" caught his eye. It was a drug called yagé—also known as ayahuasca—and the claims made of its powers were spec-tacular: the ability to see in great detail places and cities never before observed. A hallucinating narcotic stranger and more powerful than any other. Having a special interest in narcotics and after decades of personal use, including having taken peyote with Indigenous peoples in Mexico, smoking hashish in Morocco, and at various times using cocaine, opiates, and a range of other psychoactive agents, Burroughs felt he was uniquely qualified for the subjective assaying and personal appraisal of a mysterious new Amazonian drug. He was a professional. He was the "man who could dig it."[1] But for Burroughs, yagé would become more than just another drug to add to a growing repertoire. Yagé would become a quest for redemption.

Although he would later become an icon of the Beat Generation of writers, penning the postmodern cut-up classics *Naked Lunch* and

The Ticket That Exploded, in 1951 he was relatively unknown outside of a small literary circle that included poet Allen Ginsberg and outlaw novelist Jack Kerouac. A longtime heroin user and small-time dealer with a possible two-year stretch in Angola State Prison for marijuana distribution hanging over his head, a couple of years earlier he had fled to Mexico with his wife, Joan Vollmer, hoping to return to the US once the statute of limitations had run down and the case was dismissed. On September 6, 1951, he was wandering the streets of Mexico City when he was overcome by an overwhelming sense of despair and an inexplicable yet unshakable feeling that something utterly dreadful was about to happen. It was. Already drunk and tearful, he reached the apartment of his friend John Healey, conveniently located above the bar Healey owned, armed with his Czech-made Star 0.380 automatic in a holster in his bag—a cheap gun with pitiful accuracy.

Joan was already there, already drunk and in withdrawal from a long-term addiction to the stimulant Benzedrine, and the conversation soon turned to drugs. Burroughs suggested that the best way to get off heroin would be to maroon oneself on an island with a summer tide such that it would be impossible to escape until the water rose again. Joan scoffed at the idea. Burroughs would surely die of starvation, unable to hunt for his interminable shaking. He was having none of this: "Put that glass on your head, Joanie, let me show the boys what a great shot old Bill is."[2]

Following his orders, Joan steadied the glass on her head, giggled, and looked away as Burroughs steadied his shooting arm. He fired and put a nine-millimeter hole through her brain, killing her almost instantly. He was initially arrested and charged with murder but was released on September 21 and eventually convicted of manslaughter and sentenced in absentia to two years suspended.[3]

Burroughs was fully aware of his shortcomings: his propensity for addiction, and his compulsive drinking and irrational behavior while drunk, which found its most tragic expression in that fatal William Tell act. But Burroughs didn't believe that he was entirely responsible. Since the age of five, he believed he was possessed by what he came to call the Ugly Spirit—an amorphous creature that held permanent residency in his brain, manifesting its presence with bouts of deep depression, anxiety, and loss of self-control. "I live with the constant threat of possession, a constant need to escape from possession, from Control."[4]

He believed the Ugly Spirit to be responsible for his decades of addiction and irrational behavior, including the death of his wife, and yagé was his chance to exorcise it for good. Perhaps yagé would be the final fix.

Although he spent most of his time scoring drugs on the streets, he wasn't entirely unfamiliar with psychoactive plants used by Indigenous peoples. Having completed graduate studies in anthropology at Harvard in 1938 and then at Colombia, he'd no doubt come across accounts of Amazonian drug use in the anthropological literature. But his book smarts would only get him so far, and in 1953, as his debut novel, *Junkie,* was about to be published, he left Mexico City and headed for the jungle.[5]

Toward the end of January 1953, he had arrived in Bogotá, Colombia, and without anything even approaching a strategy to locate the jungle drug, headed directly to the Institute of Natural Sciences, where he hoped someone might at least be able to point him in the right direction. "In a vast dusty room full of plant specimens and the smell of formaldehyde, I saw a man with an air of refined annoyance. He caught my eye."[6]

He could hardly have stumbled upon a better person to help him in his quest. A classmate of JFK, whom he despised,[7] Richard Evans Schultes completed his bachelor's degree in biology at Harvard—his major thesis on the use of the peyote cactus by Kiowa Indians of Oklahoma—in 1938, and by the time Burroughs bumped into him, had become the world's preeminent authority on the toxic, medicinal, and psychoactive plants of Amazonia. As a seven-year-old child bedridden in a hospital, Schultes's father had read to him from Spruce's field notes and as an adult, he had deliberately modeled his life and work on that of the peerless British botanist. After completing his Ph.D. in 1941, he traveled to Colombia where, for twelve years, he lived and worked among the native peoples of the area, collecting over 24,000 plant specimens and discovering six psychoactive plants new to science, all of which he also consumed. If there was a psychoactive plant he hadn't tried, it was because it hadn't yet been discovered.[8]

In 1942, Schultes headed into the Putumayo region of Colombia, home to the Kofan people known for their extraordinarily potent arrow poisons, known locally as *curare*. Here he identified and documented over seventy distinct plants used to make the lethal paste, the key components being plants of the *Chondrodendron* and *Strychnos* genii, later shown to contain the neurotoxin strychnine. Among the additional plants, he also observed nontoxic plants of the pepper family being added to the curare preparation. Although the rationale for including these ostensibly superfluous plants was unknown to Schultes, they would later be shown to contain the alkaloid piperine which, by acting as a general inhibitor of drug metabolism, enhances the absorption and stability of the toxic strychnine alkaloid,[9] increasing its potency and hastening its paralyzing action.[10] This pharmacological synergy, in which the combined effect of two or more drugs is greater than the simple sum of their individual effects, was an early intimation that indigenous plant mixtures weren't simply thrown together, but were jungle technologies developed and refined over long periods of time. Pharmacological synergy would later be shown to play a crucial role in the action of another drug preparation Schultes studied while living among the Kofan: yagé.

By the time Burroughs wandered into his office, Schultes was a world authority on the yagé decoction, also known as *ayahuasca*, *nateema*, *nepi*, and, of course, *caapi*. What Schultes didn't know about this potion wasn't known outside of the Indigenous communities that prepared and used it. So, when he advised the Putumayo region as the most accessible area where he'd be likely to find the drug, Burroughs knew exactly where he needed to go, and just a few weeks later found himself in the small town of Mocoa, the capital of the Putumayo. From here, he traveled to Puerto Limon by truck, a settlement on the south bank of the Caquetá River, where he quickly managed to locate a local who gave him an armful of the yagé (caapi) vine, but who refused to prepare the brew, stating that it must be done by a *brujo*—a medicine man. Fortunately, there just happened to be such a man in town. Unfortunately, however, this brujo turned out to be an "old drunken fraud" who insisted he couldn't possibly work his magic unless thoroughly liquored up.[11] When Burroughs entered the brujo's hut, he was already well juiced, leaning over some poor chap sweating and shivering with malaria while slurring incantations designed to drive the evil spirit from the man's body. As soon as the cure was complete, the man was kicked into the streets and Burroughs had the medicine man to himself. Naturally, things couldn't proceed any further until the requisite pint of aguardiente—a powerful local spirit with up to 60 percent alcohol by volume—was delivered and for another quart, he agreed to prepare the yagé brew.

After stealing half the vine, the medicine man shaved the bark from the remainder before briefly soaking it in water—a simple cold-water infusion not dissimilar to the one Spruce first drank a century earlier. Burroughs was eventually presented with about a pint of liquid comparable in appearance to a three-day-old urine sample.[12] And it might as well have been urine for all the good it did him; barring some particularly vivid and colorful dreams that night, he noticed no effects whatsoever from the decoction. This was most certainly not the yagé he'd come halfway across South America for. But despite being a complete failure from Burroughs's perspective, this first experience was actually of significant scientific value. Since he both procured the vine from a presumably knowledgeable local source and witnessed the preparation of the decoction in its entirety, we can be sure that what he drank was an infusion of the caapi vine and the caapi vine alone. And since it had already been established that some vivid dreams were about all one could expect from a low dose of the constituent caapi alkaloids— already known to be harmine and harmaline—his lackluster experience was precisely what we would have expected.

Although somewhat dejected, he wasn't ready to give up and decided to press farther into the Putumayo in the hope of reaching Kofan territory, where he knew the real yagé artists could be found. Unfortunately, fate had other ideas, and after being collared by one of the ubiquitous and meddlesome federal cops for a clerical error on his tourist visa, he was eventually escorted back to Bogotá with nothing accomplished.[13] Fortuitously, however, Schultes was still in Bogotá and happened to be embarking on an expedition to the Putumayo—where Burroughs had intended on traveling—accompanied by two Colombian botanists and two English members of the cocoa commission. So, Burroughs decided to join them as they retraced his steps back to Mocoa, where he quickly managed to procure twenty pounds of the caapi vine from a friend of Schultes, and an appointment with a local medicine man was arranged.[14]

Hopeful that this man would be an improvement on the drunken hack he'd encountered a few weeks earlier, he arrived at the dirt-floor thatched shack to find the baby-faced seventy-year-old waiting hand outstretched for the obligatory bottle of liquor that would allow the proceedings to commence. The man took an impressively long swig before squatting in front of a cloth-covered bowl set before a shrine decorated with the accouterments of the Catholic faith: a picture of the Virgin Mary, a crucifix, a wooden idol, and other such knickknacks.

"You've come to the right place," he assured Burroughs.

Then the singing began; a series of sacred chants interrupted only by the occasional swig from the liquor bottle. Finally satisfied that the incantations had worked their magic, the medicine man uncovered the bowl to reveal a dark oily liquid—visually, at least, much more impressive than the weak piss the other one had knocked up.

Forgoing any further ritualistic pretensions, about an ounce of the black liquid was unceremoniously scooped up with a dirty red plastic cup, which was then passed to Burroughs: "Just drink this straight down."

He knocked it back—"bitter foretaste of nausea."[15] Within two minutes it became obvious that this was an entirely different species of decoction to what he'd drank a few weeks earlier. Similar to a decent lungful of ether, the room began to spin as he became overwhelmed by dizziness and vivid blue forms flashed before his eyes. The hut itself then became transfigured, taking on an archaic Pacific look with Easter Island heads carved in the support posts. Paranoid before he even arrived, he was now convinced that the "old drunken fuck of a witch doctor" was trying to kill him, perhaps by slipping a healthy dose of strychnine or even rat poison into the mix.[16] But there was no time to consider his options. A sudden wave of intense nausea hit him with immense force and he staggered outside, his legs of only minimal assistance in getting him to a tree against which he vomited violently and repeatedly before falling to the ground as his limbs convulsed. Entities in the form of "larval beings" then made an appearance, passing before his eyes and offering little sympathy, but each merely "an obscene, mocking squawk."[17]

Fortunately, he was no stranger to overdoses and had sequestered a bottle of the sedative and anticonvulsant barbiturate Nembutal in his pocket for just such an eventuality. However, crippled by unrelenting spasms in his arms, it took him several minutes to shake the pills from the bottle, and even when he did eventually get them into his mouth, it was too dry to swallow. With the postural grace of a marionette being operated by an arthritic farmhand, he somehow managed to maneuver his body to a nearby stream and press his face into the water, sucking up just enough to wash down the pills. A few minutes later, the convulsions mercifully began to subside and he was able to crawl back to the hut and cover himself with a blanket. Suddenly very drowsy, he slept.

Despite his paranoia that the "old bastard . . . who specializes in poisoning gringos" might have slipped a little something extra into his brew, the effects of the decoction on Burroughs were strikingly similar to those experienced by German psychiatrist Karl Beringer's laboratory assistant after a high dose of the isolated caapi alkaloids. He also appeared "drunken,"[18] struggled to walk, and shook uncontrollably. Also, as reported by other scientists investigating the alkaloids earlier in the century, his visions were poorly formed and, barring some larval beings, generally limited to blue forms that flashed before his eyes. Yet again, despite receiving a much more concentrated variant of the brew, his experience fell short of his expectations.

The following day, he fully recovered and was able to make his way back to Mocoa, where he joined Schultes's crew on an expedition to Puerto Asís. Under the informal tutelage of Schultes and by his own observations, he had already become familiar with two distinct methods of preparation of the yagé potion, which he referred to as the Vaupes method and the Putumayo Kofan method.

"In the Vaupes, the bark is scraped off about three feet of vine to form a large double handful of shavings. The bark is soaked in a liter of cold water for several hours, and the liquid strained off and taken over a period of an hour. No other plant is added."[19]

This simple cold-water infusion is what he received with the first medicine man and is likely similar—albeit not identical—to what Spruce first drank with the Tukano people along the Vaupes River in 1852. While Schultes was busy collecting plant specimens in the rain forest, Burroughs attempted to manufacture a quantity of yagé himself using this method. But despite drinking a quart of the light red liquid, he described the experience as not dissimilar to cannabis: blue flashes, nausea, enhanced mental imagery, and general silliness. And as with his very first experience with a brew prepared in a similar manner, there were no visions. He became further convinced that the yagé he was looking for was prepared using what he referred to as the Putumayo Kofan method: "The pieces of vine are crushed with a rock and boiled with a handful of leaves from another plant—tentatively identified as *ololiuqui*—the mixture is boiled all day with a small amount of water and reduced to about two ounces of liquid."[20]

Ololiuqui is an Aztec name referring to the seeds of the vine *Rivea corymbosa* (now *Ipomoea corymbosa*) used as a ritual psychedelic in Mexico. Ololiuqui had been identified by Mexican botanist Manuel Urbina in 1897,[21] and in 1960, Albert Hofmann—inventor of lysergic acid diethylamide (LSD)—would isolate the hallucinogenic alkaloid lysergic acid amide from the seeds.[22] Although these psychoactive alkaloids have been detected in the leaves of *Rivea corymbosa*,[23] they are much more concentrated in the seeds, which are used traditionally. However, this is moot, since there's no evidence that either the leaves or the seeds were ever a component of the yagé decoction. But despite this error, Burroughs was closer to working things out than he realized at the time. However, unsurprisingly considering his prior experiences, he was somewhat blinded by his contempt for the medicine men who prepared the potion, whom he dismissed as a "bunch of con artists" working in an Amazon "infested with bullshit."[24] He wasn't even remotely convinced that they possessed any kind of special powers or secrets, but pretended to do so to maintain their monopoly on its production. "The brujos say they are the only ones competent to prepare it: two other secret plants must be cooked into the mixture; the brujo has to croon over it and spit in it and shake a whisk broom over it otherwise the yagé is nowhere. . . . The truth is, anyone can cook up a pot of yagé in an hour or so."[25]

Despite his cynicism, he had at least noticed—and his first two experiences certainly suggested—that perhaps yagé wasn't all about the caapi vine, but other plants might also have a role in its visionary effects. Just as the string of scientists had established earlier in the century, he had at least convinced himself that crude extracts of the caapi vine alone were effectively inactive or, at least, lacking the visionary powers he was expecting. After separating from Schultes's group, he ended up back in Bogotá armed with his crate of caapi vine, where he subsisted by stealing alcohol from the Institute laboratory and, each evening, sitting in cafes drinking the lab-grade spirit mixed into bottles of Pepsi. While visiting the Institute, he also managed to acquire basic instructions on using the lab alcohol to make an extract of the vine, in the hope that he could separate the active alkaloids from the "nauseating oils and resins." But the extract merely made him sleepy. Not surprisingly in retrospect, considering he was merely repeating the work of Zerda-Bayón and others a few decades earlier, there were no visions of cities, no discarnate entities, not even any colors or sharpening of mental imagery.

With his visa expiration date drawing near, Burroughs decided to leave Colombia and head to Peru, intending to reach the Peruvian Amazon, where he hoped his luck in finding the most powerful variants of yagé would improve. After being waylaid for a week in Lima with neuritis, likely caused by his consumption of copious quantities of a strong local cane spirit, he eventually landed in Pucallpa, a small city on the banks of the Ucayali River, the main headstream of the Amazon.[26] As soon as his plane touched down, he could feel his fortunes begin to change. The manager of Hotel Pucallpa, where he was staying, was well-informed about yagé—known as ayahuasca in this region—and immediately connected him with a local shaman called Saboya, who ran small group ayahuasca ceremonies and was more than happy to bring Burroughs into the fold.

When he arrived at Saboya's hut on the outskirts of the town, a group of six locals had already gathered under a tree ready for the ceremony to begin. The young shaman then brought out the ayahuasca—a dark brown liquid that he poured into a plastic cup from a beer bottle—whistled a quick tune, and then passed to each in turn. Everyone remained silent and waited. A few minutes later, the effects began to take hold. "I experienced at first a feeling of calm and serenity like I could sit there all night. I glimpsed a new state of being."[27]

Then, soon after, the visions began: "A blue substance seemed to invade my body. I saw an archaic grinning face like a South Pacific mask. . . . Everything stirs with a writhing, furtive life. The room is Near Eastern and South Pacific and in some familiar-but-undefined place. . . . There is a feeling of space time travel that seems to shake the room."

After several convulsive and nauseating but ultimately disappointing attempts, Burroughs was convinced he had finally discovered the true yagé he'd been searching for. And like any good scientist, he was happy to change his mind about the medicine men as new evidence presented itself. "Hold the presses! Everything I wrote about yagé subject to revision in the light of subsequent experience. It is not like weed, nor anything else I have ever experienced. I am now prepared to believe the brujos do have secrets, and that yagé alone is quite different from yagé prepared with the leaves and plants the brujos add to it. . . . It is the most powerful drug I have ever experienced. That is it produces the most complete derangement of the senses. You see everything from a special hallucinated viewpoint."[28]

There's little doubt that this variant of the brew was distinctly more visionary than his previous attempts, and indeed much closer to the fantastical reports from Spruce and others. The drink wasn't merely altering the appearance of the world around him but was actually transporting him to somewhere else—to a different world. Following the session, he learned why, when Saboya let him into a trade secret: "He mashes pieces of the fresh-cut vine and boils two hours with the leaves of another plant."[29]

He managed to slip a few of these leaves into his pocket, and with the help of a Peruvian botanist, was able to make a tentative identification: A New World species from the *Palicourea* genus of the *Rubiaceae* family. Although Burroughs's botanist didn't quite get this right (although he was close), his discovery was a breakthrough and would later turn out to be of critical importance in understanding how this mysterious potion could have such dramatic effects on the conscious world.

Burroughs certainly wasn't the first to notice that, in some variants of yagé, plants other than the *Banisteriopsis caapi* vine were added to the decoction. In his field notes, Richard Spruce mentioned, almost in passing, that the leaves of another plant "painted with strong blood-red veins"[30] were sometimes added along with the caapi vine. He never identified this other plant, however—he wasn't convinced it was that important. A few years after Spruce's first encounter with the caapi potion, travel writer Alfred Simson reported that Indigenous groups in Ecuador "drink ayahuasca mixed with yagé" in addition to at least two other botanicals, suggesting that ayahuasca and yagé actually refer to two different plants.[31] And in 1921, the Parisian medical doctor and anthropologist Pierre Reinburg reported that, while working among an Indigenous group in the Peruvian Amazon, he observed ayahuasca being prepared as an infusion of the ayahuasca vine and the "leaf of yagé," again suggesting that the vine wasn't the only important component of the brew.[32] And perhaps most tellingly, in the same year, the Belgian botanist Florent Claes observed ayahuasca being prepared by boiling pieces of the vine and then later, the leaves of another plant, which he wasn't permitted to see—it was a secret, and secrets are kept for a reason.[33]

Almost certainly entirely unaware of the continuing debate and confusion among the professional botanists over the identity—and even the existence—of this secret, professional drug user William S. Burroughs had been able to pinpoint a single admixture plant that he hypothesized contained an unidentified component necessary for the visionary effects: "The other leaf is essential to realize the full effect of the drug. Whether it is itself active, or merely serves as a catalyzing agent, I do not know. This matter needs the attention of a chemist."[34]

Despite lacking any formal scientific credentials, his insight was momentous. While the caapi vine was the principal component of the yagé (ayahuasca) decoction, the vine alone with its constituent harmala alkaloids was insufficient to achieve the effects recounted by Spruce and others (as had already been well demonstrated earlier in the century).

Another molecule—perhaps another alkaloid—derived from an entirely separate plant was essential to complete the decoction. In other words, the ability of ayahuasca to gate access to the discarnate Other likely depended not on a single psychoactive molecule, but on the synergistic interaction between at least two entirely different molecules. Like the curare arrow poison studied by Richard Schultes throughout the previous decade, ayahuasca wasn't simply a drug—it was a technology.

3

THE LITTLE PEOPLE

So they had gone at their subjects with metronomes, serpents, Brechtian vignettes at midnight, surgical removal of certain glands, magic-lantern hallucinations, new drugs, threats recited over hidden loudspeakers, hypnotism, clocks that ran backward, and faces.

—Thomas Pynchon

In the early 1950s, William Burroughs wasn't the only American with an interest in peculiar technologies to manipulate the human mind. And not all such technologies were manufactured in the South American rain forests. On April 15, 1953, just as Burroughs had returned to Bogotá, Colombia, following his second ayahuasca experience, CIA Chief Allen Dulles approved a top-secret program to study unconventional techniques for modifying an individual's behavior by covert means: wired interfaces to control the brain like a computer; electroshock treatments; forced lobotomies; and, of course, drugs. The program was christened with the now infamous code name MK-ULTRA.[1]

The intelligence arms of the US government had been experimenting with methods of covert mind control since the creation of the Central Intelligence Agency in 1947 and had already tried and ultimately rejected a number of prospective "truth drugs," including the psychedelic peyote alkaloid mescaline, the deliriant scopolamine, potent extracts of cannabis, as well as a range of sedative barbiturates. And, not surprisingly, when Albert Hofmann's extraordinarily potent ergot derivative, LSD, appeared in the early 1950s, the Agency was keen to add this new drug to its repertoire. The techniques employed (or at least proposed) by the Agency have since become the stuff of legend: Dropping LSD into the water supply of an enemy city to render its population unable—or unwilling—to defend itself;[2] testing the effects on Special Operations Division officers by spiking their Cointreau during a three-day retreat (leading one man to commit suicide shortly after);[3] setting up "safe houses" where men would be enticed by prostitutes and wind up drugged with LSD while being watched by agents behind two-way mirrors; as well as slipping the drug into the drinks of random members of the public in bars, clubs, and restaurants and observing their reactions. At the height of their covert LSD program, Sandoz, the sole manufacturer of LSD at the time, was supplying the Agency at a rate of 100 grams per week—enough to dose up to a million people—allowing them not only to monopolize the supply of the drug but also to dominate research into its effects.[4]

But the Agency wasn't satisfied with only testing drugs that were likely already on Soviet radar—they wanted something entirely new. So, when they caught whiff of a mysterious mushroom cult rumored to be operating in Southern Mexico, the Agency dispatched a young scientist to Mexico City to locate and collect samples of the magical fungi to test on its willing—or, in some cases, entirely unwitting—human subjects back in the States. He eventually returned with samples of *Psilocybe* "magic" mushrooms, as well as ten pounds of the psychedelic LSA (lysergic acid amide)-containing seeds of *Rivea corymbosa* (ololiuqui).[5] All the Agency needed now was a suitably qualified and morally ambiguous individual to perform the experiments on human subjects.

One such scientist on the Agency payroll was pharmacologist Harris Isbell, director of the Addiction Research Center in Lexington, Kentucky. Unlike other scientists who would have to go through a protracted period of recruitment to gather volunteers for research into novel pharmaceuticals, Isbell had privileged access to a practically inexhaustible supply of test subjects from a—quite literally—captive population. It was a matter of sheer coincidence that Isbell's Addiction Research Center just happened to share its campus with the Federal Bureau of Prisons who, in 1953, was responsible for the custody (and, *ahem*, care) of over twenty thousand federal inmates. Recruitment from this population was straightforward: The word was discreetly injected into the Bureau's prison network that anyone who volunteered for Isbell's research would be rewarded with either reduced time or a limited supply of top-notch heroin that wouldn't have raised an eyebrow had it found its way into the president's own personal stash. They almost always chose the latter. The only catch was that, while inmates were told they would be required to ingest one or more experimental drugs, they weren't privy to any further information: neither the name or type of drug, nor any possible effects. The obligatory "informed" consent forms were signed, legal waivers granted, and Isbell had complete carte blanche.[6]

Inmate volunteers would be awoken early, denied breakfast, and the drug administered at precisely 8 a.m., either mixed with raspberry syrup to disguise the taste or, in the case of LSD, a few drops of the solution were simply soaked into a graham cracker.[7] Any attempts to create a relaxed, comfortable, or reassuring environment were entirely foregone. The inmates lay on a standard hospital bed and as the effects of the drug took hold, would be at the mercy of the doctors' prods, pokes, and interrogations, but most of all, at the mercy of their own minds. Although their experiences were occasionally pleasant, even fantastical—"trips to the moon or living in gorgeous castles"[8]— considering the less-than-optimal setting for a psychedelic trip and given that the subjects invariably had absolutely no prior experience with these highly unusual states of consciousness, more often than not they were marked by nervousness, anxiety, and outright paranoia, with some inmates fearing insanity or believing their minds to be controlled by the investigators.

Although Isbell seemed to delight in his work, the inmates understandably grew fearful of the doctors in the experimental wing of the institute. But the draw of first-rate heroin was too much to resist so, slippered and hungry, they marched to the "special ward" for their treatment, with no more of an idea as to what might befall them that day than Isbell himself. And if they were at least expecting some kind of compassion or concern for their welfare, they most certainly would

have been disappointed. One of Isbell's most notorious experiments involved keeping seven inmates high on LSD for eighty-five days without interruption, gradually increasing the dosage—"double, triple, and
quadruple"—as the weeks passed by so as to "break through" their
growing tolerance.[9] Naturally, he was also more than happy to feed his
inmate subjects any other obscure psychoactive drug preparations procured during the Agency's secret expeditions to Mexico. Once a new
drug landed on his desk, it wouldn't be long before it found its way into
an inmate's bloodstream, and he made it quite clear to his CIA contacts
that he wouldn't dilly-dally on such matters: "I will write you a letter as
soon as I can get the stuff into a man or two."[10]

"The stuff" might have referred to any one of a long list of drugs Isbell
administered to his captive volunteers throughout the 1950s: a string of
novel ergot alkaloid derivatives,[11] exotic cannabinoids, amphetamines,[12]
super-potent synthetic opioids,[13] as well as a series of drug combination
experiments with the powerful deliriant scopolamine aimed at intensifying the mind-twisting effects of LSD.[14] The results of his experiments
with the plant-derived drugs procured by the CIA agent from Mexico
were mixed. While he found psilocybin isolated from the *Psilocybe*
mushrooms to produce similar effects to LSD, he was less impressed
after feeding spoonfuls of the ground ololiuqui seeds to his subjects,[15]
who became so sick that he struggled to assess their psychological
state.[16] But there was one other South American drug, more obscure
than either of these, that Isbell was keen to get into a man or two.

In the late fifteenth and early sixteenth centuries during the Spanish
conquest of the Americas, the priests who accompanied the troops began to hear alarming stories from natives across South America of their
regular encounters with monstrous creatures not of this world, which the
priests obviously identified with the devil: "The Indians told of strange beings who appeared to them in the shapes of monsters armed with pointed
fangs, terrifying beings with glowing eyes and roaring voices who presented themselves in thunder and lightning and were recognized by the
Indians as their overlords and masters. They were afraid of the monsters,
it is true, but at the same time, they respected and obeyed them."[17]

What was particularly alarming wasn't their mere belief in these horrifying supernatural beings, but that the natives were apparently able to summon them at will by entering a trancelike state achieved by inhaling a fine powder not dissimilar in appearance to ground cinnamon. During his second voyage to the Americas between 1493 and 1496, Christopher Columbus observed the Taino people of Haiti using this visionary snuff, which they called *cohoba* and inhaled using a Y-shaped tube placed inside the nostrils to induce a state of intoxication during which they talked wildly and incoherently while claiming to hear voices and see visions.[18]

This account from Spanish Jesuit priest Father Juan Rivero who, in the early eighteenth century, spent many years working among the Achagua people along the Meta River in Colombia and Venezuela illustrates the kind of state induced by this visionary powder: "They talk in loud and shrill shouts like mad men, making hideous grimaces, and even if many of them are gathered together, they do not converse one with another, but each one talks only to himself, with gestures and shakings, questions and cross-examinations, all of which demonstrates that they are talking with the devil."[19]

In 1802, German naturalist and explorer Alexander von Humboldt was able to observe the preparation of a similar snuff, referred to as either *niopo* or *yopo*, while living among the Otomac of the Orinoco Basin. The seeded pods of a tree were first broken up and left to soften in water before being mixed with flour and lime and kneaded to form a dough, which was then baked until hard and then pulverized in a pestle and mortar to form the final finely powdered product, ready for inhalation.[20]

And in 1854, just two years after he identified the caapi vine, while exploring the Orinoco Plains, Richard Spruce came across a group of nomadic Guahibo people who also used the visionary niopo snuff. As Humboldt had also observed, the snuff was prepared from the ground seeds of a leguminous tree—a new species that Spruce christened *Piptadenia niopo* (now *Anadenanthera peregrina*). However, in 1916, American botanist William Safford demonstrated that cohoba and niopo/yopo were, in fact, different names for the same snuff, which was found to be used by practically all Indigenous groups encountered across the Orinoco Plains, where the tree grew wild.[21]

When self-administered in small quantities, yopo (niopo, cohoba) acts as a mild stimulant. However, there is also a much more intensely visionary "shotgun" mode of administration that requires a partner: A tube up to a yard long is packed with up to a teaspoon of yopo and one end inserted firmly into a nostril. The partner then blows forcefully on the opposite end, exploding the powder deep into the nasal passages. Not surprisingly, this is an extremely painful procedure and the immediate response is to fall to the ground trembling as blood begins discharging from the nose. Then, once the initially unpleasant effects subside, the visions begin.[22] Just like the ayahuasca potion, yopo is not merely an intoxicant, but a tool for communication with beings invisible to the sober mind.

Once the identity of cohoba and niopo/yopo had been pinpointed to a single tree, it was commonly assumed that any and all of the many visionary snuffs observed across the Orinoco and Amazonia were prepared from the same species. To preeminent ethnobotanist Richard Schultes, however, this made little sense, since the *Anadenanthera peregrina* tree grows only on open savannahs, while accounts of ritual snuff use extended well into deep rain forest regions where the tree is neither cultivated nor to be found growing wild.[23] An account from German ethnologist Theodor Koch-Grunberg, who described a "magical snuff" used by the Yekuana people of Venezuela to communicate with the spirit world, only added to his confusion: Unlike yopo, this snuff was apparently prepared from the bark of a tree known as *hakudufha*.[24] Spruce and others had quite clearly identified the yopo snuff as being prepared from seeds, whereas Koch-Grunberg specifically mentioned the use of a tree's bark. Was this another snuff entirely?

Schultes's confusion wouldn't be resolved until 1951, when he was surveying the forests of the Orinoco Basin with a group a rubber workers and happened upon a small flowering tree that he immediately identified as a species of *Virola*, a genus native to rain forest regions of South America. A small boy—the son of a shaman—examined the bark and turned to Schultes: "This is the tree that gives *ya-kee*. My father uses it when he wants to talk to the little people."

Schultes was stunned and immediately pulled the boy aside for interrogation. Despite apparently similar visionary effects to yopo, this snuff was prepared not only from a separate species, but an entirely different genus.[25]

The following morning, the young boy demonstrated to Schultes how to prepare the snuff. The bark was peeled from the tree and a thick red liquid soon began to bead on the inner surface. In a manner not dissimilar to the preparation of ayahuasca, the bark was then pulverized in cold water and strained. The liquid was then slowly boiled off to yield a thick syrup that was then allowed to dry in the sun before being ground into a fine powder. Although Schultes took the opportunity to sample the young boy's product and despite noting a "general feeling of lassitude and uneasiness," he experienced little else beyond a headache that didn't relent for two days—he certainly didn't meet any little people.[26]

Several years later, Schultes was trekking along the banks of the Río Loretoyacu in Colombia, having been commissioned by a pharmaceutical company to collect 100 kilograms of bark from a *Virola* tree shown to have promising anti-inflammatory properties. As they were stripping bark from the trees, his young Witoto assistant remarked: "This tree is the one my father made little pellets from. He ate them when he wanted to speak with the little people."[27]

Schultes could hardly believe what he was hearing. An entirely different species. The same little people.

These little people were quite obviously more than an idiosyncratic vision of a single *Virola*-ingesting shaman. The first boy who remarked of his father using *Virola* to see the little people was a member of the Puinave people, who live mainly along the banks of the Inírida River in Colombia, as well as in smaller communities along the Orinoco River near the Colombia–Venezuela border. The second boy was a Witoto, who lived much farther south, along the Putumayo River in Southern Colombia and Northern Peru. However, these *Virola* snuffs are used by many Indigenous groups across the tropical rain forest regions of western Amazonia and the Orinoco Basin, where at least seventy-five species of the genus grow wild. And wherever you find *Virola* snuffs, you will find the little people.

One of the largest Indigenous groups in South America, and

prodigious users of both yopo and *Virola*-based visionary snuffs, are the Yanomami, who live in the rain forests of northern Brazil and southern Venezuela.[28] For the Yanomami, the little people, known as *xapiri* (or *hekura*), form an integral part of a rich otherworldly ecology of normally invisible beings that populate the forests. Described as tiny, luminous humanoid creatures with an immense propensity for singing and dancing—"The xapiri's songs follow each other endlessly"—and who "shine brightly, like stars moving through the forest," the xapiri operate in such numbers that you "can never come to the end of them!"[29] And while it's often convenient to refer to the xapiri as "spirits," Yanomami shaman Davi Kopenawa makes it clear that they are neither human nor animal nor spirit: They are "other." As in other Indigenous groups, the only way to see the xapiri is to inhale either yopo or a snuff produced from the resin of *Virola elongata* known as *epéna* or *yãkoana*, similar to what Schultes first identified.[30]

The importance of the xapiri (hekura) in Yanomami cosmology can hardly be overstated: "Hekura are the intangible and immortal nuclei of all material components of the Yanomami cosmos."[31] Even the shaman himself is considered to be "a multiple being, a micro-population of shamanic agencies sheltered in one body."[32] The xapiri are first called during a grueling shamanistic initiation lasting up to a month, during which epéna powder is constantly blown into the young initiate's nose: "When they answer the neophyte's call, glowing hekura arrive in innumerable multiplicities, dancing along their shining paths and moving to the rhythm of a shapori's [shaman] songs."[33] The xapiri then take up residence in the young shaman's chest, where they will remain as his assistants and allies until he passes them onto another person or, when close to death, they finally abandon him and return to the forest.[34]

The appearance of these little people seems to be an almost universal feature of intoxication with yopo and epéna snuffs. American ethnobotanist and Schultes protege Mark Plotkin describes his first experience with a visionary epéna snuff while working among the Yanomami: "The force seemed to propel the drug from the shaman's tube directly into my bloodstream and then into my very soul. . . . At the edge of my field of vision, tiny figures began to appear . . . began to dance . . . multiplied in number as they danced faster and faster. . . . I asked the shaman who the little men were."

Of course, the shaman answered without hesitation: "They are the hekura . . . the spirits of the forest."[35]

Although the innumerable dancing and singing little people are their most common manifestation, a multitude of different types of xapiri, varying in both form and character, can also be seen while intoxicated with the snuffs: the Warusinari giant insects who became other; the Hakohakori vulture beings; the Yapimari butterfly beings; and the Koimari, who appear as birds of prey and enjoy cutting up children—and even shamans on occasion—to feast on their fat. Kopenawa describes a particularly gruesome attack by this most fearsome of xapiri: "They silently drew close to me at the end of their presentation dance. They did not seem threatening. Yet suddenly I felt their blades violently hitting me. They cut my body in half in a single stroke down the middle of my back! The impact drew a long moan of pain out of me. But that did not stop them! After they had cut me in two, they sliced off my head."[36]

Although the names given to particular types of beings vary, across all Indigenous Amazonian cultures we find the same kinds of entities in the same types of relationships with humans.[37] Likewise, the same modes of communication and interaction with these beings are employed: powerful visionary plant preparations. The Matsigenka people, for example, who live on the eastern slopes of the Andes in Peru, choose ayahuasca as their preferred means of communication with the little people, whom they call *saankariite*.[38] Like the xapiri beings who take up residence in the chest of the Yanomami shamans, the Matsigenka form a close relationship with their saankariite, who remain with them and protect them until death, including when threatened by other beings. Whichever plant preparation might be preferred, these visionary tools are "the basic instrument of shamanistic technology, being used as a kind of visual prosthesis" with which to see and communicate with these beings.[39] What Schultes's young assistants had remarked upon so casually wasn't merely an intriguing drug-induced hallucination, but a living, intimate interaction with beings far older, far wiser, far more intelligent and powerful than the rain forest people themselves and absolutely central to their view of life and reality.

While Harris Isbell back in Lexington did manage to procure some seeds of *Anadenanthera peregrina*—used to make yopo—he had less luck in coaxing the little people out from hiding. He had the Laboratory of Chemistry of Natural Products at the National Heart Institute in Maryland convert the raw seed to snuffs of various types: "Roasted snuff, fermented snuff, limed snuff, fermented and roasted snuff, fermented and limed snuff, and as fermented, limed, and roasted snuff."[40] Unfortunately, despite convincing his plucky recruits to inhale up to a gram of snuff every thirty minutes—presumably until they could take no more—barring an awful lot of coughing and sneezing and general discharging, the little people—or indeed any type of entity—failed to make an appearance. In fact, his volunteers experienced no effects whatsoever—either physical or psychological.[41] So what went wrong? It's quite plausible that his inmates were understandably less than enthusiastic in their efforts to force gram after gram of the powder up their noses and it's highly unlikely that Isbell employed the painful two-man shotgun technique to ensure maximal delivery deep into the nasal passages. However, the explanation is probably much simpler: Much like the scientists studying the caapi vine earlier in the century, Isbell simply underestimated the sophistication of the techniques required to produce and use an active visionary snuff. It turns out that preparing yopo is a little more complicated than simply roasting and grinding the seeds. Or was he perhaps missing some vital catalyzing component of the yopo preparation?

As with ayahuasca, the method of preparation of yopo, epéna, and similar snuffs varies between Indigenous groups and often includes admixture plants that can modulate or potentiate their effects. One of the most common preparations of epéna includes a mixture of the dried *Virola* tree resin and the powdered leaves of a tree known as *mashihiri* (*Justicia pectoralis*), a type of water-willow. It used to be assumed, somewhat naively, that mashihiri was added merely as an aromatic, since it has a particularly pungent but pleasant aroma when dried.[42] However,

Justicia pectoralis has a long history of use as a traditional medicine, particularly as an expectorant in the treatment of coughs and other respiratory conditions. The leaves of *Justicia* contain a group of chemicals called coumarins, which have been shown to relax smooth muscles and open the airways,[43] as well as causing small blood vessels in the nasal passages to dilate. Overall, this increases the surface area for absorption of any alkaloids in the snuff, hastening their entry into the bloodstream. Just like the curare arrow poisons studied by Richard Schultes, the epena snuff is not simply a plant preparation, but a plant-derived technology employing pharmacological synergy to maximize the snuff's potency and efficacy.

Not surprisingly, many yopo snuff preparations also contain important admixture plants. However, what's particularly interesting about yopo is its curious connection to ayahuasca. In 1854, just two years after discovering and naming the *Banisteriopsis caapi* vine, Richard Spruce reported in his field notes meeting an old Guahibo man while exploring the Orinoco basin who carried a pouch of yopo (niopo) together with a piece of dried caapi bark around his neck.

"With a chew of caapi and a pinch of niopo, one feels so good!" he told Spruce.[44]

It wasn't clear to Spruce whether this was a simple drug combination—as we might combine alcohol and nicotine—that the Guahibo enjoyed, or something more interesting. Another Indigenous group of the Orinoco Basin, the Piaroa, have only ever prepared a drink using the caapi vine alone—never with any admixture plants. However, when they want to experience particularly strong visions, they will often follow the caapi drink with yopo snuff. The Piaroa also prepare a particularly potent version of yopo by blending the ground *A. peregrina* seeds with ground caapi vine. Their reasoning is quite clear, as expressed by this Piaroa shaman: "The force of yopo and the force of caapi work together. . . . Caapi extends yopo and makes it stronger. Without caapi, yopo only lasts a short time. The visions are weak."[45]

This shaman is unequivocally alluding to a type of pharmacological synergy, in which two or more drugs together produce a much greater—or entirely different—effect than either drug alone. This is precisely what Burroughs concluded from observing the preparation of ayahuasca in Peru. The caapi-only brew yielded little more than convulsions and projectile vomiting, whereas the addition of the "secret" admixture plant completed the decoction, yielding a highly visionary potion capable of transporting the drinker through space and time to an entirely new world. So it seemed that the caapi vine, while not the primary psychoactive component of either ayahuasca or the yopo snuff, played a central pharmacological role in either activating or potentiating their effects. Although CIA recruit Harris Isbell saw yopo as simply another drug to add to a growing repertoire of prospective tools to twist the minds of his inmate test subjects, among the scientists and botanists working closely with the Indigenous peoples of South America, an entirely different picture was beginning to emerge. The yopo snuff and its close cousin epéna, just like the ritual decoction ayahuasca, were not merely plant-derived visionary drugs that happened to induce visions of little people and other strange creatures, but psychoactive drug technologies, developed over many centuries, if not millennia, and all designed to perform that same function—to render the Hidden Ones visible; to allow humans to communicate and develop lifelong relationships with the countless forms of discarnate intelligence that populate the forest and the world beyond. Of course, recognizing a technology is one thing. What none of the scientists yet understood was how these technologies worked and what nobody, scientist or otherwise, could have imagined was what they would reveal as they were carried from their tropical home and into the high-tech laboratories of the West. The little people were about to escape the rain forest and enter a world populated by people entirely unprepared for their arrival.

4

BREAKTHROUGH

A lot can be said for the infinite mercies of God, but the smarts of a good pharmacist, when you get down to it, is worth more.

—Philip K. Dick

As Harris Isbell's inmate volunteers were busy clearing their nasal passages of the multiple grams of seemingly inactive snuffs he'd induced them to inhale, the chemists at the National Heart Institute were busy with a detailed chemical analysis of the yopo seeds themselves. Despite Isbell's failure to elicit any psychoactive effects from the snuffs they'd prepared, the Institute was hoping to find an alkaloid that would explain the powerful visionary effects of the snuffs reported by the many Indigenous groups that used them. They found two.[1]

The most prominent of this pair, bufotenine, wasn't a new molecule, having been isolated more than thirty years prior as a minor component of the skin secretions of the common toad, *Bufo vulgaris*, from which it received its name.[2] The toxic properties of frogs and toads have been known for centuries, with their skin and gland secretions known to be highly complex mixtures of alkaloids and bioactive peptides.[3] As such, when bufotenine was first isolated, it was thought to be just another potentially useful pharmacological tool. Experiments on decapitated rabbits showed that it contracted smooth muscle in blood vessels and increased blood pressure.[4] Perhaps if they'd left the heads on they might have seen something more interesting, but anyway . . . The chemical structure of bufotenine was established in 1934 by German chemist and Nobel Laureate Heinrich Wieland. It belonged to a family of alkaloids known as the tryptamines, derived from the amino acid tryptophan.[5] At the time, this wasn't a particularly noteworthy observation, and bufotenine was added to an already long and growing list of naturally occurring alkaloids and largely forgotten about.

The following year, across the German border at Sandoz Laboratories in Basel, Switzerland, natural product chemist Albert Hofmann was at the tail end of a decade-long research project isolating the chemical components of the Mediterranean squill—a coastal plant containing potent cardiac toxins—and was looking for a new avenue of research. His boss, Professor Arthur Stoll, had isolated the alkaloid ergotamine from the parasitic rye fungus ergot, *Claviceps purpurea*, in 1917, but further research was abandoned after ergotamine found a role in obstetrics and in the treatment of migraines. Hofmann felt it time to pick up the mantle and obtained permission from Stoll to continue where he'd left off, studying the alkaloids of the ergot fungus. Although ergot was known to contain a mixture of bioactive alkaloids, none of them, barring ergotamine, were fully chemically characterized. However, American chemists had recently discovered the chemical nucleus common to all the ergot alkaloids, which they named lysergic acid. Crucially, it was possible to derive this lysergic acid molecule by chemically cleaving off a generally much larger and more complex structure from any of the ergot alkaloids. This gave Hofmann a steady supply of lysergic acid from which he was able to quickly and relatively easily synthesize a range of chemical analogs known as the lysergic acid amides, in the hope that one or two might show interesting pharmacological properties. The twenty-fifth derivative in this series was the molecule the CIA would soon be eager to get their paws on for their MK-ULTRA program, the lysergic acid diethylamide analog, LSD-25.[6]

Owing to its structural similarity to a known central nervous system stimulant nicotinic acid diethylamide, Hofmann hoped that LSD-25 would display similar properties. And although LSD-25 was found to be effective in causing uterine contraction, it "aroused no special interest in our pharmacologists and physicians; testing was therefore discontinued."[7] But Hofmann just couldn't shake the feeling that there was more to this molecule than the initial tests had suggested, and five years later decided to return to LSD-25, but during the final stages of purification of the molecule, began to feel unusual. He described his experience in a letter to Stoll the following week:

> Last Friday, April 16, 1943, I was forced to interrupt my work in the laboratory in the middle of the afternoon and proceed home, being affected by a remarkable restlessness, combined with a slight dizziness. At home I lay down and sank into a not unpleasant intoxicated-like condition, characterized by an extremely stimulated imagination. In a dreamlike state, with eyes closed (I found the daylight to be unpleasantly glaring), I perceived an uninterrupted stream of fantastic pictures, extraordinary shapes with intense, kaleidoscopic play of colors. After some two hours, this condition faded away.[8]

Making the obvious connection to the LSD-25 he'd been synthesizing at the time, Hofmann weighed out the smallest dose he could possibly imagine being active—a quarter of a milligram (250 micrograms)—and dissolved the crystals in water: "tasteless." What followed has since become arguably the most famous psychedelic experience in history—the world's first acid trip. Experiencing similar but more intense effects than the previous week, Hofmann asked his laboratory assistant to escort him home by bicycle. As he laid on the sofa, he began to experience the peak effects of what turned out to be a hefty dose of the peerlessly potent psychedelic, now known to be active at doses as low as 50 micrograms: "My surroundings had now transformed themselves in more terrifying ways. Everything in the room spun around, and the familiar objects and pieces of furniture assumed grotesque, threatening forms. They were in continuous motion, animated, as if driven by an inner restlessness. The lady next door, whom I scarcely recognized, brought me milk. She was no longer Mrs. R., but rather a malevolent, insidious witch with a colored mask. . . . A demon had invaded me, had taken possession of my body, mind, and soul."[9]

Hofmann and Stoll immediately recognized the potential of LSD-25 in both the study and possible treatment of psychiatric disorders, and in 1947, Sandoz began distributing LSD under the trade name Delysid. By 1949, scientists in the US were made aware of Hofmann's uniquely potent mind-altering ergot derivative,[10] which couldn't have arrived at a more opportune time, since psychiatrists had long been searching for some kind of connection between the chemical milieu of the brain and the profound cognitive disturbances of schizophrenia. Unfortunately, although LSD was initially thought to induce a state similar to an acute, albeit temporary, psychosis, nobody had any inkling as to how it achieved these effects. However, fortuitously, scientists in the US had recently made a landmark discovery that would provide that crucial chemical connection between this exogenous ergot alkaloid and endogenous neurochemistry.

In 1946, three years after Hofmann discovered LSD in Switzerland, American chemist Maurice Rapport was hired by the prominent physiologist Irvine Page at the Cleveland Clinic, Ohio, to isolate and characterize a potent vasoconstrictor principle that had been interfering with his experiments aimed at determining the causative factors underlying hypertension. Rapport immediately began the unenviable—and somewhat gruesome—task of extracting and purifying the bothersome molecule from more than 7,000 liters of blood procured over several months by daily excursions, armed with a stack of four-gallon buckets, to the local slaughterhouse.[11] Almost two years later, Rapport succeeded in reducing the thousands of liters of raw cow's blood to a few "thin, rhomboid pale-yellow" crystals[12]—a tiny sample, but sufficient for him to fully ascertain its chemical structure. It was an alkaloid, 5-hydroxytryptamine, which he provisionally named serotonin. The name stuck.

Pretty soon, serotonin seemed to appear almost anywhere a biochemist looked: in the gut secretions of dogs, rabbits, and mice; in the skin secretions of various frogs; in the venom of wasps and scorpions; and even in the salivary glands of the octopus. But it wasn't until American biochemist Betty Twarog developed a highly sensitive technique for its detection in mammalian tissue that its now most famous residence was revealed: the brain.[13] Naturally, neuroscientists immediately became keen to uncover a role for serotonin in human neurochemistry, but none

Serotonin, DMT, and bufotenine are all based on the tryptamine parent mole-cule, the central feature of which is a pair of fused carbon rings called an indole group. Attached to the 3-position on the indole is a two-carbon side chain which terminates in an amine group (NH2). To generate N,N-dimethyltryptamine (DMT), two methyl (CH3) groups are attached to this amine. Serotonin simply adds a hydroxyl (OH) to the indole 5-position. Bufotenine includes both the dimethyl group and the hydroxyl group.

more so than Canadian-American biochemist Dilworth Wayne Woolley, working at Rockefeller University in New York. Despite being almost completely blind as a complication of type 1 diabetes, it didn't escape Woolley's attention that Albert Hofmann's novel ergot derivative LSD displayed curious structural similarities to the newly discovered brain chemical.[14]

Like bufotenine, serotonin belongs to the tryptamine family of alkaloids. The parent molecule of this family, tryptamine itself, contains a pair of connected rings—a six-membered ring of carbon atoms and a five-membered ring containing a single nitrogen atom—known as an indole system, with a two-carbon side chain terminating in an amine group (NH_2). In serotonin, this basic tryptamine skeleton is decorated with a single hydroxyl group (OH) at the 5-position on the indole ring, and so has the chemical name 5-hydroxy-tryptamine. If you look carefully, you can also see this tryptamine skeleton embedded in the more elaborate four-ring structure of LSD. This commonality prompted Woolley to wonder whether LSD might interfere with serotonin's pharmacological activity. And indeed it did: When applied to isolated carotid arteries, LSD blocked serotonin's ability to contract the smooth muscle and thus constrict the artery.[15] In neural tissue, things were a little more complicated. Sometimes LSD blocked the activity of serotonin and sometimes it mimicked it.[16] It would be a few decades before the biochemistry underlying this complexity would be worked out. However, despite lacking a deep understanding of the mechanisms involved, these early experiments were some of the first intimations that LSD's pharmacology was connected to serotonin, and Woolley surmised that its powerful mind-altering effects might be due to disruption of serotonin's function in the brain.[17]

Realizing that he was onto a potentially extremely important avenue of research, Woolley then directed his attention to other alkaloids bearing the basic tryptamine skeleton. An obvious choice was bufotenine, which is simply serotonin with two extra methyl groups (CH_3) attached to the side chain amine, giving it the chemical name 5-hydroxyl-N,N-dimethyltryptamine (N,N-dimethyl-serotonin is also a perfectly valid name for bufotenine). However, unlike LSD, when applied to isolated

Lysergic acid amide (LSA) is found in seeds of plants of the morning glory family, Convolvulaceae (such as ololiuqui, Ipomoea corymbosa). Lysergic acid diethylamide (LSD) is the semi-synthetic diethyl derivative of LSA. All lysergic acid derivatives are based on the four-ring ergoline parent molecule.

blood vessels, rather than blocking serotonin's activity, bufotenine actually mimicked serotonin and caused smooth muscle contraction. This
didn't necessarily mean that bufotenine's effects in the brain would also
be the opposite of LSD's effects. How a drug interacts with serotonin
on isolated blood vessels doesn't necessarily predict how it will interact
with serotonin in the brain, if at all. However, this simple experiment
demonstrated that, in blood vessels at least, like LSD, bufotenine and
serotonin shared some kind of pharmacological connection. Unlike
LSD, however, bufotenine's effects in humans had never been tested
experimentally. So, when bufotenine was isolated from the Indigenous
snuff yopo, known to elicit powerful visionary effects, it was immediately assumed that this long-neglected frog alkaloid was responsible. It
just needed to be proved.

Initial animal tests were promising. Both LSD and bufotenine displayed similar effects on electrical activity in the visual system of the
cat[18] and effects on monkeys were also comparable. Immediately following injection of either drug, the animals laid flat on the bottom of their
cages with limbs splayed before apparently recovering twenty minutes
later and circling the cage in a somewhat drunken manner for the next
few hours.[19] In dogs, the effects were somewhat more startling. Immediately upon injection of bufotenine, the experimental canines began
to emit "an unearthly howling" and continued to do so for up to two
hours.[20] These intriguing effects in animals soon caught the attention of
a psychiatrist operating a private practice in Cincinnati, Howard Fabing,
who hoped that the howls of dogs would translate to interesting psychological effects in humans. He just needed some willing volunteers.
Unfortunately, however, it seemed that members of the public happy to
be injected with an experimental drug known to induce such terrifying effects in dogs weren't particularly forthcoming. But Fabing didn't
always work alone and had, in fact, recently completed a study on LSD
in collaboration with none other than Harris Isbell of the Addiction Research Center in Lexington. So rather than attempt to cajole members
of the public to be injected with this experimental tryptamine, he drew
inspiration from his dear colleague and turned to a population likely to
have less of a say in the matter: inmates at the Ohio State Penitentiary.

Staff at the correctional institute readily agreed to provide four young male convicts for Fabing's bufotenine experiments, and after being denied breakfast, each was injected with the drug. Disappointingly, even at the highest dose levels, none of the convicts were greeted by the little people or any of the hidden ones that usually make their appearance following inhalation of the yopo snuff. In fact, beyond seeing brightly colored dots and a "pleasant Martini feeling,"[21] effects were largely negative: a crushing pressure in the chest; intense nausea; a tingling feeling all over the body. Bearing in mind Woolley's prior work showing that bufotenine acts as a powerful blood vessel constrictor, these effects shouldn't have been overly surprising. However, not to be discouraged, Fabing doubled the highest dose and injected one of the convicts for a second time that morning. The man immediately reported a burning sensation in his mouth, began sweating profusely, and despite his empty stomach, wretched and vomited violently as his face turned a startlingly vivid purple described by Fabing as "the color of an eggplant." Fabing ended his report by promising that his studies with bufotenine would be expanded. Fortunately for the inmates at the Ohio State Penitentiary, they never were.[22]

Although there was little in Fabing's report that would suggest bufotenine was anything beyond mildly mind-altering, his claim that the drug induced effects were reminiscent of LSD and mescaline was apparently enough to convince most members of the scientific community that, as he and others had assumed, bufotenine was indeed responsible for the psychoactive effects of the yopo snuff. A young Hungarian physician with a newly kindled interest in the pharmacology of psychedelic drugs, however, was unconvinced.

Anyone with even a passing interest in psychedelics will likely be familiar with the story of Albert Hofmann's discovery of the psychedelic effects of LSD, but far fewer are likely to know of Dr. Stephen Szára, who, in 1955, had recently set up a biochemistry lab at a psychiatric hospital in Budapest. Szára's forays into the brand-new—to the West, at least—world of mind-altering drugs had actually begun several years earlier. Having read Aldous Huxley's most famous contribution to the psychedelic trip report literature, *The Doors of Perception*, an account of his first experience with the peyote cactus alkaloid mescaline, Szára was struck by the beauty of Huxley's description of the drug's effects, and after a few more reads, became more and more convinced of his desire to begin his own research program focused on these extraordinary new molecules.[23] News of the remarkable mind-bending effects of Hofmann's new lysergic acid derivative had already spread throughout the European medical community, and so Szára decided he'd start there, penning a letter to the home of LSD, the Sandoz company in Switzerland, requesting a sample for his clinical research. Unfortunately for Szára, in 1953, Hungary was still very much on the wrong side of the Iron Curtain and Sandoz was reluctant to risk delivering the drug into Communist hands. His request was politely refused. Szára needed an alternative.[24]

"At this point, I sent an order to a British pharmaceutical house to purchase 10 grams of mescaline. To my surprise, and delight, the drug arrived in December 1955. I remember weighing out 400mg of mescaline in the laboratory a few days before Christmas and took it home."[25]

Szára had his very first psychedelic experience, with the mescaline procured from England, on Christmas Day:

> I took it about 3 p.m. After about one hour I felt nothing, so I decided to go to the church on the top of the Castle-Hill in Budapest. On my way, on the bus, I started to feel that my vision had started to change; I was looking out through the window to the familiar landscape and seeing the trees moving in a strange way. When I got to the church I managed to get in, already full with people, standing room only. The ceremony had already started, loud organ music filled the air. . . . To my surprise, as I was looking down to the marble floor, it was enlarging around me into a large circle, my neighbors seemingly far away, while I knew that I could touch them.[26]

Szára was hooked and began to consider possible entry routes into the nascent field of psychedelic research, turning his attention to the flurry of research papers that had followed Hofmann's discovery in the prior decade. Of course, Sandoz had already vetoed any kind of research working with LSD. Mescaline was certainly a possibility. But Szára soon came across a recently published paper that didn't seem to make any sense or, at least, left him feeling that something important had been overlooked. Howard Fabing's article on the effects of bufotenine on the Ohio inmates did little to convince him that bufotenine was indeed the psychoactive alkaloid responsible for the purported powerful visionary effects of the yopo snuff. To Szára, it was perfectly obvious that those seeking communion with the gods were hardly likely to be impressed by the flashes of color coupled with the dangerously hypertensive, choking, and nauseating side effects of this minor frog alkaloid. But so focused was Fabing on bufotenine that he completely neglected the other major alkaloid detected alongside it in extracts of the yopo seeds. Szára wasn't going to make the same mistake.

That other alkaloid of the pair isolated by the chemists at the National Heart Institute, N,N-dimethyltryptamine (now usually referred to simply as DMT), like bufotenine, wasn't exactly new and had been synthesized in 1931 by German-Canadian chemist Richard Manske.[27] As a Ph.D. student at Manchester University, Manske was part of the team that originally characterized and synthesized the harmala alkaloids—harmine and harmaline—in 1927. He then returned to Canada to work at the National Research Laboratories in Ottawa, where he became interested in the highly toxic calycanthine alkaloid mainly found in plants of the genus *Calycanthus*. Based on his analysis of the chemical structure of calycanthine, Manske felt that the then entirely unknown alkaloid, DMT, might prove useful in its synthesis. However, he found the synthesis of DMT, an ostensibly simple molecule, to be more challenging than he had anticipated, and although he was eventually successful in generating enough for full structural characterization, his yields left a lot to be desired. So, after publishing his synthetic procedure, Manske moved onto more promising avenues of research and DMT was abandoned as little more than a chemical curiosity—if that.

Chemically, DMT is perfectly unremarkable. The most that could be said in its favor is that, like bufotenine, it bears an obvious similarity to the neurochemical serotonin. As bufotenine can be described as serotonin with two additional methyl (CH_3) groups attached to the indole side chain, DMT is simply bufotenine minus the hydroxyl (OH) group on the indole ring. There's nothing else striking about its structure, especially compared to the beautifully elaborate four-ring architecture of LSD. In contrast, DMT appears to be something of a blunt instrument. But since it was the only other major alkaloid detected alongside bufotenine in the yopo seed extracts, it made sense for Szára to pursue it. Fortunately, he didn't have to rely on Richard Manske's challenging and inefficient 1931 synthesis to produce enough DMT to begin his work. Less than two years prior, inspired by both LSD and the recent discovery of serotonin, a pair of chemists at the Upjohn Company, Merrill Speeter and William "Bill" Anthony, had published a simple method—now known as the Speeter-Anthony synthesis—for synthesizing bufotenine, but which could readily be applied to other tryptamines, including DMT.[28] Armed with this new synthetic technique, in the spring of 1956, Szára decided to make some and was able to produce ten grams in just a couple of days.

The first tests in experimental animals were promising. A cat, which appeared afraid at first, became "quiet and very friendly" after being injected with the molecule. This effect lasted less than thirty minutes so, if DMT was psychoactive, it seemed to be a rather short-acting drug. After a series of first experiments with increasing dosages in rats, Szára was satisfied that the drug was unlikely to be toxic and was ready to begin the world's first experiments with DMT in human volunteers. First test subject: Dr. Stephen Szára.[29]

Mindful that Albert Hofmann had considered a quarter of a milligram of LSD a conservative first dose and ended up, in Szára's words, "bombed out,"[30] he opted for the same tiny amount, which he ingested orally. Nothing happened. Over the next few days, he gradually increased the dose up to about three quarters of a gram. Still, no effect. Somewhat discouraged and ready to abandon DMT, a colleague suggested that he might try injecting it:

In April of 1956, I tested three doses intramuscularly, paced at least two days apart to allow the drug to clear my body. The first dose (30mg, around 0.4mg/kg) elicited some mild symptoms—dilation of the pupils and some colored geometric forms with closed eyes were already recognizable. Encouraged by these results, I decided to take a larger dose (75mg, around 1.0mg/kg), also intramuscularly. Within three minutes the symptoms started, both the autonomic (tingling, trembling, slight nausea, increased blood pressure and pulse rate) and the perceptual symptoms, such as brilliantly colored oriental motifs, and later, wonderful scenes altering very rapidly.[31]

Although Szára was unable to recall more details of this first experience, it was perfectly obvious that this was a psychedelic of an entirely different order to the largely disappointing bufotenine: "My consciousness was completely filled by hallucinations, and my attention was firmly bound to them."[32]

Szára's first experience displayed the features that would later come to typify the DMT trip: a rapid onset with complex and highly dynamic geometric patterns that soon gave way to fully formed, immersive, and captivating hallucinations. As he slowly returned to normal conscious awareness over the next few minutes, all doubt as to the true identity of the alkaloid responsible for the psychoactive effects of the yopo snuff faded.[33] It was clear to Szára that the afore neglected DMT was the molecule everyone else had been looking for but missed: "I remember feeling intense euphoria at the higher dose levels that I attributed to the excitement of the realization that I, indeed, had discovered a new hallucinogen."[34]

Szára wasted no time in beginning the very first study of the effects of DMT in human subjects, recruiting thirty volunteers, mainly doctors from the National Institute for Mental and Nervous Diseases in Budapest where he worked. All received about 50mg of DMT intramuscularly and their experiences were carefully recorded. Although only a handful of these early DMT trip reports survive, it immediately became clear to Szára that his own experience was far from idiosyncratic. A 28-year-old male physician was one of the first to receive his 50mg dose: "The room is full of spirits. . . . The images come in such profusion that I hardly know where I want to begin with them! I see an orgy of color, but in several layers one after the other. . . . Everything is so comical. . . . One sees curious objects, but nevertheless everything is quickly gone, as if on a roller coaster."[35]

Just like Szára, the physician was overwhelmed by visions that swept over him in a seemingly endless procession. The significance of the curious objects and the uncannily comical aspect to his experience would become clear in the decades that followed, but what was most striking about this early report was the presence of a multitude of discarnate beings that filled the room—it was perhaps a reflection of the time that these entities were described as "spirits."

And this wasn't the only report to describe an encounter with non-human entities. Immediately following some typical initial auditory effects, often described as a high-pitched buzzing or whistling sound, this 27-year-old female physician, Dr. E, describes breaking through into a new realm: "The whistling has stopped; I have arrived. In front of me are two quiet, sunlit gods. They gaze at me and nod in a friendly manner. I think they are welcoming me into this new world. . . . One of the gods—only his eyes are alive—speaks to me: 'Do you feel better?'"[36]

Dr. E couldn't help but feel that she'd entered a world more real than the one she'd left behind and, sadly, the one she would soon return to:

The dimensions are strange, still. The whole world is frightfully realistic. This is the true color and shape of things. Dangerous game; it would be so easy not to return. I am faintly aware that I am a doctor, but this is not important; family ties, studies, plans, and memories are very remote from me. Only this world is important; I am free and entirely alone.

Back, back, I urge myself. I must find the way back to the real world. On the way home, I meet an acquaintance on the bus. I begin to chat with him, in order to get back the feeling of reality. The trees along the streets look gray and faded. Life is dull, unfriendly, and monotonous.[37]

Unfortunately, Szára was largely unaware of the significance of the appearance of these entities in his first cohort of test subjects, and as such, his subjects weren't pressed to elaborate on their experiences and the reports can seem terse compared to those that would emerge later. However, it was immediately clear that DMT was unlike any of the other known psychedelics. Whereas reports of LSD, mescaline, and *Psilocybe* mushroom intoxication described sensory distortions, enhanced color perception, alterations in time perception, and other shifts in the structure and dynamics of the experienced world, DMT seemed to transcend this, not only eliciting fully immersive and overwhelming visions, but apparently transporting the user to an entirely different world—a world populated by nonhuman discarnate beings.

As well as healthy volunteers, Szára was also keen to observe the effects of DMT in some of the psychiatric patients at the hospital. There was a growing belief in psychiatry that these new "psychotogenic" agents, specifically LSD and mescaline, might be useful in the treatment of psychosis, or at least as tools to study the disease. Szára selected twenty-four female inpatients, the majority with a diagnosis of schizophrenia, and all were given 1mg/kg DMT intramuscularly.[38] Only three case reports were featured in the resulting publication and these were objective accounts of the patients' behavior after DMT administration, as recorded by the physician—any insight into the subjective experiences of the patients could only be gleaned from their spontaneous utterances. Despite this, one of the case reports is particularly salient. The patient was a 30-year-old female with "persecutory delusion and paranoid behavior." A few minutes after the DMT was administered, the typical auditory effects began: "She complains of a strange feeling, tinnitus, buzzing in the ear."

A period of agitation and confusion followed—"she keeps asking, 'Why do I feel so strange?'"—and then, after about thirty minutes, she seemed to indicate some loss of body awareness, also common in DMT users, which is echoed later in the session: "As if my heart would not beat, as if I had no body, no nothing."

Then, around thirty minutes after the injection, her head began to clear and she was able to recount her visions: "I saw such strange dreams, but at the beginning only . . . I saw strange creatures, dwarfs or something; they were black and moved about."[39]

Although this is only a single case study, its significance ought to be obvious. Just as the Yanomami and other Indigenous groups consistently report visions and interactions with a multitude of lively "little people" following inhalation of yopo and epena snuffs, here we have a report of dynamic diminutive beings under the influence of one of the major alkaloids isolated from the primary plant component of at least one of these snuff variants. The visionary properties of the jungle technology had been reduced to a single, simple alkaloid capable not only of inducing profound mind-altering effects, but of replicating the original function of the technology: to render normally hidden discarnate intelligences visible to conscious awareness. Szára had quite obviously made a tremendous breakthrough in our understanding of how at least one of these visionary plant technologies worked. But even in these early reports there seemed to be an indication that DMT in its pure form had the ability to transcend even the most potent versions of the Amazonian plant-derived preparations, dissolving the normal waking world and replacing it with an entirely new, far stranger one. Szára's breakthrough was just the beginning, as William Burroughs was also about to discover. The little people had not only escaped the tropical rain forests of Amazonia but had already found their way to a Soviet psychiatric hospital on the outskirts of Budapest. And they were just getting started.

5

NIGHTMARE DRUG

It is difficult to describe what is impossible to imagine.
—Cristina Rivera Garza

In the summer of 1956, shortly after Stephen Szára discovered the remarkable visionary effects of DMT, William Burroughs penned a letter to the British Journal of Addiction, providing a personal survey and appraisal of a medley of psychoactive and narcotic drugs—from morphine to cocaine to peyote—he'd consumed over a career spanning more than two decades.[1] Naturally, this somewhat unusual monograph also included his unique insights into the ayahuasca brew gleaned during his recent expeditions through South America. Although more than a century had passed since Richard Spruce first choked down that repulsive green soup on the banks of the Vaupes River, the source of ayahuasca's visionary powers remained largely a mystery. The harmala alkaloids, which by then had been isolated and purified from the *Banisteriopsis caapi* vine by numerous scientists, certainly didn't appear to elicit anything beyond a rather unimpressive drunkenness and a subsequent urge to lie down and sleep. Having confirmed this for himself as he ambled from shaman to shaman, leaving a trail of vomit between them, Burroughs finally made a breakthrough when he was let into the trade secret of the Peruvian shamans: Along with the stripped bark of the caapi vine, a handful of the leaves of a second plant—tentatively identified as a *Palicourea* species from the *Rubiacecae* family—must be added to the boiling mixture, leading Burroughs to speculate on another catalyzing component within the leaf essential to realize the full visionary effects of the brew. The identity and even the existence of this other component, however, remained unknown.

But Burroughs's speculations didn't stop there: "Since the crude extract is such a powerful, hallucinating narcotic, perhaps even more spectacular results could be obtained with synthetic variations. Certainly the matter warrants further research."[2]

He had no idea how right he was.

The following year, a pair of medicinal chemists working at the Pfizer company, Frank Hochstein and Anita Paradies, were about to make a rather bold claim. They were working on caapi vine collected by a botanist in Peru, with the botanical identity of the samples confirmed by eminent Peruvian botanist Ramon Ferreyra at the University of San Marcos in Lima. As several others had before them, they were able to isolate harmine and harmaline, as well as some minor analogs, from extracts of the vine—nothing to get too excited about. However, they also received in the same shipment about two liters of a dirty green liquid, claimed to be an aqueous extract of a plant called "yagé," used as an admixture in the ayahuasca brew alongside the caapi vine. In 1922, anthropologist Pierre Reinburg and Belgian botanist Florent Claes had independently reported the addition of a "secret" plant to the ayahuasca decoction, also called "yagé," but which they were unable—or weren't permitted—to collect and identify. But the aqueous extract of yagé received by Hochstein and Paradies *had* been identified: *Prestonia amazonicum*, a member of the *Apocynaceae* or dogbane family.[3]

Recognizing the potential ethnobotanical importance of this liquid, the pair eagerly set to work separating the alkaloids, reducing the two liters down to about three grams of a colorless oil that crystallized spontaneously. Half expecting the extract to merely be another source of harmala alkaloids, they first tested its melting point. Crystals of harmine melt at just over 260 degrees Celsius, but these crystals began to melt at only 46 degrees. This was something else. Further chemical analyses confirmed that both harmine and harmaline were completely absent from the extract. They had, in fact, isolated and purified an entirely different alkaloid: N,N-dimethyltryptamine (DMT).

In light of Stephen Szára's recent publication on the psychedelic effects of DMT isolated from the seeds of *Anadenanthera peregrina* (used to make the yopo snuff), finding DMT in a plant used to make the ayahuasca decoction was of exceptional significance, and soon after their report was published, it inevitably caught the attention of peerless ayahuasca expert Richard Schultes. But rather than celebrating the discovery of the elusive visionary component of the potion, Schultes's response could best be described as a mixture of skepticism and confusion. Firstly, Schultes knew *Prestonia amazonicum* to be a rare plant with an extremely limited geographical range, so it seemed unlikely that natives would be employing it in abundance across all regions that used ayahuasca. Secondly, if *Prestonia* was a source of DMT, it would be the only plant in the *Apocynaceae* family to contain any simple indole alkaloids at all.[4] It all seemed quite improbable, so Schultes wrote to Ramon Ferreyra, who had apparently identified the botanical samples sent to Hochstein, for clarification. His response wasn't encouraging: Although Ferreyra had indeed identified the caapi vine, he had nothing to do with, and was completely unaware of the existence of, the dirty green liquid claimed to be an extract of *Prestonia amazonicum*.[5] In the absence of any vouched plant specimens to accompany the aqueous extract, Schultes could only conclude that the plant had most likely been misidentified, and while the sample obtained by Hochstein most certainly contained DMT, it was unlikely to be an extract of *Prestonia amazonicum*. So what was it? Frankly, nobody had a clue.

Whatever the true identity of the "*Prestonia amazonicum*" extract, the word was out that the elusive missing piece of the ayahuasca brew had been identified and, most significantly, that it contained Stephen Szára's recently discovered psychedelic alkaloid, DMT. And although its veracity remained very much in doubt, this word soon reached the ears of a young chemistry lecturer at Imperial College London. Dennis Evans, as well as making several important contributions to nuclear magnetic resonance spectroscopy, also maintained a keen extracurricular interest in exotic pets—including scorpions, a Cayman Islands alligator, and a five-foot snake called George—and exotic psychoactive molecules, which he would synthesize and personally bioassay in his basement lab. He also happened to be a friend of none other than William S. Burroughs, who would regularly visit Evans's lab to test his products, including optimizing a blend of heroin and cocaine with the aim of producing the perfect speedball. Not surprisingly, when Evans caught wind of Hochstein and Paradies's breakthrough discovery of DMT in the ayahuasca brew, he soon added it to his basement lab product line.[6]

Burroughs received a sample of the DMT from Evans, which he referred to as "Prestonia"—after the plant from which Hochstein claimed to have isolated the alkaloid—while staying in the international zone of Tangier, Morocco, in March of 1961.[7] There's no evidence from his writings that Burroughs ever made the connection between Prestonia and the trade secret he'd observed being added to ayahuasca in Peru in 1953, but based on the work of Richard Schultes and others, it's highly likely that both Burroughs's and Hochstein's suppliers had misidentified the same plant. In other words, the secret component of the ayahuasca brew was indeed a DMT-containing plant, but its true identity remained unconfirmed. So, whether or not he realized it, Burroughs was about to test his hypothesis that "even more spectacular results could be obtained with synthetic variations" of ayahuasca.

The Prestonia—DMT—arrived as a white powder, and in the company of his friend—composer, author, and longtime Tangier resident Paul Bowles—Burroughs settled in for his very first experience with the then rare and exotic Amazonian psychedelic. Unsure whether to inhale or inject the powder, Bowles opted for the less invasive nasal route—he wanted nothing to do with needles—while Burroughs obviously had no issues with the latter mode of administration. After sprinkling a little of the powder onto the table for Bowles, Burroughs excused himself and went to the kitchen to prepare an injection. Bowles arranged the unknown quantity of powder into a small cone, then lowered his head to the table and sniffed sharply. Almost immediately the DMT exploded in his brain as his skull cracked and flew open, hurling his entire being thousands of miles into the air, neither here nor there nor anywhere, and utterly alone. Shocked, astonished, and terrified, Bowles didn't recall the details of the visions that followed over the next few minutes. All he knew was that he had absolutely no idea or conception of what had just happened to him.

Burroughs returned just as Bowles was coming down from his trip: "How was it?" Burroughs asked.

"I don't know," was all Bowles could offer in reply.[8]

Burroughs's first experience after injecting around 60mg of the powder was less explosive than Bowles's, and he compared its effects to those of *Psilocybe* mushrooms,[9] albeit only lasting about half an hour. Over the following month, he injected the drug close to a dozen times, hoping that his experiences would generate material for a new novel, and while he admitted that his trips were occasionally unpleasant, he always felt in complete control. But that would soon change.

Barely a month after his first injection—which was probably the first time anyone outside of a clinic or research institute had injected DMT—Burroughs decided to push his usual dose of 60mg to almost 100mg which, in retrospect, was most decidedly on the heavy end. Things didn't go as expected:

> A blast of pain and hate shook the room as the shot of dim-N hit, and I was captured in enemy territory Power of Sammy the Butcher. The Ovens closed round me glowing metal lattice in purple and blue and pink screaming burning Hash flesh under meat cleaver of Sammy the Butcher and pitiless insect eyes of white-hot crab creatures of The Ovens . . . No place to go trapped here cut off tried to slip out on The Gray into mirrors and spoons and doorways of the Fish City, but by my smoke escape was cut off by white-hot metal lattice in this soulless place of The Insect People. Place of Dry Air shriveling envelopes of larval flesh—white-hot blue sky—Insect eyes of The Alien Species—the Soulless Insect People.[10]

After several weeks of relatively tame and manageable trips, Burroughs had crossed a threshold and broken through into some kind of hell realm; a decidedly menacing netherworld populated by equally menacing nonhuman entities. It's hard not to make the connection between the "Soulless Insect People" and the vicious Warusinari insect beings so feared by the Yanomami people and occasionally encountered after inhaling yopo or epena snuff. The Yanomami make it quite clear that the Hidden Ones form a diverse invisible ecology of beings of varying form and character, from the friendly and jovial to the wicked and ferocious, so it isn't so surprising that Burroughs should eventually encounter beings from the more objectionable end of that spectrum. Yet there was something uncanny about his experience. Something strikingly unearthly. Something quite distinctly alien.

Unsurprisingly, Burroughs was both shocked and horrified by this encounter with The Alien Species and DMT immediately became "strictly the nightmare hallucinogen."[11] But then, in March of 1961, no doubt with the very best of intentions, he unwittingly released the Insect People into the wild by penning a breathless letter of warning to the budding high priest of the psychedelic revolution, Dr. Timothy Leary: "I would like to sound a word of urgent warning with regard to the hallucinogen drugs with special reference to N-Dimethyltryptamine (sic). . . . It was completely and horribly real and involved unendurable pain. . . . I think you will readily see the danger involved."[12]

The 38-year-old tweed-jacketed Harvard psychologist was still very much a psychedelic neophyte, having had his first life-transforming experience with *Psilocybe* mushrooms just the previous summer while staying in the town of Cuernavaca, south of Mexico City.[13] He wouldn't take the drug to which his name is most famously attached—LSD—until the fall of 1961, but such was the impact of that first mushroom experience, he had already decided to dedicate his life to the study of psychedelics. Leary soon began to make a name for himself among the burgeoning hippie and underground literary cultures, as well as making use of his stellar Harvard credentials to ingratiate himself with the likes of Albert Hofmann and *The Doors of Perception* author Aldous Huxley. Earlier in 1961, beat poet Allen Ginsberg had urged Leary to write to Burroughs and bring him into the psilocybin project Leary was planning at Harvard, and they soon began a regular correspondence.[14] Perhaps predictably, in retrospect, given Leary's already blossoming romance with this novel class of mind-altering drugs, when Burroughs's letter of "urgent warning" arrived, it didn't quite have the effect Burroughs intended.

By the fall of 1962, Leary and a core group of researchers and acolytes had begun living in a communal house in Newton Center, not far from Leary's Harvard office, where they worked mainly with psilocybin and later LSD.[15] But apparently more intrigued than disturbed by Burroughs's reports of being tortured by insectoid aliens while trapped in latticed white-hot ovens, Leary was keen to also begin working with DMT. The Newton Center house was remodeled to include a secret room accessible only from the basement within which to conduct one of the world's first underground research programs with Burroughs's nightmare hallucinogen. Although Leary hadn't actually experimented with DMT himself, he had to some extent absorbed Burroughs's paranoia, referring to the drug as "the horror-show drug of the psychedelic family" with a pronounced tendency to catapult "the voyager into strange and decidedly unfriendly territory."[16] This reputation was cemented during a conversation with a Los Angeles psychiatrist, Oscar Janiger, who claimed to have already given DMT to over a hundred subjects, only four of whom had positive experiences. Janiger was an early advocate for the use of psychedelics, especially LSD, as tools for mind expansion and for enhancing human creativity, and would regularly give his clients the drug in his LA private practice until the US government began clamping down on psychedelic researchers in the early 1960s.[17] When Stephen Szára began publishing his early work with DMT, Janiger's interest was piqued. Although less horrifying than Burroughs's insectoid episode, Janiger's first experiment with an unknowingly high dose of DMT injected in his rear elicited some distinctly unearthly effects: "Man, I was in a strange place, the strangest. I was in a world that was like being inside of a pinball machine. The only thing like it, oddly enough, was in a movie called *Zardoz*, where a man is trapped inside of a crystal. It was angular, electronic, filled with all kinds of strange over-beats and electronic circuits, flashes, and movements. It looked like an ultra souped-up disco, where lights are coming from every direction. Just extraordinary."[18]

This was yet another early indication that, at least in the higher dose ranges, DMT had an unusual ability to gate access to realms that seemed inorganic, nonhuman, alien, and weren't exactly what was expected from the reports of the alkaloid's effects in traditional Amazonian plant preparations.

By this point, Leary had already formulated his so-called "set and setting" hypothesis, by which the nature and content of a psychedelic experience was said to be a function of both the internal mental state of the tripper and their external environment. Janiger's claims that DMT elicited entirely negative experiences in more than 90 percent of subjects seemed to be a direct challenge to this model. Challenge accepted; the first DMT session was arranged.

On the appointed day, Timothy Leary and clinical psychologist Richard Alpert arrived at Janiger's house, together with a Vedanta monk and two female friends. It seems Leary might have taken Burroughs's letter of warning to heart after all and offered the couch first to Alpert. Sixty milligrams was administered intramuscularly and within a couple of minutes, much to Leary's relief, Alpert's face took on an almost angelic countenance as he began to gasp and murmur with joy. Twenty-five minutes later, he grinned, sat up, and said: "It lasted for a million years and for a split second. But it's over and now it's your turn."[19] Reassured by Alpert's glowingly positive reaction to the drug, Leary replaced him on the couch, the injection was administered, and Leary closed his eyes and waited. Five minutes later, the visions began:

> The room was celestial, glowing with radiant illumination . . . light . . . light . . . light . . . the people present were transfigured . . . godlike creatures . . . we were all united as one organism. Beneath the radiant surface I could see the delicate, wondrous body machinery of each person, the network of muscle and vein and bone—exquisitely beautiful and all joined, all part of the same process. There was never a second of fear or negative emotion.[20]

Leary was both thoroughly awestruck and now quite satisfied that, despite Burroughs's stark warning and contrary to the experiences of Janiger's subjects, with the appropriate set and setting, the DMT trip could not only be entirely positive, but positively beatific. However, it should be noted that the dose both Leary and Alpert received, 60mg by intramuscular injection, was much lower than that both Burroughs (around 100mg) and Janiger (he doesn't specify, but claimed it was an "enormous dose"[21]) injected when they lost complete awareness of their surroundings and broke through into an entirely new, entirely alien, world. While Leary's trip was most certainly highly visual, he maintained the ability to observe his surroundings with his eyes open, even comparing the first few minutes to LSD. Now we would call Leary's first trip "sub-breakthrough," but at the time, it was an indication that pushing to a higher dosage doesn't merely increase the intensity of the experience, but that, beyond some kind of threshold, DMT has the ability to completely "switch the reality channel" as all contact with the environment is lost and the user is transported to an entirely novel alternate world.

Leary was now keen to study the nature and content of the DMT state much more thoroughly and having secured a steady supply of the molecule from a local drug company, plans to put the Newton House basement room—dubbed the "Time Chamber"—to its intended use were initiated.[22] For the first of these sessions, Leary enlisted the guidance of fellow Harvard psychedelic enthusiast psychopharmacologist Ralph Metzner to act as "interrogator," and at precisely 8:10 p.m. one evening, Leary lay back on a mattress, and just like the first time, received 60mg of DMT by intramuscular injection and closed his eyes: "Suddenly, as if someone touched a button, the static darkness of retina is illuminated . . . enormous toy-jewel-clock factory, Santa Claus workshop . . . not impersonal or engineered, but jolly, comic, lighthearted. The evolutionary dance, humming with energy, billions of variegated forms spinning, clicking through their appointed rounds in the smooth ballet."[23]

Leary's account of this early phase of his second trip is strikingly similar to one from Stephen Szára's very first study several years earlier: "Everything is so comical . . . one sees curious objects, but nevertheless everything is quickly gone, as if on a roller coaster."

Curious as to how the outside world might appear, Leary then opened his eyes and was greeted, not by Metzner, but by something quite unexpected: "There squatting next to me are two magnificent insects . . . skin burnished, glowing metallic, with hammered jewels inlaid . . . richly costumed, they looked at me sweetly . . . dear, radiant Venutian crickets. . . . One has a pad on his lap and is holding out a gem-encrusted box with undulating trapezoidal glowing sections. . . . Questioning look. . . . Incredible."[24]

Incredible indeed. Again, he closed his eyes: "Back to dancing workshop . . . joy . . . incredible beauty . . . the wonder, wonder, wonder . . . all hooked together . . . everything fits into the moist, pulsating pattern . . . a huge gray-white mountain cliff, moving, pocked by little caves and in each cave a band of radar-antennae, elf-like insects merrily working away, each cave the same, the gray-white wall endlessly parading by . . . infinity of life-forms."[25]

Far from a nightmare, Leary had entered a magical realm bursting with energy, intelligence, and life, all suffused with a jovial, comical ambience: the "*magnificent insects*" proffering strange but beautiful objects; the merry elfin beings busily working away within the endless passages and anterooms of this most wondrous of worlds. This time, despite receiving the same dose as the first time, Leary had broken through, not only into a new world but a vast alternate universe that hummed and pulsated in perfect crystalline clarity "that made ordinary reality seem like an out-of-focus, tattered, jerky, fluttering of peep-show cards, tawdry and worn."[26] This was no nightmare drug. This was a wonder drug. This was pure neurochemical magic.

Buoyed by the ineffable beauty of his second experience, Leary, together with Alpert and Metzner, would go on to perform over a hundred DMT sessions from the Time Chamber over the following months, with over 90 percent of the subjects having positive experiences with the drug. However, despite Leary's excitement over the potential of this marvelous medicine and the steady stream of both experienced and novice psychedelic explorers who drifted in and out of the Time Chamber, DMT remained, at least for the following few years, a niche psychedelic entirely eclipsed by its much more famous tryptamine cousin, LSD, which was both orally active and so extraordinarily potent that several hundred doses could be dispersed into the fibers of a single sheet of blotting paper. DMT, on the other hand, as Stephen

Szára had learned as he came close to abandoning the molecule, was completely inactive when taken by mouth and needed to be formulated as an injectable solution to be administered either intramuscularly or intravenously—an obvious obstacle to the spread of its use among the needle-wary majority of psychedelic drug users. But as so often seems to be the case in the history of scientific discoveries, a moment of serendipity would soon change all that.

By the fall of 1963, Leary and his crew had left Newton House and relocated to the 2,300-acre Millbrook Estate in Upstate New York, where their work with LSD continued.[27] One of the many visitors to the estate was the talented young psychedelic chemist Nick Sand, who would later become known for producing the legendary batch of highly pure LSD known as "Orange Sunshine." When Richard Alpert first met Sand following a lecture at Brooklyn College where Sand was a student, Sand was running his own clandestine laboratory in the basement of his mother's house. Alpert was invited to see his operation and, deeply impressed by his work, invited Sand up to Millbrook, where he would eventually become Leary's chief chemist.[28] During his time at Millbrook, in the summer of 1965, Sand was introduced to fellow clandestine chemist Owsley Stanley, who would later be dubbed the Acid King by the media, producing upward of five million doses of LSD in little more than a couple of years between 1965 and 1967. Although Sand had already succeeded in synthesizing DMT before meeting Owsley—and was in fact the first underground chemist to do so—his product didn't have a particularly good reputation. Rather than being a pure white crystalline powder, Sand's DMT was more of a yellowish-orange paste. It also stank.[29] It isn't clear which synthetic route to DMT Sand used, but the most popular method pioneered by Speeter and Anthony (and used by Stephen Szára) uses a molecule called indole as a starting material, which can impart a pungent mothball aroma to a poorly purified product. Other synthetic routes have the potential to produce skatole—the indole derivative that gives feces its smell—as a side product, and if this isn't properly removed during purification, there's a real possibility of the final product smelling, quite literally, like shit. And who in their right mind wants to inject a drug that smells like shit? Under the tutelage of Owsley, Sand upped his game tremendously, however, and later became an exemplary chemist producing some of the finest DMT available anywhere in America, with between 20 and 30kg of the molecule exiting his laboratory during his clandestine chemistry career. But even with Sand's product on the up, there was still the needle issue. Few people liked to mess with needles.

Sometime during 1965—the exact date unknown—Sand was purifying DMT in his laboratory when a few of the crystals happened to fall on a lab hot plate, instantly melting and bubbling before emitting a cloud of white vapor, leaving no trace whatsoever on the metal surface. As the distinctive indolic aroma tickled Sand's nasal passages, a question crystallized in his mind: *Can we just smoke this stuff?*[30]

In retrospect, the idea that the hypodermic needle might be avoided altogether and DMT simply smoked seems obvious. Even in 1965, smoking as a mode of drug administration was hardly new—think tobacco and opium. But for some reason, it had never occurred to anyone that DMT might also be consumed in this way. Whether or not a drug—particularly an alkaloid, such as cocaine, morphine, or DMT—can be smoked often depends on how it's formulated during production. Alkaloids come in two basic forms: a salt form and a freebase form. The salt form can usually be dissolved in water for either intramuscular or intravenous injection. DMT fumarate is the most well-known salt of DMT and is likely what everyone had been using up until that point. However, when heated, salts will generally pyrolyze—burn—before they vaporize, destroying the molecule. The freebase, on the other hand, is generally insoluble in water and cannot be injected. However, unlike the salt, the freebase will tend to melt and then vaporize; the vapor can then be inhaled. In this moment of perfectly quotidian carelessness, Nick Sand had done something revolutionary, transforming the consumption of DMT from a rather fiddly and unpleasant affair requiring special equipment and skills to something anyone with access to a glass pipe and butane lighter could perform at home or pretty much anywhere. But smokeable freebase DMT wasn't only more accessible and convenient—the experience itself was dramatically different.

When a drug is injected intramuscularly, absorption into the bloodstream depends on small vessel blood supply to the muscle and is surprisingly slow and often erratic and incomplete—recall the difference between Leary's first and second trips with the same dose. The initial effects of intramuscular DMT begin only several minutes following the injection and then build gradually as the drug is slowly flushed from the injection site into the circulation. The subjective effect is a gradual immersion into the experience, which lasts for around thirty minutes. Compared to the muscles, the lungs have a much richer blood supply, so when vaporized DMT is inhaled, it enters the circulation much more rapidly, causing a sharp increase in blood concentration that peaks at a much higher level. This makes it much more likely that a cleanly vaporized hit of DMT will push the blood and brain concentration past the "reality switching" threshold experienced by both Burroughs and Janiger. The subjective effects begin before the pipe even leaves the lips and rather than the gradual dissolution of the normal waking world, vaporized DMT obliterates it, firing the person taking it across an invisible veil with such force that the immediate psychological response is one of shock and astonishment. Mercifully, although more intense— cataclysmic, ferocious, unyielding—the trip is much briefer, and by the time you've gotten over the shock and oriented yourself within the space, you're already being dragged back into the old familiar world.

Following his discovery, both Sand and Owsley, although focused on LSD, also maintained a small-scale production of freebase DMT, with their convenient smokeable product spreading rapidly across the West Coast of America, including among the Hell's Angels, who were plied with the drug in return for the raw materials for LSD manufacture.[31] Their product also found its way into the hands of the young chemistry student Rick Watson who, in 1965, had his first taste of LSD courtesy of Merry Prankster Ken Kesey, but soon found his attention drawn toward the short-acting powerhouse of psychedelics that had by then become known in psychedelic circles as the "businessman's trip." One rainy February evening in 1967, Watson decided to visit a friend in Berkeley, carrying a sample of freebase DMT he'd acquired from Kesey's circle—likely the product of Owsley Stanley.[32] Terence McKenna answered the door and Watson fished the DMT from his pocket: "Here's something that you might be interested in."

The twenty-year-old McKenna had recently enrolled at the University of California at Berkeley and was already something of an intellectual well-versed in matters of the mind. He'd immersed himself in the works of psychologist Carl Jung since he was a teen, he'd read *Finnegans Wake* as well as all of the works of Aldous Huxley and, in recent years, had become acquainted with the unusual states of consciousness reached with seeds of the morning glory plant and, of course, Albert Hofmann's semisynthetic lysergic acid derivative, LSD. All of this, naturally, on a background of daily cannabis consumption. He was as ready as anybody, which is to say: entirely unprepared.

"Well, what is it?" McKenna examined the curious material similar in appearance to "orange mothballs"—if it was Owsley's, it wasn't one of his cleanest batches.

"Well, it's short-acting—it's a flash. . . . It's called DMT."

"OK, we'll do it."[33]

Whatever McKenna might have been expecting or anticipating, what followed a few seconds later wasn't it:

> There was a something, like a flower, like a chrysanthemum in orange and yellow that was sort of spinning, spinning, and then it was like I was pushed from behind and I fell through the chrysanthemum into another place that didn't seem like a state of mind, it seemed like another place . . . a brightly lit, inhabited, non-three-dimensional, self-contorting, sustained, organic, linguistically intending modality that couldn't be stopped or held back or denied. I sank to the floor—I couldn't move. I had a hallucination of tumbling forward into fractal geometric spaces made of light, and then I found myself in the sort of auric equivalent of the Pope's private chapel, and there were insect elf machines proffering strange little tablets with strange writing on them.[34]

The entirely DMT-naive McKenna who, five minutes earlier, had never even heard of this molecule, had suddenly and quite inexplicably found himself among the elfin beings observed by Leary a few years earlier. But these ones had something to say—of sorts: "They were speaking in some kind of—there were these self-transforming machine-elf creatures—were speaking in some kind of colored language which condensed into rotating machines that were like Faberge eggs, but crafted out of luminescent super-conducting ceramics, and liquid crystal gels, and all this stuff was so weird, and so alien, and so 'un-Englishable' that it was a complete shock."[35]

Following Burroughs, Leary, and Janiger—among many others—McKenna had been propelled into an alternate dimension that was not merely a strange or enchanted realm populated by dancing forest imps or angels of the astral planes, but a thoroughly alien universe entirely disjointed from the mundane three-dimensional world he'd left behind. In that moment, the entire ontological foundation of his reality had been extirpated: "I can't believe it. It's impossible. It's impossible. . . . I was aghast, completely—appalled—because the transition had been a matter of seconds and my entire expectation of the nature of the world was being shredded in front of me. I've never gotten over it."[36]

Later that same year, Terence and his younger brother Dennis, then only sixteen, were lying in a park in Berkeley enjoying the sun, passing around a joint, and pontificating on the mysteries of the universe. Naturally, the conversation soon turned to "the ultimate metaphysical reality pill" that Terence had first experienced on that rainy evening in February. With his effortless eloquence, Terence had Dennis captivated—he had to try this stuff. Unfortunately, Terence wasn't carrying, but later that year, he would get the chance. Terence managed to procure a few grams of the waxy orange paste and Dennis took some home. His first experience with smoked DMT was typical: "On the second toke, I struggled to hold in the foul-tasting smoke as I watched reality dissolve before my eyes into a billion scintillating fractal jewels, all transforming and squirming before my eyes like iridescent jellyfish while a buzzing, burbling, ripping sound like cellophane being torn to shreds echoed through my aural space; there was a feeling of literally tearing loose, accelerating, falling forward, faster and faster into a twisting, writhing tube or tunnel lined with glistening jewels, a supersonic roller coaster careening through the intestines of God."[37]

As now seemed to be the standard course after a couple of lungfuls of cleanly vaporized freebase DMT, the rapid procession of highly complex geometric imagery soon gave way and McKenna the Younger broke through to the other side: "There was definitely a feeling of movement, and of crossing a threshold of some kind, of briefly poking one's head into a parallel dimension where the most astonishing things imaginable were going on, all in a frenetic, circus-like atmosphere of hilarious ecstasy. It's almost as if this dimension is always there, just a toke away, and these things, these entities, are bouncing around and cheering, 'So happy to see you, so happy to meet you, meat-worm, welcome to our world, won't you join the fun?' It was the ultimate carnival ride: Climb aboard and away we'll go!"[38]

Having had time to reflect on this first trip, Dennis was unequivocal in his appraisal of what and whom he had encountered: "I encountered other creatures whose environment was this alien universe that I had broken through to. I became aware of, perhaps entered into communication with, actual distinct and separate consciousnesses, members of a race of beings that live in that place, wherever that place may be. . . . I can say no more as to the nature of these beings except that they do exist."[39]

Whether or not these beings truly exist, for each of the McKenna brothers, that first visit to the DMT realms was an event of unimaginable import. But it was more than that: Their experiences, and the experiences of Burroughs, Leary, Janiger, and others, were confirmation that DMT, if ingested at a sufficient dose level, was able to do something to the human mind that nobody could have anticipated—something that didn't make any sense. This wasn't supposed to happen. This was a simple tryptamine alkaloid isolated from a pair of Amazonian plants used to communicate with the Hidden Ones of the forests. We were promised "birds with radiant plumage," "all the wonders of the Arabian Nights," a glowing chorus of hekura in feathered headdresses, playing flutes, and dancing to a lilting pentatonic air. Not self-transforming machine elves crafting syntactical structures from liquid crystal gels. Not Soulless Insect People. Not alien intelligence. Were these really the little people Schultes's young Witoto assistant had spoken of? Were these odd creatures what the Yanomami called the hekura? Whatever this place was, it appeared to have nothing to do with the rain forests or its people—or indeed any people. It had nothing to do with anything on Earth, or this universe, or any other place we might or might not want to imagine. It was beyond our ability to imagine. It was completely and utterly alien.

6

THE SECRET

You see, a secret is not something untold. It's something which can't be told.

—Terence McKenna

For both the McKenna brothers, and for anyone else with the courage and respiratory fortitude to hold a couple of lungfuls of its vapor in their lungs, DMT was no longer a secret. It was *the* secret. And the secret was out. By the mid-1960s, dozens of circles, sects, brotherhoods and sisterhoods centered on the newly discovered mind-expanding medicines that had emerged, with Timothy Leary's League for Spiritual Discovery, founded at Millbrook, being the largest and most influential.[1] However, while these sects primarily focused on LSD and *Psilocybe* mushrooms as quasi-religious tools for spiritual transcendence, following the publication of Leary's earliest experiences with the drug, it wasn't long before DMT was also elevated to sacramental status. Also founded at Millbrook by psychologist-turned-psychedelic-activist Arthur Kleps, the much smaller sect, the Neo-American Church,[2] produced and distributed a small booklet, *The Psychedelic Guide to Preparation of the Eucharist in a Few of its Many Guises*, which provided detailed—and highly technical—procedures for the chemical synthesis of a range of psychedelic molecules, including LSD, psilocybin, mescaline, and DMT.[3] Although this likely inspired some clandestine chemists to begin adding DMT to their product line, there was little incentive for them to divert their resources from an already wildly popular and extraordinarily potent lysergic acid derivative yielding ten thousand doses per gram to one that yielded barely three dozen. Despite Nick Sand's breakthrough discovery that DMT could be smoked (or, more correctly, vaporized), there was no way it could compete with LSD, and it remained relatively rare on the underground drug market. And even armed with the Neo-American Church's guidebook, anyone but the most serious of chemists attempting to make it for themselves would likely have struggled to execute the fairly advanced chemistry required to complete the synthesis, even if they were able to obtain the requisite chemical precursors.

So, while more and more people were beginning to hear about this extraordinary new psychedelic, very few actually had the opportunity to try it for themselves, and if "the secret" was to spread beyond the small clutch of committed psychedelic enthusiasts with a penchant for the more exotic members of this drug class, together with the necessary connections to procure it, it would need another little push. This would eventually come, not from the clandestine chemists of West Coast America, however, but from the ethnobotanists working deep in the rain forests of South America. Likely entirely ignorant of the strange elfin creatures bouncing around the brains of the McKenna brothers and Leary's acolytes, the ethnobotanists were still arguing among themselves about the jungle technology that, partly thanks to Hochstein and Paradies's controversial "*Prestonia amazonicum*" paper, had by then become most closely associated with DMT: ayahuasca.

Despite the impact of Stephen Szára's discovery of the uniquely visionary properties of DMT, coupled with Hochstein and Paradies's isolation of the alkaloid from a key plant component of the brew, many scientists remained unconvinced that DMT had anything to do with ayahuasca. Firstly, Richard Schultes had been quite vocal in expressing his doubts over the identity of the plant extract obtained by Hochstein. And secondly, it was by then perfectly well known that DMT was completely inactive when consumed orally, so it made little sense that it would form the central psychoactive component of a visionary *drink*. But then again, it seemed to stretch credulity that Hochstein might have received a plant extract that, while having no psychoactive role in the ayahuasca brew, just happened to contain high concentrations of a powerful visionary alkaloid. It made little sense, and making it make sense was no simple business. Rather than a single standard ayahuasca recipe to analyze and deconstruct, ethnobotanists were faced with a plethora of different variants of the potion complicated by a gamut of admixture plants. Almost a hundred different species from around three dozen plant families have been documented being added to the ayahuasca decoction alongside the caapi vine.[4] The Siona people of the Putumayo in Colombia recognized at least seventeen varieties of the ayahuasca brew, and the Barasana people of the Rio Piraparana boasted no less than thirty distinct variations, each with its own name and admixture plant components.[5] And to complicate matters even further, since each admixture plant often went by several different names depending on a particular Indigenous group, their location, and the local tongue, even formally identifying each plant in a particular ayahuasca recipe was a formidable task, let alone delineating its role—if any—in the brew's psychoactive effects. Although more than a century had passed since Richard Spruce first tasted the ayahuasca potion on the banks of the Rio Vaupes, and despite the remarkable progress made in deconstructing the alkaloid composition of the caapi vine, everyone seemed as confused as ever, prompting Schultes to lament: "Here we are still standing on the threshold with one hand on the knob of a door just set ajar, not yet opened."[6]

That door was finally kicked off its hinges when ethnobotanist Homer Pinkley, a graduate student of Richard Schultes, arrived in the small village of Dureno, Ecuador—home of the Kofan people and some of the greatest ayahuasca artists in South America.[7] William Burroughs had previously described what he referred to as the "Kofan method" of ayahuasca preparation that required the leaves of a secret second plant essential for the full visionary effects. During his work with the Kofan, Pinkley also caught wind of an additional plant added along with the caapi vine that allowed drinkers of the decoction to see beings known as *oprito*, meaning "small heavenly people."[8] A plant that allowed you to see little people—surely this must have been a clue?

One evening in the spring of 1966, following the death of a tribal chief, a group of around twenty Kofan men and boys gathered in the ceremonial house to perform an ayahuasca ceremony. Pinkley was permitted to join them. The following morning, hoping to uncover evidence of this secret admixture plant, he fished around in the empty cauldron used to prepare the brew. He was in luck: A few leaves and seeds somehow managed to escape the hours of ferocious boiling intact—just about sufficient to make a formal identification. Latin name: *Psychotria viridis*, more commonly known as *chacruna*, but known to the Kofan as *oprito*—the same name given to the small heavenly people whom these magical leaves made visible.[9]

Coincidentally, during the summer of the same year, American anthropologist Kenneth Kensinger was collecting plant specimens used in the production of ayahuasca in the village of Balta, on the Rio Curanja in Peru. Among the samples collected was the plant Pinkley had, just a few weeks earlier, identified across the border in Ecuador, *Psychotria viridis*, which was shipped to pharmaceutical chemist Ara Marderosian at the Philadelphia College of Pharmacy and Science for analysis. After decades of confusion, speculation, and debate among the greatest minds in ethnobotany, the elusive secret admixture plant of the ayahuasca potion had finally been identified. And like the yopo and epena snuffs, its power derived from a simple molecule. Marderosian's analysis revealed only one major alkaloid component: DMT.[10] Although Homer Pinkley is usually given the credit for this monumental discovery—that *Psychotria viridis*, chacruna, was the elusive missing but essential component of the ayahuasca decoction—it turns out that, in all fairness, someone else got there first.

When William Burroughs was let into the "trade secret" by the medicine man Saboya in Pucallpa, Peru, on returning to Mexico City in 1954, he wrote to Richard Schultes to announce his discovery, enclosing a few of the leaves he'd pocketed:

Dear Dick,

I enclose sample of leaves used in preparation of Yage-Ayauska there-by Peru Indians. They boil the macerated vine with a large portion of these leaves for two hours. Yagé prepared in this way is a great deal more powerful and quite different in effect from yagé prepared in the same manner alone or from a cold infusion.[11]

To Burroughs's disappointment, Schultes never replied and it seems didn't bother to examine or attempt to identify the leaves. However, almost twenty years later, upon hearing of his student's discovery of chacruna, he finally decided to look over the specimens. Burroughs's Peruvian botanist friend had identified the plant as a species from the *Palicourea* genus of the *Rubiaceae* family. He had made an error: Although the plant was indeed from the *Rubiaceae* family, it wasn't a species of *Palicourea*—it was, in fact, a species of *Psychotria*. Specifically, *Psychotria viridis*—precisely the same plant that would be collected and identified by Homer Pinkley as the key DMT-containing ayahuasca admixture plant more than sixteen years later.[12] Burroughs had been right all along—there *was* an additional component in the ayahuasca brew necessary for the full visionary effects. It was an alkaloid. It was the gateway to the soulless place of The Insect People. It was his nightmare hallucinogen.

Not only did Schultes fail to recognize the importance of Burroughs's discovery in 1954, twelve years prior, in 1942, he'd also come across another plant that held the same secret. Chacruna is mainly used in Amazonian Peru, parts of Ecuador, and Brazil, but in other parts of Amazonian Ecuador and in Colombia, the natives use a different "secret" admixture plant.[13] While working among the Ingano people in Puerto Limón in 1942, a settlement in the Putumayo region of Colombia—where William Burroughs first obtained the caapi vine—Schultes was informed that the ayahuasca potion could be enhanced by the addition of the bark of another vine closely related to *Banisteriopsis caapi*, which he identified as *Banisteropsis rusbyana*, and known to the natives as *chacropanga*.[14] So, in the spirit of scientific enquiry, Schultes decided to test this claim. One night he tried the potion prepared with the caapi vine alone and then, a few nights later, with the addition of chacropanga. With the first caapi-only preparation, he experienced "slow undulating waves of color," but with the addition of chacropanga, the effect was "electric"—"reds and golds dazzling in diamonds that turned like dancers on the tips of distant highways."[15] Since chacropanga was so closely related to the caapi vine, it was plausible that it too contained harmala alkaloids that provided an additive effect. After all, in high enough doses, the harmala alkaloids are at least moderately psychoactive. Unfortunately, analysis of the chemical composition of the bark wasn't performed and chacropanga was largely forgotten. But more than two decades later, during his stay with the Kofan, Homer Pinkley, as well as (re)discovering chacruna, also collected samples of chacropanga. But this time the samples were distributed to a pair of chemists for independent chemical analysis. Both analyses revealed the presence of a single, now familiar, alkaloid: DMT.[16] In retrospect, it seems likely that Hochstein and Paradies's "*Prestonia amazonicum*" was, in fact, an extract of either chacruna or chacropanga. We'll never know, but whatever the truth, it was now clear that Indigenous groups across South America were all turning to one of a pair of plants containing high concentrations of DMT to complete their versions of the ayahuasca decoction. This suggested the existence of a minimal binary decoction that invariably must include the caapi vine plus the leaves of a DMT-containing plant. Other admixture plants were optional and only used to modulate the effects, much to the confusion of the botanists studying the potion.

While the discovery of chacruna and chacropanga brought some welcome clarity to the ayahuasca decoction, it left a major question yet to be answered: If DMT, derived from the leaves of chacruna or the bark of chacropanga, was the active psychedelic component of the brew, what was the caapi vine for exactly? Why was it considered a primary essential component of the decoction? Why was it added to the brew at all? Richard Spruce's encounter with the Guahibo people of the Orinoco Plains in 1854 provided the first clue to solving this mystery. As well as enjoying yopo in relatively small doses as a stimulant, the Guahibo people also chewed the dried caapi vine along with the snuff, perhaps suggesting some kind of pharmacological synergy between the DMT in the yopo snuff and the harmala alkaloids in the vine. This idea was supported by the Piaroa people's employing of a similar technique, although they drank an infusion of the caapi vine prior to inhaling larger doses of yopo to potentiate the visions.[17] But yopo apparently wasn't the only visionary snuff that could be enhanced this way.

In 1965, Swedish physician Bo Holmstedt performed chemical analyses on a variant of epéna snuff obtained from the Surara people of

northwestern Brazil. These are the visionary snuffs that Schultes had previously identified as being derived from the resinous exudate of various
Virola species, and which twice he'd been informed were used to speak
to the little people. Bearing in mind the propensity of synthetic DMT
to induce encounters with such beings, it should come as little surprise
that Holmstedt's analysis of the epéna snuff revealed the presence of high
concentrations of this visionary tryptamine. But Holmstedt also detected
two other, entirely unexpected, major alkaloids in the extract: harmine
and harmaline.[18] Since these alkaloids aren't produced by any *Virola* species, they could only result from the addition of another admixture plant,
possibly the caapi vine. So, again, the Indigenous manufacturers of this
particular epéna snuff seemed to be exploiting some kind of pharmacological synergy to enhance the visions elicited by the principal alkaloid
DMT. Of course, both yopo and epéna snuffs are active without the addition of any admixture plants, since DMT can be readily absorbed through
the mucosal membranes of the nasal passages. The caapi vine is used only
to potentiate the effects of the DMT. But what is the mechanism of this
potentiation and how does it relate to the caapi vine's use in the ayahuasca
decoction?

When Burroughs began his experiments with synthetic DMT in the
early 1960s, he employed the mode of administration that had served
him well throughout his life as a chronic morphine user: He injected it.
Timothy Leary and others had followed suit, with mind-blowing results.
Stephen Szára, on the other hand, initially opted for a more cautious
approach, swallowing the best part of a gram but without experiencing
any effects whatsoever. It was only after his colleague suggested he try
injecting it that Szára discovered DMT's astonishing psychedelic effects.
The lesson was clear: DMT was completely inactive when consumed
orally. Or, at least, DMT alone was inactive orally. But why?

As early as 1913, the Scottish virologist Sir Patrick Playfair Laidlaw
showed that, when passed through isolated rabbit livers, tryptamine—
the parent molecule of DMT and bufotenine—was rapidly broken
down,[19] and two decades later, the liver enzyme responsible for the
metabolism of tryptamine was identified.[20] However, this so-called
monoamine oxidase enzyme was soon found to be widely distributed

in mammalian tissues, including the brain and, crucially, the gut, provoking speculation as to whether it might play a role in metabolizing and detoxifying potentially harmful molecules before they can enter the circulation.[21] By the mid-1950s, it was clear that monoamine oxidase was important in the metabolism of serotonin but was also able to break down bufotenine and, most pertinently, DMT.[22] This seemed to provide a simple explanation for why DMT, when consumed orally, was completely inactive: The monoamine oxidase enzyme present in the gut was rapidly metabolizing the DMT before it could reach the circulation and, ultimately, the brain. But this didn't explain why, when present in the ayahuasca decoction, DMT was able to elicit such powerful visionary effects.

The solution to this problem was already embedded in the work of Karl Beringer in the 1920s, who had demonstrated striking improvements in motor control when Parkinson's patients were given alkaloids extracted from the caapi vine, now known to be identical to harmine and harmaline. Parkinson's disease is caused by the progressive destruction of dopamine-producing cells in the brainstem, leading to a gradual depletion of dopamine levels in the brain. Dopamine, which is essential for the brain's ability to control movement, is also broken down by monoamine oxidase. In 1958, American biochemist Sidney Udenfriend discovered that the harmala alkaloids were potent inhibitors of the monoamine oxidase enzyme.[23] So, injection of harmine or harmaline prevented the metabolism of dopamine and increased its levels in the brain, thus relieving the symptoms of Parkinson's disease. Now it was all starting to make sense. When DMT was ingested alone, it was rapidly metabolized by monoamine oxidase in the gut. However, when harmala alkaloids— from the caapi vine—were consumed at the same time, they inhibited this enzyme and protected DMT from metabolism, allowing it to pass into the circulation and reach the brain.[24] It was a beautifully elegant idea—it just needed to be proved.

In 1978, the American ethnobotanist Jeremy Bigwood decided to put the hypothesis to the test, by ingesting a capsule containing 100mg of DMT freebase together with a similar quantity of pure harmaline. And it worked! Bigwood soon began experiencing "DMT-like hallucinations very similar to a DMT- and harmaline-containing ayahuasca brew that I had previously experimented with."[25] And just a few years later, in the early 1980s, a more formal biochemical test of the hypothesis was performed by none other than Terence McKenna's brother, Dennis, who, following his revelatory DMT experience in 1968, had decided to devote his life to the scientific study of plant-derived psychedelics. McKenna analyzed the alkaloid levels in several samples of a Peruvian ayahuasca decoction and found that a typical 100ml dose contained around 650mg of harmala alkaloids and 60mg of DMT—well into the psychedelic dosage range—as well as demonstrating that even diluted samples of the potion were potent inhibitors of monoamine oxidase.[26]

So, not only was ayahuasca powered by DMT, but was also, as William Burroughs had speculated, a true pharmacological technology, exploiting the synergistic interaction between the constituent harmala and tryptamine alkaloids. Naturally, this immediately raised questions as to how the Indigenous peoples of South America, without any knowledge of the underlying biochemistry, could possibly have discovered, from the tens of thousands of plant species that filled the rain forests, that combining this particular pair of plants, neither of which produced any significant psychoactive effects when consumed orally alone, would elicit one of the most profound visionary experiences produced by any substance. It seemed almost miraculous in its implausibility, with ethnobotanist Jonathan Ott later calling it "conceivably the most sophisticated pharmacognostical discovery ever made in the archaic world."[27]

Since some groups still prepare a decoction using the caapi vine alone—with limited visionary effects—it's likely that this potent synergistic combination was discovered after a long period of trial and error, with different plants added and tested over perhaps hundreds of years.[28] Eventually, the minimal binary decoction of the caapi vine plus chacruna or chacropanga was discovered. This in no way detracts from the brilliance of the discovery, but if anything, demonstrates the Indigenous people's tenacity in developing this technology over many centuries, such was its value in making the Hidden Ones visible. A technology of this importance was worth the effort.

As the old saying goes: Once is happenstance, twice a coincidence,

thrice a pattern. With the discovery of three ostensibly unrelated Indigenous visionary technologies, all designed to enhance and optimize the
absorption of DMT into the body and brain, it became clear that this
simple plant alkaloid had been—and indeed still was—of central importance as a tool for making visible and communicating with the hidden
discarnate intelligences of the forest long before it found its way into the
clinics of the US and Europe and into the hands of William Burroughs,
Timothy Leary, and those that followed shortly after. But this pattern
was just the beginning, and somewhat echoing serotonin research in the
1940s, once DMT had been identified as the psychoactive component
of yopo, epéna, and ayahuasca, it seemed to be everywhere the chemists
and botanists looked. In the decades that followed, aside from the rain
forest plants used in these three primary technologies, DMT would be
detected in dozens of unrelated plants across several continents, from
Europe to North America to Australasia to Africa and Asia, including
the giant river reed, the Illinois bundleflower, eight species of *Phalaris*
grass, five species of mimosa, twelve *Delosperma* species, confirmed in
at least twelve Australian and Asian *Acacia* species and reported in several dozen more and, most surprisingly, in the skin of several species of
citrus fruit.[29] This simplest of plant-derived psychedelic molecules was
likely scattered across more plant species than most people could count,
let alone identify. DMT wasn't merely common, it was ubiquitous.

    In one sense, this shouldn't have been that surprising. After all,
DMT can be derived in two simple enzymatic steps from the amino
acid tryptophan, and the enzymes responsible for these chemical trans-
formations are found in practically all living organisms. But what was
remarkable—almost unnerving—was that such a simple and common
plant alkaloid, in a pure form, would also just happen to gate access to a
bizarre hypercomplex alternate universe teeming with apparently intelligent nonhuman—alien—beings. While the closely related psychedelic
alkaloid psilocybin can be found in mushrooms in habitats across the
globe, it is limited to certain species of the *Psilocybe* and related genii.
Likewise, the ergolines—including the lysergic acid derivatives and
ergot alkaloids from which LSD is derived—are to be found only in
a small number of species from the morning glory (*Convolvulaceae*)

family and fungi from the ergot (*Claviceps*) family. But DMT, on the other hand, is so common in the natural world that Dennis McKenna would later quip that "nature is drenched in DMT," before further speculating not only of ubiquity but complete botanical universality: "DMT could be found in all plants, at tiny but detectable levels if anyone bothered to look."[30] On a Sunday morning stroll through the park, you might well pass half a dozen or more plant species silently but busily manufacturing the world's strangest drug—a gateway to densely populated alien worlds beyond your imagination. What could this mean? Nobody could say for sure, but it was hard to shake the feeling that it meant something. Perhaps something of immense significance.

Whatever it meant, the doorway to the strange alien landscapes of the machine elves had been located, not in an isolated patch of virgin rain forest, but scattered across the natural world and available not only to those boasting advanced degrees in organic chemistry or with connections to a clandestine psychedelic in-group, but to anyone willing to seek out any one of its countless botanical sources. DMT's time as one of the rarest and most exotic of psychedelics would soon be over. The entrance to elf land was about to be democratized. But first, the scientists still had unfinished business.

7

EXPEDITIONS I—THE CLINIC

This insect really seems to be a machine with highly advanced parts, which can operate automatically.

—Léon Binet

In the early 1980s, Rick Strassman, a young American psychiatrist at the University of New Mexico, had just completed his clinical training and was looking for a research project that would connect the altered states of consciousness achieved during deep meditation, of which he'd been a keen practitioner for several years, and human neurochemistry. Since human research with psychedelics was all but impossible in the US at the time, he turned his attention to the pineal gland, deep in the center of the brain. Since ancient times, this enigmatic organ had occupied an exalted position in Eastern mysticism as a connection between the material and spiritual worlds, and speculating that the pineal's primary secretion, the sleep hormone melatonin, might be responsible for certain mystical states, Strassman began a two-year project to investigate its psychoactive properties in human subjects.[1] Unfortunately, melatonin turned out to be far less interesting than he had hoped, and in 1986, just as he was beginning to wonder whether he needed to look elsewhere for the keys to the mystical realms, he was invited to speak at a conference at Esalen in Big Sur, California. It was an invitation that would change the direction of his research and his life forever.

Following his lecture, he was approached by another conference speaker, Terence McKenna, who asked him: "You're talking about DMT, but have you ever tried it?"

"No, but I'd like to," Strassman replied.

McKenna directed Strassman to a room in the big house. He'd track down some DMT and meet Strassman there in an hour. Recounting this first DMT experience more than three decades later, Strassman recalls a "being" speaking to him "in a singsong voice" and saying, "Now do you see? Now do you see? Now do you see?"

"It shook me to my ontological roots," he later recalled.[2]

The course had been set by that experience and he immediately returned to the University of New Mexico Hospital in Albuquerque, abandoned his work on melatonin, and began developing a funding proposal for his own research into the effects of DMT—the first US study of the effects of a psychedelic drug in humans in more than two decades. Once permission and funding had been very much hard won (the long bureaucratic process would later serve as a roadmap for other psychedelic researchers), he began recruiting the five dozen volunteers for what would become the world's largest study of the effects of DMT in human subjects.[3]

Strassman's aim was to replicate as closely as possible the experience of using DMT in a nonclinical setting. By that time, Nick Sand's vaporization technique had long been standard among amateur DMT enthusiasts, but Strassman wasn't convinced this would be appropriate for the clinic. Not only does DMT have a pungent aroma, but cleanly vaporizing a precisely measured dose is no easy task. Add to that concerns about possible difficulties some volunteers might have had in holding a full dose in their lungs, and the vaporization approach was quickly abandoned. Strassman needed an alternative. All of the human studies with DMT earlier in the century had employed intramuscular injection. However, DMT administered this way enters the bloodstream rather slowly and erratically, resulting in a much more variable and drawn-out experience. So instead, he opted for a more efficient mode of administration: intravenous injection directly into the bloodstream. The intensity and time course of a vaporized DMT experience is very similar to that administered by intravenous injection, with effects building rapidly and peaking after just a few minutes before subsiding just as quickly.

After completing various screening tests for physical and psychological health, accepted volunteers were each given a unique code name: DMT-##. Each would receive several doses of DMT, usually on separate days, with 0.05mg/kg being the lowest (around 3–4mg for an average person), which elicited barely detectable effects. The highest dose, 0.4mg/kg (around 30mg), was almost invariably a full breakthrough dose that rapidly transported the volunteer from the normal waking world into the alternate DMT worlds. On the appointed dosing day, volunteers would arrive at the hospital, give their code name, and be escorted to hospital room 531, where Strassman and an attending nurse waited. The volunteer would then lie down on a bed and be fitted with a cannula to receive the drug.[4] All volunteers were then given a simple instruction: "Remember everything you can and tell me what happened."[5]

Despite his own personal, albeit limited, experience with the molecule, Strassman wasn't prepared for what his volunteers would find—what he would be forced to confront. One by one, as they emerged from their sojourns in the DMT worlds, the reports of encounters with strange and intelligent life-forms began to accumulate.

Strassman's first volunteer, DMT-01, given the alias Karl, arrived at the clinic on January 13, 1991, for his high-dose—0.4mg/kg—experience, accompanied by his wife. As the forty-five-second infusion of the drug began, he closed his eyes and his wife rested her hand on his leg. Barely two minutes later, it was clear the drug was beginning to take effect: "This is really strange."[6]

Karl smiled and then laughed before opening his eyes briefly. Eyes closed again, the smile faded, and he remained quiet as he was propelled further into the depths of the DMT state. As the effects subsided just a few minutes later, he was able to speak: "That was real strange. There were a lot of elves. They were prankish, ornery, maybe four of them appeared at the side of a stretch of interstate highway I travel regularly . . . I heard a giggling sound—the elves laughing or talking at high-speed volume, chattering, twittering . . . They held up placards, showing me these incredibly beautiful, complex, swirling geometric scenes in them. One of them made it impossible for me to move. There was no issue of control; they were totally in control. They wanted me to look!"[7]

Almost exactly forty years since Richard Schultes first heard about the little people of the Orinoco Basin invoked with the DMT-containing epéna snuffs, more than three decades since one of Stephen Szára's first subjects reported similar beings after receiving pure synthetic DMT by intramuscular injection, and at least a couple of decades since Terence McKenna was first left reeling by their bizarre linguistic gymnastics after smoking the drug for the very first time, the typically dynamic and diminutive members of the transdimensional chattering class made their first appearance in the very first subject of the world's first large-scale human DMT study.

And Karl wasn't the only volunteer to meet the little people. Chris, a thirty-five-year-old computer salesman with extensive prior experience with LSD, but none with DMT, was also greeted by a multitude of impish beings eager to communicate in the limited time available: "They were trying to show me as much as possible. They were communicating in words. They were like clowns or jokers or jesters or imps. There were just so many of them doing their funny little thing . . . There were blue hands, fluttering things, then thousands of things flew out of these blue hands. I thought, "What a show!"[8]

These kinds of comical madcap scenes populated by elves, imps, jesters, and the like engaged in some kind of performance are typical of relatively low-dose DMT trips (although not exclusively so). Twenty-two-year-old Cassandra volunteered for the project with no expectations beyond "I want to see what DMT feels like," but having been sexually abused as a teenager, Strassman was worried about the resurfacing of traumatic themes during her sessions. He needn't have been concerned as she was treated to the wildest of performances: "Something took my hand and yanked me. It seemed to say, 'Let's go!' Then I started flying through an intense circus-like environment. I've never been that out-of-body before . . . We went through a maze at an incredibly fast pace. I say 'we' because it seemed like I was accompanied. It was cool. There was a crazy circus sideshow—just extravagant. It's hard to describe. They looked like jokers. They were almost performing for me. They were funny-looking, bells on their hats, big noses. However, I had the feeling they could turn on me, a little less than completely friendly."[9]

Strassman followed up with Cassandra over the telephone the day after her final dose of intravenous DMT. Reflecting on her experiences, she remarked: "On DMT, I saw and felt myself as a good person, as loved by the DMT elves."

Strassman was startled: "Elves?" he asked.

Cassandra replied, "There was a sense of many visitors. They were jovial, and they had a great time giving me the experience of being loved."[10]

The little people. Again.

Despite their regular attempts to steal the show, it would have been a major error to assume that these (usually) friendly little folk were all you could expect after a decent hit of DMT. Reminiscent of Burroughs's first high-dose, breakthrough experience with those menacing "Soulless Insect People," forty-six-year-old Aaron—DMT-14—was met by similar insectoid beings during his first high-dose experience: "An insect-like thing got right into my face, hovering over me as the drug was going in. This thing sucked me out of my head into outer space. It was clearly outer space, a black sky with millions of stars. I was in a very large waiting room or something. It was very long. I felt observed by the insect-thing and others like it. Then they lost interest. I was taken into space and looked at."[11]

Also like Burroughs, Aaron couldn't help but feel that there was something less than friendly about these creatures: "There is a sinister backdrop, an alien-type, insectoid, not-quite-pleasant side of this, isn't there? It's not "we're going to get you, motherfucker," it's more like being possessed. During the experience there is a sense of someone, or something else, there taking control. It's like you have to defend yourself against them, whoever they are, but they certainly are there. I'm aware of them and they're aware of me. It's like they have an agenda. It's like walking into a different neighborhood. You're really not quite sure what the culture is."[12]

As the volunteers' reports began to accumulate, it was becoming increasingly clear that, beyond the comical, outlandish, and madcap world of the elves, imps, and jesters, DMT had the propensity—often at higher dose levels—to fire the tripper into decidedly alien territory—a realm that could only be described as some kind of supremely advanced nonhuman civilization. Consciousness researcher Aaron's experience was fairly typical: "I was in a huge infinite hive. There were insect-like intelligences everywhere. They were in a hypertechnological space."[13]

But one of the most unambiguously alien-like reports was that of "Dmitri," which read more like some kind of abduction scenario than a spiritual voyage, complete with the technological apparatus of beings far more advanced than any earthly intelligence. A couple of decades later, I managed to track down Dmitri—real name Spiros—a self-described "acid head" of Greek heritage who, prior to the study, was also living in New Mexico working as a writer and editor.[14] He agreed to an interview. Although Spiros had extensive experience with free-base DMT prior to Strassman's study, he found the vapor extremely irritating and struggled to draw enough into his lungs to achieve a deep breakthrough experience. So when he caught wind of a study where he'd receive pure, clinical-grade DMT injected directly into his veins, it seemed like a "fairy-tale" opportunity, and after applying and answering a few questions about his mental and physical health, was given his code name: DMT-40.

Although he had encountered strange creatures in the DMT realm on several occasions prior to the study, he was entirely unprepared for the direction the drug would take him as he arrived at the clinic. In one of his earlier sessions during the study, rather than passing cleanly through into the alternate realm, he was frustrated to find his entire field of vision obscured by an instrument that was not merely advanced, but from his perspective at least, entirely impossible: "It held up this control pad. . . . I felt for sure it was showing me a reality synthesizer. . . . It had knobs and sliders. . . . I tried mentally and verbally to ask how to use this thing. . . . I had no idea how to use it or what it was trying to say to me by having it right in my face. . . . I couldn't see past it."[15]

The entities' attempts (almost always in vain) at communication using some kind of technological device—recall the "gem-encrusted pad" proffered by the elf-insects met by Leary—seemed to be a fairly regular feature of the state. Fortunately, during a later high-dose session, the entities had apparently given up on that rather importunate and entirely fruitless communication strategy, and instead whisked him straight to the center of the action:

> I felt like I was in an alien laboratory . . . A sort of landing bay or recovery area. There were beings. I was trying to get a handle on what was going on. I was being carted around. It didn't look alien, but their sense of purpose was. . . . They had a space ready for me. They weren't as surprised as I was. It was incredibly unpsychedelic. I was able to pay attention to detail. There was one main creature, and he seemed to be behind it all, overseeing everything. The others were orderlies, or dis-orderlies. . . . They went through different zones in my imaginal body and cleaned them up or tuned them. . . . They activated a sexual circuit, and I was flushed with an amazing orgasmic energy. A goofy chart popped up like an X-ray in a cartoon, and a yellow illumination indicated that the corresponding system, or series of systems, were fine. They were checking my instruments, testing things. When I was coming out, I couldn't help but think "aliens."[16]

The instruments used by the beings were particularly striking, not merely in being technologically advanced, but in being far more so than the technology of the time: "They were smoother and didn't have all the dials and wires of the technical instruments of that era. . . . It was an advanced technology but it was simple. It did advanced things, but it didn't look complicated in structure."[17]

Confused, awed, and left in a state of complete shock, Spiros struggled to make sense of this encounter, even emailing Terence McKenna in the hope he might at least be able to offer some kind of speculative explanation, but even this veteran explorer of elf land was unable to provide any answers: "It befuddled him as much as me," Spiros recalled. Even now, almost three decades after the study was concluded, Spiros's interpretation of the beings encountered in that alien laboratory remains "a big unknown" and he's still not ready to dismiss the experience as something cooked up by his brain: "It does seem to have enough agency, some parts that feel outside of my own construction. And that's a big deal."[18]

But as strange and startling as Spiros's experience was, it appears somewhat tame when compared to what the following pair of volunteers had to endure—a far bigger deal than either of them had bargained for.

Although Rick Strassman published a representative selection of the reports of his volunteers in his book *DMT: The Spirit Molecule*, naturally, not all of them made the cut. Rick was kind enough to give me access to his original bedside notes recorded during the study, and as I made my way through the hundreds of reports, the experiences of two volunteers stood out, as each was confronted by a reality so far beyond human experience and so utterly and horrifyingly alien that it shook them to the very core of their being.

When DMT-20—Strassman didn't give him an alias, but we'll call him Peter—entered room 531 on the morning of January 14, 1993, for his high-dose DMT injection, Strassman noticed Peter seemed more nervous than usual—perhaps a presage of what lay ahead. Strassman left him to go downstairs and fetch the drug.[19] When he returned, he was pleased to see that Peter seemed a little more relaxed.

"How are you feeling about getting started with this big dose?" Strassman asked as he prepared the injection.

"Less nervous than twenty minutes ago. Fairly ready," he replied.

He lay down on the bed, slipped on the eyeshades, and at 9:18 a.m., Strassman began the infusion.

"Feels real cold," Peter said. He grew a little pale and sighed. He seemed restless, jostling his legs about before curling up in a fetal position. Five minutes after the injection, he was breathing rapidly and heavily.

"Jesus Christ!" he suddenly cried. "I had no idea what it would do to me!"

He bolted upright, slamming his head into his hands and trembling before retching several times into his gown as Strassman watched Peter's heart rate and blood pressure abruptly and markedly plummet. Perhaps

McKenna's warning of the risk of "death by astonishment" wasn't hyperbole after all. Fortunately, to Strassman's immense relief, Peter's vital signs began to recover a few minutes later and he was able to speak again: "Boy! Most of it I have forgotten already; it was futuristic. It was not funny. It was malevolent. I wouldn't say it was destructive or demonic, but it wasn't anything I wanted to look at for very long. . . . There was something like a space station. It was pretty frightening, the suddenness. It was too bizarre."

Still shaking, he managed a nervous laugh: "Nothing like that has ever happened to me before, nothing even close to that. I am glad it is quick. . . . You have to ask yourself, 'Is that reality?' It's so totally alien."

"How about the space station? Was it inhabited?" Strassman asked.

"Yeah, yeah. There is nothing that can prepare you for this. There is a sound, there is a *bzzzz*. It started off and got louder and louder and faster and faster and then *pow!* I was totally unprepared. It was so fast; I was so confused! The suddenness. There was a feeling of others there. They weren't human."

Intrigued, Strassman continued to probe: "How about fleshing out the trip a bit?"

"There was this buzz, which increased in intensity, and then there were some interesting patterns developing, like computer-chip circuits vibrating, but there was more texture to them. It was coming on and coming on and then *pop!* There was a feeling of the space ship; it wasn't exactly like that, it's just the closest thing to it. I didn't see, but sensed, two presences that started taking me somewhere, and then the nausea came."

Although he seemed to have physically recovered somewhat by this point, he was still quite obviously shaken and confused:

What is this? How can such a reality exist? There was time sense of being in the future. It was very, very strange. It was hundreds, if not thousands, of years from now. It was a combination of an intimation plus an image. They weren't human beings. They were like robots; they were very busy and machinelike. It's not like the imagination; I couldn't have imagined this. . . . I was participating. They were like technocrats dialing knobs, working on machinery. There were two orders of beings there. There were the busy guys and then there were the others. There was more than one. They were taking me somewhere.

"You look pretty stunned."

"Yep, stunned. My guess is that it was shock that put me into that low blood pressure state. It's another reality, I'll say; it's there," Peter said.

Wherever "there" might have been, it was quite obviously not here or indeed anywhere else this side of normal human experience.

Things didn't become any more comfortable or familiar for DMT-41—we'll call him Paul—who had several intriguing early insectoid encounters, but like Peter, was in no way prepared for what he would confront when he arrived at Strassman's clinic on April 20, 1994.[20] At 9:51 a.m., a moderate dose—0.2mg/kg—was injected. Thirty seconds later, Paul's body jerked and continued to do so every thirty seconds or so with increasing frequency until he jerked almost with every breath. Fifteen minutes after the injection he finally became quiet and seemed to relax.

"Well, how did it go?" Strassman asked.

"It was the worst trip I've ever had. There was nothing human. There was nothing human. Everything was totally alien without . . . "

"Without what?" Strassman prompted.

"Without any concern, recognition, or interest in me. It was like hell because there was nothing human. No human concerns whatsoever. It was like some alien creatures from an unknown place devouring me with no awareness that I WAS! Maybe that's why I'm cold because of how cold and lifeless and drained of reality that was. It was like I was a mountain being mined by machines."

"How do you feel now?" Strassman asked.

"Really, really sad."

"It sounds bleak and impersonal," Strassman said.

"Yeah, like there is a state in this universe where nothing gives a damn at all. It doesn't even recognize humanity," Paul replied.

He lifted his eyeshades and put his hand to his eyes as the attending nurse tried to comfort him.

"You are back among friends now, at least," the nurse said.

"I was being mined, devoured by such strange alien forces. The only analogy I can think of is like how people breathe in air without knowing that the air is being breathed. It's like robots mining a mountain without knowing the mountain is there. Totally impersonal and unaware and unacknowledging. It is what hell must be like . . . being devoured without anything familiar."

"Did you see those aliens, or were they mostly just a feeling?" Strassman questioned.

"Yeah, I could see. In a way, if you took the god Ganesh and started making real far-out versions of that, that would give you a sense of how strange it was. It was that kind of feeling," Paul said.

"Lots of them?"

"I don't know. 'Them' is a pronoun referring to things we know of. This wasn't anything I knew."

Reading Peter and Paul's reports, I was reminded of my own first experience with DMT and how the world that I had somehow been fired into not only transcended humanity entirely, but seemed far beyond any normal conception of reality—a thoroughly alien domain that came from nowhere. For Strassman, too, it was becoming perfectly obvious that this molecule wasn't just a catalyst for bright colors and complex geometric visions, nor merely a doorway to an enchanted realm populated by spritely elfin beings. No, this was a gateway to a world teeming with an inordinately complex hyperdimensional ecology of discarnate intelligences of every unimaginable form. How and why could this simple and ubiquitous plant alkaloid possibly have such effects on the human mind?

Two of Strassman's more insightful volunteers began to intimate that DMT was more than just a naturally occurring drug that happened to induce complex visual hallucinations of discarnate entities. There was something more to DMT than this—something special, profound, and unique.

Strassman regarded freelance writer Sara as one of his "most content and insightful research subjects," who volunteered with the intention of developing a "deeper understanding of myself and my relationship to the universe and unseen worlds."[21] Following an earlier circus-like experience, Sara's later journey would take on a more serious form. Not only were the entities aware of her presence intruding into their world, but they clearly had an active interest in her. Immediately following the initial complex geometric visual stage, Sara broke through to "the other side": "Suddenly, beings appeared. They were cloaked, like silhouettes. They were glad to see me. They indicated that they had had contact with me as an individual before. They seemed pleased that we had discovered this technology."[22]

This technology? Sara's use of this word, apparently prompted by the beings, is particularly striking. If DMT is somehow gating access to a normally inaccessible domain occupied by highly advanced discarnate intelligences, then perhaps "technology" is indeed a more fitting term than "psychedelic drug." Certainly, the beings encountered by Sara were far removed from any typical mythological or mystical fare: "I always knew we weren't alone in the universe. I thought that the only way to encounter them is with bright lights and flying saucers in outer space. It never occurred to me to actually encounter them in our own inner space. I thought the only things we could encounter were things in our own personal sphere of archetypes and mythology. I expected spirit guides and angels, not alien life-forms."[23]

Sara wasn't alone in sensing that there was something about DMT that was decidedly unlike that of a drug. Armed services veteran Jeremiah also found himself in a distinctly technological environment, occupied by beings not only aware of his presence, but actively manipulating his brain/mind: "There was one big machine in the center, with round conduits, almost writhing—not like a snake, more in a technical manner. . . . The machine felt as if it was rewiring me, reprogramming me. There was a human, as far as I could tell, standing at some type of console, taking readings or manipulating things. He was busy, at work, on the job. I observed some of the results on that machine, maybe from my brain. It was a little frightening, almost unbearably intense."[24]

And, like Sara, he couldn't help but feel that his experience was no hallucination, but rather the result of interfacing with another aspect of reality via some kind of technology:

DMT has shown me the reality that there is infinite variation on reality. There is the real possibility of adjacent dimensions. It may not be so simple as that there's alien planets with their own societies. This is too proximal. . . . You can choose to attend to this or not. It will continue to progress without you paying attention. You return not to where you left off, but to where things have gone since you left. With other psychedelics, you can change it. This is independent. It's solid, stable. It makes one believe it's not a hallucination, but an observation. I'm not intoxicated. I'm lucid and sober. . . . It's more like an experience of a new technology than a drug.[25]

This stability and lucidity of the DMT experience mentioned by Jeremiah is one of its most intriguing features and one of the most challenging to explain. It's also one that was regularly noted by Terence McKenna: "One of the most puzzling things about DMT is it does not affect your mind. . . . It simply replaces the world 100 percent with something completely unexpected. But your relationship to that unexpected thing is not one of exaggerated fear or exaggerated acceptance as in 'Oh great, the world has just been replaced by elf machinery!' Your reaction is exactly what it would be if it happened to you without DMT. You're appalled!"[26]

With a dose sufficient to propel you past the threshold of complex and dynamic geometric imagery—a breakthrough dose—the experience entirely lacks the feeling of being stoned or intoxicated. It's as if the normal sober waking world has simply been switched to a new channel with all the other faculties left mercilessly intact. There's a kind of clinical razor-sharp efficiency with which DMT achieves this neurological transition—almost as if it were designed for this purpose. One moment you're enjoying the stable mundane world of everyday life and the next you find yourself immersed in the world of a supremely advanced alien civilization either going about its business unaware or apathetic to your presence or, in some cases, waiting for you. It's more stable, and in that sense, closer to normal waking reality than a dream. Whereas dreams are often unstable, poorly rendered, and shift from scene to scene, the DMT state feels more like an observation. You're catapulted into this realm that's been going on before you arrived and will continue to do so after you leave just a few minutes later. And aside from a euphoric afterglow, once the DMT begins to clear the brain, you're just as quickly back to baseline consciousness, shaken and awed but entirely lucid with no hangover or dizziness or other physical or psychological aftereffects. Rather than simply perturbing or disrupting the brain, DMT seems to slot like a molecular device with engineered precision into your neural machinery to exert its effects. If this wasn't some kind of molecular alien communication technology, it sure looked like one. But unsurprisingly, not everyone was convinced.

8

EXPEDITIONS II—UNDERGROUND

I happen to believe myself that we're all explorers in our way. But exploration is much more than naming and describing. An explorer's task is to postulate the existence of a land beyond the known land. Whether or not he finds that land and brings back news of it is unimportant. He may choose to lose himself in it forever and add one more to the sum of unexplored lands.

—Gerald Murnane

At 5:35 p.m. on May 25, 1995, more than five years since his first volunteer, DMT-01, laid down on the bed in room 531 of the University of New Mexico Hospital, his final volunteer, DMT-60, slipped on the eyeshades, lay back, and for the very last time, Dr. Rick Strassman began infusing the DMT into his veins. As the alkaloid slipped silently into his central nervous system, he occasionally sighed but was otherwise quiet.

"I felt like I was peeking into a party that you didn't get to go into."[1]

At just 0.05mg/kg, it was the lowest of the dose levels in the study, and while DMT-60 didn't get to gatecrash that party, most of Strassman's five dozen volunteers—and Strassman himself—were now fully aware of what lay beyond the threshold. It was a party unlike any other, and for many of them, one they'd be unlikely to accept another invitation to anytime soon.

Ten minutes after the infusion began, DMT-60 cleared his throat. "It's almost over."

As far as this research project was concerned, it was indeed over. But for Strassman, it was only the beginning. Throughout the prior five years, as each of his intrepid volunteers had carefully recounted their extraordinary expeditions in this weirdest of alternate worlds, DMT had revealed itself to be something far stranger and far more challenging to explain than he could have anticipated when he first conceived of his study almost a decade earlier. It was now abundantly clear that there was something very special—something seemingly miraculous—about this simplest of alkaloids scattered throughout the plant kingdom with an unrivaled ability to rapidly and efficiently dismantle the world and replace it with one that transcended the imagination and the apparent limits of conceivable reality—to switch the brain's reality channel to a bizarre hypertechnological domain filled with advanced and thoroughly alien intelligent beings. If you wanted to design a molecular tool to perform this neural reconfiguration, it would be hard to improve on DMT. As two of his volunteers had intimated, DMT was beginning to look less and less like a drug and more like some kind of neuro-molecular technology. But a technology designed by whom and to what end?

On January 1, 2001, almost five years after the study was concluded, Strassman published his magnum opus, *DMT: The Spirit Molecule*, detailing his work with the five dozen volunteers, as well as attempting to explain—albeit in a highly speculative manner—how and why this molecule elicited such profound effects on the conscious world. And it's fair to say that he wasn't afraid to step outside the boundaries of what might be considered orthodox science in doing so. In fact, he had little choice. His major thesis—from which he derived the term "spirit molecule"—was that DMT is released by the pineal gland in the center of the brain at the point of death, providing the conduit by which the soul exits the body and enters the afterlife.[2] However, the frequency with which aliens, insectoids, and other nonhuman discarnate intelligences from advanced civilizations appeared in his volunteers' reports remained a challenge to explain. In the end, Strassman felt compelled to accept that perhaps DMT really did allow his volunteers access to some normally hidden dimension of reality and to contact with intelligent beings resident therein. But hardly surprisingly, not everyone was convinced and certainly didn't intend to let Strassman get away with such seemingly outlandish speculations.

Having spent decades as a fugitive and several years in both the Canadian and American prison systems as reward for his tireless work keeping the citizens of the US supplied with millions of doses of some of the finest LSD available outside of the Sandoz laboratories, it's hard to blame Nick Sand—who first discovered DMT could be vaporized—for his distrust of anyone he believed to be connected to "the system," which included, in his mind at least, Strassman. In an article for the *Entheogen Review*, a now defunct quarterly publication on the use of visionary plants and drugs founded by American epidemiologist and author Jim DeKorne, Sand certainly didn't sugarcoat his disdain—bordering on outright contempt—for Strassman's approach to studying DMT: "These are experiments being done by government agencies examining the use of these psychedelic substances in the pursuit of more power, money, and success."[3]

Strassman represented the establishment from which Sand and the others of the first psychedelic revolution of the 1960s had been seeking emancipation. Strassman was, in a sense, the enemy or, at least, in cahoots with the enemy. Although Sand's attitude was to some extent understandable, in Strassman's defense, he was merely doing his best to work within the parameters set by the system, and it was a stretch to claim that he was working toward any kind of nefarious ends beyond his genuine curiosity surrounding this thoroughly unique variety of human experience. Politics aside, it was Strassman's interpretation of his volunteers' reports that Sand took particular issue with, and his dismissal of the apparent "alien intelligences" encountered by many study volunteers was unambiguous: "First off, DMT is not a rerun of *The X-Files*. There are no aliens squiggling through psychospace to do experiments on us. That idea is just plain silly."[4]

Appealing to Timothy Leary's "set and setting" hypothesis, it was quite obvious to Sand why so many of Strassman's subjects reported being "examined, discussed, measured, probed, and observed" in "alien laboratories." It was simply an artifact of his "highly artificial and agenda-driven environment" in which his subjects were indeed being "examined, discussed, measured, probed, and observed."[5] Change the setting and instead of "reptiles, aliens, and robot doctors, you have gods, magicians, celestial and magical beings."[6] Although at first blush, his argument seems reasonable—perhaps even compelling—things would turn out to be not quite as simple as Sand so stridently insisted, as the reports of Strassman's volunteers would soon be dwarfed by a much larger dataset.

Although at the time of the New Mexico study DMT remained relatively rare on the underground drug market, thanks to the labors of the botanists and chemists throughout the twentieth century, we now knew that this marvelous molecule was not only common but ubiquitous across the plant kingdom. It was only a matter of finding suitable plants from which to isolate the alkaloid, and as Strassman's study got underway, underground psychedelic enthusiasts were already beginning to explore sources of DMT that didn't require advanced degrees in organic chemistry or access to a well-stocked dealer. One such psychedelic enthusiast of immense repute, American ethnobotanist Jonathan Ott, began attempting to recreate the so-called "ayahuasca effect"—the synergistic combination of DMT and a monoamine oxidase inhibitor—using alternative botanical sources of both DMT and the harmala alkaloids. In a series of auto-experiments (that is, on himself), Ott was able to produce highly visionary ayahuasca analogs by combining the ground seeds of Syrian rue—*Peganum harmala*, the original botanical source of the harmala alkaloids—with the dried and powdered root bark of the Illinois bundleflower (*Desmanthus illinoensis*), a common shrub found across many areas of South Central and Midwestern US, with DMT concentrations quantified at around 0.18% of the dried bark (comparable to chacruna, *Psychotria viridis*). Similar success was achieved with the leaves of the Australian Mount Buffalo wattle (*Acacia phlebophylla*), known to contain DMT at almost double the concentration of chacruna and rivaling that of the more potent chacropanga (*Banisteriopsis rusbyana*).[7]

Ott's experiments unequivocally demonstrated that the visionary power of ayahuasca didn't require access to the traditionally employed botanicals but could be replicated with any DMT-rich plant coupled with another containing sufficient concentrations of the harmala alkaloids acting as monoamine oxidase inhibitors. Of course, any such DMT-rich plant could also, in theory, be used to isolate the alkaloid in a pure form for vaporization and indeed, Ott was also successful in extracting an acceptably pure DMT freebase from the Illinois bundleflower root bark. However, while extracting alkaloids from plant material is far simpler than synthesizing DMT from scratch, it wasn't necessarily an entirely foolproof endeavor. Although a particular plant species might sport high concentrations of DMT, it will often also contain a rich cocktail of other alkaloids, as well as other molecules, some of which might have entirely different psychoactive effects or could even be toxic. It takes some level of skill—and some would say artistry—in practical chemistry to separate DMT from these other bothersome molecules. So if DMT was to become accessible to entirely inexperienced chemists using simple kitchen chemistry, it would require a plant source that was easy to source or cultivate, as well as boasting high levels of DMT and little else. One such contender for this title of holy grail of DMT botanicals began making its case early in the 1990s, although it had been bothering antipodean sheep farmers since long before then.

At least as early as the first half of the twentieth century, Australian farmers began noticing unusual neurological symptoms in their sheep when allowed to graze on the young shoots of a particular species of grass, *Phalaris aquatica* (a.k.a. *Phalaris tuberosa*). Known as the "Phalaris staggers," affected ovines would suddenly become unstable on their feet, begin nodding their heads and grinding their teeth and then, in the most severe cases, fall to the ground before swiftly fulfilling an early appointment with the Good Shepherd.[8] Obviously, waking up to find their pastures littered with half the flock in various stages of rigor mortis was both a horrifying and expensive problem, and the farmers were more than keen to get to the bottom of it. And once the vegetal culprit had been collared, it was naturally assumed that some toxic molecule peculiar to this species of grass was responsible for killing the sheep. But quite unexpectedly—for the chemists at the time, at least—extracts of the grass were found to contain relatively high levels of several tryptamine alkaloids, the most prominent of these being DMT. However, while scientists were able to replicate many of the (nonlethal) neurological symptoms of *Phalaris* staggers by injecting sheep with pure synthetic DMT, it's now thought that a closely related alkaloid found in some variants of the grass—gramine—was likely responsible for the ovine fatalities.[9] DMT was off the hook. Although this chemical analysis data was published (in a fairly obscure Australian chemical journal) in 1964,[10] it wasn't until almost three decades later that it caught the attention of a clandestine chemistry community with an eye to transposing the rasping squeals of dying sheep to a more melodious refrain: the pitter-patter of tiny elf feet.

In 1992, an industrious psychedelic enthusiast and amateur chemist going by the (presumed) pseudonym Johnny Appleseed penned a letter to the *Entheogen Review* detailing a simple procedure for extracting DMT from the leaf blades of *Phalaris aquatica*, as well as describing the strains most likely to contain high levels of the alkaloid.[11] One strain in particular, discovered by Italian ethnobotanist Giorgio Samorini near Bologna—which he named AQ1—appeared to be nothing short of a botanical DMT factory, with levels quantified at over 1 percent of the dried leaf biomass—more than five times the level in chacruna and double that measured in chacropanga—making it a strong contender for the richest source of naturally occurring DMT yet discovered.[12] Considering that this fast-growing grass could be cultivated with ease by "anyone anywhere on the planet outside of the polar regions," *Entheogen Review* founder Jim DeKorne described the discovery of such high concentrations of DMT in its leaf blades as a "tactical nuclear explosion" on the War on Drugs.[13] Unfortunately, the alkaloid levels in *Phalaris aquatica* were later found to be erratic and unreliable, depending strongly on growth stage, soil and climactic conditions, and sunlight exposure, and compounded by concerns about the toxic gramine alkaloid finding its way into an extract, the initial excitement over this grass species soon waned. So, while *Phalaris* grass failed to live up to DeKorne's nuclear hyperbole, the publication of these early forays into clandestine kitchen drug chemistry sparked a flurry of articles and letters in the *Entheogen Review* speculating that, given its apparent botanical ubiquity, other rich sources of naturally occurring and easily extracted DMT might well be buried in the scientific literature, just waiting to be uncovered. And they weren't wrong.

In January of 1996, Jonathan Ott joined Terence McKenna and several other big names in psychedelic ethnobotany at the Mayan ruins of Palenque in Mexico for a weeklong conference on ethnobotany and shamanism sponsored by the Botanical Preservation Corps, which McKenna co-founded. Although Ott wasn't booked to speak on ayahuasca or its analogs, he couldn't help but give "high praise" to a plant he'd recently been experimenting with—one that was so rich in DMT that a mere five grams of its dried root bark were sufficient for a full visionary "ayahuasca" journey, suggesting DMT concentrations rivaling that of Samorini's *Phalaris aquatica AQ1*.[14] And like the *Phalaris* grass, this was by no means a rare or newly discovered source of the alkaloid.

Back in 1946, Brazilian chemist Oswaldo Gonçalves de Lima visited the Pankararu people in eastern Brazil and was permitted to observe the ancient ritual of *jurema*, which involved the preparation of a visionary drink known as "vinho de jurema"—wine of jurema.[15] Its preparation would have been familiar to anyone experienced with ayahuasca. The roots of a tree were macerated in water and then strained to yield a bitter red liquid. The visions will also be familiar: "An old master of ceremonies, wielding a dance rattle decorated with a feather mosaic, would serve a bowlful of the infusion made from yurema roots to all celebrants, who would then see glorious visions of the spirit land, with flowers and birds. They might catch a glimpse of the clashing rocks that destroy souls of the dead journeying to their goal, or see the Thunderbird shooting lightning from a huge tuft on his head and producing claps of thunder by running about."[16]

Gonçalves de Lima was able to collect and identify the plant used to make the drink as *jurema preta* (*Mimosa hostilis*, also known as *Mimosa tenuiflora*), and as was now standard operating procedure for any newly discovered medicinal or psychoactive plant, immediately went looking for an alkaloid that might explain its visionary effects. He found only one, which he isolated and christened *nigerine*. After being injected with about 70mg of the alkaloid, experimental rats trembled and struggled to walk before outright convulsions and paralysis set in, with the animals succumbing after an hour or so. (It ought to be pointed out that, using standard conversion metrics, a 70mg dose in rats is equivalent to around 5g in humans—stratospherically beyond any kind of sensible dose.) Unfortunately, Gonçalves de Lima didn't venture to inject niger-ine into his own veins. Nor was he able to definitively determine its chemical structure, and it wasn't until more than a decade later that me-dicinal chemist Irwin Pachter, using samples of jurema preta provided by Gonçalves de Lima, was able to fully characterize the molecule: an al-kaloid of the tryptamine family, specifically, N,N-dimethyltryptamine, more commonly known simply as DMT.[17]

Pachter's analyses revealed that the root bark of jurema preta not only boasted levels of DMT almost unrivaled in the plant kingdom (as far as we know), but also contained detectable levels of almost no other alkaloids. Even better, the tree was as common as muck, a practically invasive pioneer species native to northeastern Brazil, but ranging as far north as southern Mexico through Colombia, Venezuela, Panama, Honduras, and El Salvador. A few months after the Palenque confer-ence in 1996, Jim DeKorne was driving down Mexico's Baja peninsula and recalls passing through "hundreds of square miles of *Mimosa hostilis* trees." After pulling over to collect a few specimens and considering how he might explain the trunk full of cuttings to the "teenaged soldiers with loaded assault rifles" manning the endless roadblocks along that stretch of highway at the time, he was no doubt wondering whether, after the recent disappointment of *Phalaris* grass, he'd finally found the holy grail DMT source he—and everyone else—had been searching for.[18]

Once the word of the jurema preta tree's peerless proclivity for DMT manufacture was out, clandestine chemists returned to their basement labs to begin developing methodologies to isolate the alkaloid from the root bark. They didn't have to work that hard, as the bark was found to give up its visionary stash with little more than a chemical tickle. In 2006, an amateur chemist going by the name Noman published an article in the *Entheogen Review* appositely titled "DMT for the Masses," in which he detailed a step-by-step procedure—known as a *tek*—for extracting smokeable freebase DMT from powdered jurema preta root bark.[19] Not only was Noman's tek high yielding, but it was also so simple that anyone could execute it using little more than sodium hydroxide (available as drain cleaner from most hardware stores) and an organic solvent, such as Zippo lighter fluid or Coleman fuel. Kitchen chemists soon began posting pictures online of their impressively fluffy white crystals obtained in yields as high as 1 to 2 percent of the dried root bark mass. Not surprisingly, dozens of online vendors soon popped up, happy to supply anyone with a credit card and mailing address with as much of the dried root bark of this common perennial tree as they desired. Although the authorities in many countries—including the US—are now well aware of jurema preta's alternative use, with increasing numbers of customers complaining of having their kilos of shredded bark seized by postal customs agents, this Brazilian tree remains by far the most widely used source of naturally occurring DMT, now transformed from a rare and exotic psychedelic that could be acquired from the overcoat pockets of only the most well-stocked of street dealers to one that practically anyone with a few hours to spare could produce with ease in their kitchen. With Ott's rediscovery of jurema preta, the holy grail was in hand. DMT had been democratized.

Eager to tell the world about the miraculous realms and the marvelous creatures and sprites they'd met on their transdimensional excursions using this jurema preta extract, it wasn't long before the internet forums and message boards—many of them devoted entirely to DMT—began to fill up with detailed accounts of their encounters. Despite being the largest of its kind in history, Strassman's New Mexico study only recruited sixty volunteers. But with the elevation of DMT to a true psychedelic for the masses, the number of human subjects grew exponentially, and if Nick Sand was correct in his claim that the types of beings encountered by Strassman's volunteers were purely artifacts of the clinical setting, these accounts from the countless DMT users across the US and beyond would surely show it. But, on the contrary, not only were DMT users having the same types of experiences in their bedrooms, back rooms, and basements as the volunteers in room 531 of the University of New Mexico Hospital, but many were reporting entity encounters eerily similar to those of DMT users stretching back not only through the twentieth century, but into prehistory.

Continuing the thread running from the epéna-snuffing shamans of Amazonia to Szára's first study in 1956 to Leary and McKenna in the 1960s and finally to Strassman's study in the 1990s, the little people featured regularly in these underground reports, with their characteristic multiplicity and joviality, manufacturing and proffering objects of impossible beauty, eager to import some kind of important information:

> They pulled things into existence, as if from pockets of vacuum space within themselves, like beautifully jeweled liquid light revolving eggs, that transformed into and out of themselves like rolling smoke infused with layer after layer of brightly colored electrical information.... Some of the entities held out what looked like tickets, or small flash drives, very close in front of my eyes for me to look at. "Check this out!" they giggle. "Look, carefully, SEE what this is, remember it!" "This is how it all works," they seemed to say. . . . My beautiful, playful, mischievous elfin brethren implore me to look, and to see, and to remember![20]

While Terence McKenna's claim that "everybody gets elves" was clearly an exaggeration, there was now no doubt that the little folk were making more than the odd cameo appearance, but were one of a set of main characters in a long-running show with an uncannily recurring theme. But it wasn't just the elves that were familiar. Although Nick Sand dismissed the "alien experimentation" experience reported by several of Strassman's volunteers as an effect of the clinical "agenda-driven" setting, the following report, also published on the Erowid website, is remarkably similar to Spiros's (Strassman's "Dmitri, DMT-40") alien laboratory experience, including a number of smaller entities performing the experimentation and measurements and a larger, more powerful leader overseeing the procedure. Notably, the author states that "I had my one and only dose of N,N-Dimethyltryptamine (DMT) in December 1999"—more than a year before Strassman's book was published:

> I realized I was in some kind of emergency room/holding bay for "entities like myself" who "break through" into this new world. . . . Struggling for better vision, I noticed banks of "equipment" and a number of

entities. Five to six were close to me, apparently observing and analyzing me. . . . Further back was a larger one—I instinctively knew that it was higher in the "food chain" than the ones closer to me. This larger being was far less obvious in its presence than the smaller entities. It gave off a slightly dark aura, but did not appear threatening. I sensed unimaginable power and knowledge. It seemed to briefly observe me, with relative disinterest, and then looked to the entities closer to me for any relevant feedback. . . . They presented me with what appeared to be impossible alien toys—hyperspatial Rubik's Cubes would be a good description.[21]

But in some reports the encounters seemed to closely resemble the experiences of DMT users predating Strassman's study by hundreds of years. During the initiatory ordeal of a young Yanomami shaman, "the neophyte undergoes an intense experience of death through dismemberment by the spirits and subsequent rebirth, thus overcoming the human condition and becoming an individual living spirit. But at the same time, he becomes a 'collection' of other spirits who leave their natural habitats—located on the mountaintops and in the forest—and move into the initiate's body, which becomes their abode."[22] According to the Yanomami, these "spirits"—the hekura—enter and reside in the chest where the "spirit house" is located. Remarkably, in a number of modern underground trip reports, the DMT elves often displayed this ancient and uniquely hekura-like behavior: "Immediately after 'breaking through' into the DMT zone, I encountered this group of little elves. They began leaping into my chest, one at a time. They would just jump up and land inside me somehow. Each time an elf entered into my chest, what looked like a film projection would appear from my body out, filling the scene and replacing it with the new projection. New realities seemed to be beaming out from my chest, one after another."[23]

Were these DMT users familiar with this peculiar aspect of Amazonian shamanistic mythos? Terence McKenna was certainly aware of the similarities in the behavior of the "tykes" and of the Yanomami hekura beings: "These little entities, these self-dribbling basketballs, these things that I call the *tykes*; they jump into your chest and then they jump out again. I don't know why they do that. In the Amazon, among the tribes that use DMT derived from plants, they call these spirit things hekura, and they say that they will jump into your chest and then you're supposed to have a technique to keep them from getting out. The number of these things that you trap inside your body cavity indicates how powerful a shaman you are."[24]

Although it can't be ruled out that the brains of these DMT users were primed to generate these experiences, whether by familiarity with Amazonian shamanism or, more likely, with Terence McKenna's rap, in some reports, the parallels with Amazonian shamanism go far beyond simple stereotyped behaviors, but extend to the recapitulation of the entire initiatory ordeal. Compare this description of "spiritual dismemberment" from a Yanomami shaman to a trip report from a modern DMT user posted online. First, the Yanomami:

> When (the xapiri entities) arrive, they also hurt you and cut up your body. They divide your torso, your lower body, and your head, they sever your tongue and throw it far away. . . . They seized it to remake it, to make it beautiful and able to utter wise statements. They washed it, scraped it off, and smoothed it out to fill it with their melodies. . . . Later the xapiri came to reassemble the segments of my body, which they had dismembered. They put my skull and torso where the lower part of my body goes, and they put that part where my arms and head go. It is true![25]

Although the context is clearly different, the dismemberment-reconstruction scenario in this modern report is unambiguous: "I smoked and was instantly wheeled into an operating theater where I was casually torn apart in a comical manner by several attending entities who had comic-surgeon-like appearances, who then proceeded to reassemble me with new shiny parts."[26]

And in this extraordinary report posted on the Erowid site—the world's foremost psychoactive drug information website—the user describes inhaling a massive dose of DMT (claimed to be 200mg!) before being subjected to the entire process of dismemberment-reconstruction, performed by a mantis reminiscent of the giant Warusinari insect beings described by the Yanomami. First, the dismemberment: "A giant mantis-like being had its claws in my chest! It proceeded to tear open my chest and stomach. My rib cage was opened at the sternum, each half of my rib cage was being torn outward to each side. The giant mantis-like being then proceeded removing all my organs and insides with its horrible serrated claws, flinging my organs, guts and entrails into space."[27]

During a shaman's initiation, this would be the stage at which the multitudinous hekura—the little people—begin to arrive. In this report, they appear to take the form of a swarm of beautifully iridescent small objects built from light:

> I saw a bright green light flash over my shoulder. It then stopped in front of my torn-open hollowed corpse. It then became a beautiful fractal-geometric object, morphing and color changing. This object then began to shrink until it was a mere pinprick of light. There was a swarm of these objects, all appearing then shrinking down to pins of light, shrinking down to little beautiful green glowing atoms.

And finally the body is reconstructed as these tiny objects—hekura—enter and fill the torso of the initiate: "The mantis-like creature then began to direct the swarm of these atom-sized objects into my dismembered corpse's open and hollow chest cavity and stomach. Billions of these objects, each one unique and radiating beautiful green-colored light, and the mantid-like being continued to fill my body with them, all beginning to construct new organs and insides of my mangled corpse. The green lights had become like atoms reconstructing my heart, and lungs, and rib cage, and stomach."[28]

Was this user's brain merely reconstructing accounts of shamanistic initiation ordeals he'd read or heard in the past or was he, in fact, somehow tapping into something deeper and more fundamental? Of course, it's impossible to say for sure, and it's easy to cherry-pick a handful of reports from the vast number posted on internet drug forums that bear some similarity to those of earlier users. But these few select reports at least put to bed Nick Sand's contention that the kinds of entity encounters experienced in room 531 of the University of New Mexico Hospital were entirely artifacts of the clinical setting. Several research groups have performed more quantitative analyses of these underground trip reports, confirming that encounters with powerful, interactive, and supremely intelligent beings aren't just common, but in fact, typify the DMT state. Canadian physician David Lawrence at the University of Toronto performed a quantitative analysis of all trip reports posted to the r/DMT page on the Reddit website over a ten-year period, from 2009 to 2018, inclusive—a total of 3,778 reports.[29] Comparable to Strassman's study, almost half of these reports mentioned some flavor of entity encounter. While the most common type of entity was some kind of powerful female being, large numbers of reports described encounters with a range of nonhuman beings: insectoid, arachnoid, octopoid, and reptilian aliens; elves, imps, jesters, and jokers; deities, divine beings, and gods, and many others that seemed to defy description or categorization: "I was surrounded by alien-looking entities, though trying to glimpse at them was impossible. I was being scanned and examined. No communication; I could only think to thank these entities for whatever they were showing me. It wasn't frightening, but somewhat emotionless . . . with a playful attitude. Whatever they were scanning me with made my body extremely warm and it felt like I pissed my pants."[30] (It's worth noting that a sudden feeling of warmth, as well as the illusory sensation of peeing is a common side effect of the intravascular dyes used during a CT scan.)

Most commonly, the entities seemed to welcome the tripper into their world, guiding them through the experience, ushering them on a tour while displaying objects of unspeakable beauty and complexity. And although the "alien experimentation" type of interaction only occurred in about 9 percent of entity encounters, it was hardly rare, with this report being fairly typical: "I noticed several other beings of bundled energy that resembled mechanical insects or fleas. I call them 'workers' because they seemed to be very involved in helping to control and direct my experience. They were operating on me. I became very confused and anxious that I was in some sort of hyperdimensional alien operating room, but they communicated through direct feeling that they were healing me, so I calmed down and let them do their thing."[31]

An obvious drawback to this kind of "forum mining" study is the complete anonymity of the authors and, of course, it's impossible to say how many of them were simply fabricating their experiences for on-line kudos (and, in the case of Reddit, "upvotes"). Several studies have attempted to obviate this problem by recruiting volunteers to report their experiences directly to researchers, with no promise of any kind of reward barring a minor inconvenience and drain on their time. In 2020, Alan Davis, director of the Center for Psychedelic Drug Research at Johns Hopkins, conducted an anonymous survey of DMT users, attracting 2,561 respondents, who were all asked to complete an online survey about their single most memorable entity encounter.[32] But even with this improved study design, there were few surprises: 43 percent of respondents reported encountering a being that "guided" them through the experience, with 39 percent attaching the label "alien" to this entity and 14 percent "elf." Somewhat reassuringly, devils, demons, monsters, and other menacing or objectionable beings were reported in the lower single digits percentage-wise. Unfortunately, the entity categories were predefined by Davis's team, and while this aided in generating quantifiable data, unlike in Strassman's study, respondents weren't free to describe their encounters in their own words. There was no specific category for "insectoids," for example.

Eliminating this drawback, psychologist David Luke of the University of Greenwich in the UK—one of the world's foremost experts on DMT—designed a study that was almost identical to Strassman's study: Volunteers consumed DMT and immediately afterward were asked to describe their experience in detail. However, Luke's study differed from Strassman's in one crucial aspect: the setting. Rather than a hospital room, each volunteer would use DMT in same environment as they normally took the drug, untainted by a clinical research environment with the potential to influence the experience. For this "naturalistic setting" study, Luke drafted in his graduate student Pascal Michael, who met each volunteer—all of whom had some prior experience with DMT—at a location of their choosing before being accompanied to either their home or another agreed upon location to consume the drug. To avoid obvious legal issues, volunteers used their own DMT (invariably vaporized at a dosage between 40 and 75mg—a typical "breakthrough" dose level), and were then subjected to a semi-structured interview about their experiences as soon as they were capable.[33] Remarkably, in these varied settings, almost all of the forty-five volunteers who were successful in achieving a breakthrough experience—94 percent—reported encounters with at least one "non-self entity." All of the usual suspects made an appearance: elves and imps; jokers and jesters; insectoids and octopoids; reptilians and aliens; the mischievous; the magical; the menacing; and the magnificently powerful and intelligent.

"I was with the entities. Extraordinary. I don't think I've met this one before, almost tentacled, extraordinarily beautiful. I knew this wasn't me, and I wasn't a part of it—and yet I don't know, we knew each other? Yeah, we definitely knew each other; there's not another way of saying that—this was a familiar thing somehow. So tentacled, lots of colors. . . . The closest I can get to it is either like my imagining of what synapses look like, synaptic nerves and stuff, or something a bit octopus-y—but an entity which certainly had quite a lot of things reaching out all over the place. Without any doubt and I don't even know how I know this, extraordinary intelligence, and I don't mean sophisticated technology, I just mean, beyond anything I can imagine really. Extraordinary."[34]

As now seems to be a characteristic feature of the experience, entities eager to show off their beautiful, intricate, impossible objects featured regularly:

A lot of very strange clowns and mechanical entities. And again trying to show me something, but this time . . . it was like a toy, every time they were changing those toys and pushing them in my face, but I didn't have air. I was gasping for air, and they were pushing those toys. They—the toys—were somehow alive, continuously moving and changing shapes and colors. And I saw them very clear and detailed.

Some of them had fluffy texture, some of them were mechanical . . . very strange material I can't define. . . . I felt like I was in the corner of a room, and there were several clown mechanical beings. Floating, jumping around, very happy to show me those things.[35]

The insectoid aliens also made an appearance in several volunteers: "They appeared. Kind of just beings reaching down, not precise, but as kind of purple, green, blues, they were coming down trying to work on me in a way. . . . Slightly humanoid as in they had arms and a head. . . . High foreheads and large oval eyes. More alien than insectoid. . . . And a definite sense that they were benevolent and trying to help me."[36]

And despite a setting far removed from room 531 of the New Mexico University Hospital, several volunteers even reported experiences resembling an "alien experimentation" scenario: "Very, very intelligent things that were studying me somehow. They were waiting for me. No surprise to them that I was there. We were doing something together; I can't say studying, but it was close to that."[37]

"I always get these little helpers saying 'go on, do it, breathe a bit more.' They seem very insectoid. The whole trip was in a playpen, but underneath some sort of mothlike thing, holding the space. There were various observers. And a sense of being healed, a sense of them working on my physical and psychic body, eliminating toxins. Very benevolent; some curiosity from their perspective. Mostly insectoid."[38]

In total, twenty-six of the thirty-six entity encounters (72 percent) were of nonhuman/nonanimal beings. This last statistic in particular underscores another intriguing feature of DMT entity encounters that's rarely discussed. Despite the frequency at which certain recurring entity types are encountered during a typical DMT trip, one type of entity is noticeable by its almost complete absence: humans. In Michael and Luke's study, only six trip reports featured humans, only two of whom were known to the volunteer and both deceased. And in Davis's study, humans were almost entirely absent. Considering humans are by far the most familiar of all sentient beings to our species, their reluctance to make an appearance in the presumed drug-induced hallucinations of DMT users seems nontrivial to explain.

Whether inhaling a *Virola*-based snuff deep in the Amazonian rain forests, being injected with pure synthetic DMT while lying on a hospital bed, or vaporizing DMT extracted from jurema preta while reclining on a bed at home, a DMT experience is highly likely to have little dependence on set or setting, overwhelming and transcending individual psychological idiosyncrasies, expectations, or mood. These strange worlds and their inhabitants don't appear to be characteristic to the individual user, but characteristically similar across users and characteristically nonhuman or, as many users opt to describe them, alien. If you smoke DMT, there's a very good chance you'll encounter nonhuman discarnate beings similar in form, character, and behavior to those that countless others have described. Meeting a fellow human, however, would be a rare occurrence. How do we begin to explain this? Can we so easily dismiss these entity encounters as the machinations of an intoxicated mind? Those least likely to do so are, not surprisingly, those who have been confronted by and interacted with such beings. While the DMT worlds teem with an incredibly diverse nonhuman ecology of beings, one of the most consistent features of the experience is the attitude of the user—whether Amazonian shaman, drug study volunteer, or amateur psychonaut—toward those entities. They are independent of their minds, conscious and intelligent, exist before and continue to exist in some other realm after the experience ends. In short, they're real. But are they really?

9

ARE THEY REAL?

If the outside world fell in ruins, one of us would be capable of building it up again, for mountain and stream, tree and leaf, root and blossom, all that is shaped by nature lies modeled in us.

—Hermann Hesse

In early autumn of 2023, I received an email from a Korean man—I'll call him Jee. I regularly receive emails and messages from people around the world eager to tell me all about their expeditions to elf land, but this one was different. While most are excited to share how awe-inspiring and mind-blowing their experiences had been, Jee seemed genuinely frightened and disturbed. His nightmare began soon after arriving in Iquitos, the capital of Peru's Maynas Province and what has become, in the last decade or so, the epicenter of so-called ayahuasca tourism. Now numbering in the thousands every year, foreigners flock to this port city to partake in a series of traditional ceremonies led by any of the hundreds of local medicine men who have made it their business to serve this visionary potion to anyone willing to pay the fee. Jee was one of them, and just a few days after arriving in the city, settled in for the first of three scheduled sessions and hoping, like everyone else, for a private audience with the great spirit of Mother Ayahuasca or, failing that, perhaps some lesser discarnate beings of the forest. He was hoping for a healing experience—he received quite the opposite.

Within ten minutes of drinking his first cup of the potion, he vomited and the visions began, but they were nothing like he was expecting:

"I went through a rainbow-colored tunnel—very inorganic, very technological, advanced, and computer-like—with ancient symbols of an alien dimension. There I was pinned down by insect-like aliens with triangular mantis faces and horns—they were mocking me. Then a kind of chainsaw came from another dimension and cut me in half. The aliens took my heart out, showed it to me and rejoiced. It was the most precious thing I cared for, but I couldn't do anything but give it up to them. I was a hopeless animal facing death."

Already, Jee's encounter was beginning to sound familiar—a type of dismemberment scenario performed by insectoid entities, not dissimilar to reports I'd heard in the past. But the insectoids weren't the main players in this world: "I was then taken to an alien scientist who seemed much more powerful than the insect beings. This was not a divine being, however, but a very technologically advanced being—very cold and uncaring of human life. I received a message telepathically: 'You are messing with questions you cannot handle—the nature of gods.'"

This certainly wasn't what he signed up for and Jee wanted out. Unfortunately, this blunt warning didn't signal the end of the experience, but was just the beginning:

> I went through so much torture that I lost who I was. I just kept crying and saying "OK, you win, I died, OK? I died, so can it end?" But it didn't end. My soul was torn into pieces. The alien scientist kept showing me how insignificant and powerless I am—at first, just me, and then the whole of mankind. At this point I was breathing so loud and crying that a nurse tapped on the shoulder to ask if I was OK. And when I opened my eyes, I couldn't believe that I was wearing human skin. I closed my eyes and the suffering continued. It killed everything I cherished. Finally, I was left alone so all I could do was to love myself. I shouted "I love you" to myself and it was killed too. I was left with a sense of total hopelessness and despair. I saw people and animals being abducted by UFOs, experimented on, mutilated, and killed. I felt their fear and pain. This god ruled the earth and didn't care about our will. We were simply animals in a cage, the matrix, waiting to die.

His second ayahuasca experience was less traumatic, and as he prepared for his third and final ayahuasca session, Jee was beginning to
think that perhaps the alien beings, whoever they were, had made their
point and decided to leave him alone. He was wrong:

I threw up within ten minutes and the visions started right away. Then
everything became clear to me: I wasn't having ayahuasca experiences.
I was having alien experiences. I saw how aliens come to ayahuasca
sessions to fish people's souls. The aliens intercept their target before
ayahuasca connects to them. When they capture a soul, they show you
very captivating and hypnotic images. It tries to get you to focus on the
images, which allow them to scan your brain to determine your mental
weaknesses and then use them to break your soul down. I felt as if they
had connected a cable into my brain to extract data—they came from
another dimension and these hypnotic images were a sort of program.
There was nothing purifying about these pains. I resisted them this
time, but I saw that they had captured my soul, like a fish on a hook.
Whenever I take ayahuasca or DMT, they will come and find me, or
perhaps even after I die. I don't know how to take my soul back, or how
I should continue living knowing that my soul is in their hands now.[1]

Jee was clearly horrified and frankly traumatized by this experience,
and although when we spoke, it had been several months since that
final ayahuasca session, he was still terrified that the alien beings had
indeed captured his soul. He contacted me because he hoped I'd be able
to put his mind to rest. He wanted me to tell him it wasn't real, that it
had all been a hallucination—that it was all in his head. But if I had
done that, I would have been lying. The truth is, I don't know what
happened to Jee. I don't know whether he really did come face to face
with a supremely advanced and decidedly menacing being from some
other realm beyond our normal waking world or whether it was, in fact,
merely a terrifying nightmare.

The question of the reality or otherwise of the strange worlds and
entities encountered during a DMT trip—whether in a purified form or,

as in Jee's case, one of its many other preparations—is by far the most common and, arguably, the most important one. Aren't they just hallucinations? Isn't the brain just making it up, trying to make sense of abnormal patterns of neural activity when perturbed by a psychedelic drug molecule? Many neuroscientists and psychologists would, often without thinking about it too deeply, simply assume this to be the case. Those encounters with apparently highly intelligent, purposeful, and interactive nonhuman entities? They're merely (and I quote from an academic neuroscientist who shan't be named) "illusory social events." If Jee's encounter was a social event—illusory or otherwise—I'd like to know the kinds of parties this neuroscientist frequents. I must admit to a certain level of frustration in reading and listening to the opinions of many academics on this issue, especially those who have never actually encountered the kinds of entities Jee was forced to confront. For Jee, the question of the reality of the beings that mocked and tortured him was not an academic one, nor one to be dismissed with such facility—for him it was a matter of immense personal significance. As far as he was concerned, his very soul depended on it.

Jee was far from alone in struggling to deny the reality of what he experienced during those nights in Peru. Most of Strassman's subjects and indeed, hundreds of thousands of other people across the globe who use DMT outside of research or clinical settings are equally at a loss to explain how and why such experiences are possible. To them, the DMT worlds and their inhabitants are just too complex, too coherent, and too different from any kind of normal human experience to be something cooked up by the brain. And of course, the Indigenous peoples of South America who have developed and used DMT-containing plant technologies for centuries would be unlikely to entertain such an explanation— that the intelligent Other with whom they have been communicating and interacting for centuries are purely fabrications of their brains, and that they're deluding themselves by believing otherwise. Perhaps they are. Perhaps, after a cursory analysis, we will be able to neatly tuck these encounters away in a case file marked "exotic hallucinatory phenomena," and then we can all go home and pray for nicer dreams than Jee had to endure. But perhaps not. One thing that the true believers have in their favor, unlike almost every other religious or mystical tradition, is a rapid and almost fail-safe conversion program: You don't believe in the possibility of advanced discarnate intelligences outside of normal awareness? Here's a glass pipe. See you in ten minutes. And I'd wipe that smirk off your face if I were you.

Of course, while belief in the reality of these beings, no matter how strongly held, has little bearing on the truth of the matter, it's hard to deny that the frequency with which people encounter immensely powerful and intelligent discarnate entities after ingestion of DMT at least merits a more considered explanation than what we've been offered so far by modern mainstream neuroscience. Only after careful analysis of the phenomenon should we attempt to come to a conclusion about whether we're dealing with an exotic form of hallucination or an authentic mystery that might require us, in its explanation, to step into territory others fear to tread—whether for fear of ridicule or fear of the almost unthinkable implications of discovering a panoply of advanced and supremely intelligent discarnate conscious beings accessible by inhaling a couple of lungfuls of one of the simplest and most common alkaloids on the planet.

For most of us, situations in which we have to question the reality of what we're experiencing are mercifully rare. We simply assume that we're living in a world that's real—we cannot only see the world around us, but we can hear it, we can smell it, touch it. It's a world filled with all the things and people we love, as well as perhaps quite a few we despise. But in some cases, drawing a line between the real and the unreal isn't quite as simple as we might naively assume. Before attempting to tackle the alien beings encountered by Jee and others, it might be instructive to consider a case that few would have any trouble in placing on the unreal side of that line.

Legendary British neurologist Oliver Sacks was no stranger to unusual states of consciousness, both in his patients and, in fact, himself. Having received his medical degree from Oxford University in 1958, in the early 1960s Sacks moved to the American West Coast to begin what would become an illustrious career not only as a neurologist, but as an immensely popular writer on all matters of the mind, brain, and abnormal human experience.[2] He arrived in San Francisco just at the right time and quickly embraced the psychedelic culture that was beginning to bloom, experimenting with a range of mind-altering drugs, including LSA-containing morning glory (*Ipomea*) seeds and naturally, LSD. So when a friend casually remarked, "If you really want a far-out experience, try Artane," Sacks's interest was piqued.[3] Given his specialty, Sacks was unsurprisingly familiar with this fairly common drug used to manage muscular spasms and tremors in Parkinson's patients, but which was also known, in overdose, to elicit a temporary state of delirium accompanied by vivid hallucinations.[4] The usual therapeutic dose was two or three tablets per day—Sacks's friend suggested swallowing twenty. Hopeful that the effects would at least be instructive in his ongoing quest to understand the machinations of the human mind, Sacks decided to follow his friend's questionable advice: "So one Sunday morning, I counted out twenty pills, washed them down with a mouthful of water, and sat down to await the effect."[5]

Disappointingly, that effect never seemed to arrive: "I had a dry mouth, large pupils, and found it difficult to read, but that was all. There were no psychic effects whatever—most disappointing. I did not know exactly what I had expected, but I had expected something."

Having given up on experiencing anything more interesting, he returned to his normal Sunday morning routine: "I was in the kitchen, putting on a kettle for tea, when I heard a knocking at my front door. It was my friends Jim and Kathy; they would often drop round on a Sunday morning . . . 'Come in, door's open,' I called out, and as they settled themselves in the living room, I asked, 'How do you like your eggs?' Jim liked them sunny side up, he said. Kathy preferred them over easy."

As far as Sacks was concerned, he was enjoying a pleasant and perfectly normal morning with a couple of close friends. But that quickly changed: "We chatted away while I sizzled their ham and eggs—there were low swinging doors between the kitchen and the living room, so we could hear each other easily. Then, five minutes later, I shouted, "Everything's ready," put their ham and eggs on a tray, walked into the living room—and found it completely empty. No Jim, no Kathy, no sign that they had ever been there. I was so staggered I almost dropped the tray."[6]

Few would have any problem in admitting that it probably wasn't Jim and Kathy's disembodied spirits that had manifested in Sacks's living room on that Sunday morning. Nor was he beginning to show symptoms of a major psychological disorder. No, it was clearly a (delayed) effect of the drug. They weren't real. He had simply been hallucinating. Any standard psychiatry textbook will define a hallucination as a perception that has no basis in reality. Real perceptions, on the other hand, are connected to a reality existing outside of our heads. If Jim and Kathy weren't sitting in Sacks's living room waiting for a freshly cooked breakfast, where were they? They were in his head. So, it seems obvious—at first—that we can place Jee's encounter with the insectoid aliens into the same category as Sacks's experience. Albeit induced by a completely different mind-altering drug and of a far more terrifying nature, like Sacks, Jee was simply experiencing extremely convincing hallucinations—the aliens were in his head. Unfortunately, however, it isn't quite as simple as that. While the aliens might well have been in his head, that fact alone actually tells us very little about whether or not they were a hallucination—whether or not they were real.

The eighteenth-century German philosopher Immanuel Kant understood that there's a fundamental, albeit routinely ignored, difference between the world we experience when we're conscious—the appearance of the world, which he called the phenomenon—and the world-in-itself presumably existing out there in the external environment, the noumenon. The phenomenon is your entire subjective world at each moment, but the world-in-itself "out there" is and will always remain inaccessible.[7] Another German philosopher, Thomas Metzinger of the Johannes Gutenberg University of Mainz, expresses this idea clearly: "Consciousness is the appearance of a world. The essence of the phenomenon of conscious experience is that a single and unified reality becomes present: If you are conscious, a world appears to you. . . . The fact that there is a reality out there and you are present in it is unavailable to you. . . . The whole idea of potentially being directly in touch with reality is a sort of romantic folklore."[8]

This way of thinking about our subjective world isn't merely the purview of philosophy, but is also fundamental to how modern neuroscience considers the world that appears whenever we are conscious. While there is clearly an important relationship between the world we experience, the phenomenon, and the world "out there," the noumenon, they are not the same. This isn't particularly difficult to demonstrate, since we can quite easily manipulate our phenomenal world while leaving the external—noumenal—world intact. Ingesting a hundred micrograms of LSD will usually do the trick. A massive overdose of Artane is apparently an (ill-advised) alternative. Directly stimulating certain regions of the brain with pulses of electricity can also generate perceptions entirely independent of the senses, from flashes of color to complex geometric patterns to fully formed scenes.[9] So, what then is the usual relationship between the phenomenal world within which you live out your entire conscious life and the external noumenal world to which you never have direct access? In short, your subjective phenomenal world is a model of that noumenal world—the environment—constructed by your brain. Your brain is a builder of worlds. The purpose of this world model is to provide you with what Metzinger calls a "simulational space"—an interface—that allows you to navigate and survive whatever is "out there": to avoid predators, feed yourself and, hopefully, find a mate to pass on a sterling set of genes to the next generation. But your brain isn't like a video camera, taking snapshots of the external world and then somehow presenting them to consciousness. The problem the brain faces is that, while being charged with constructing a world as a functional model of the environment, it only ever has access to it via noisy patterns of electrochemical signals arriving via the sense organs. So how does your brain overcome this problem and construct a phenomenal world model that actually does what it's supposed to?

Just a few days after receiving Jee's email, I was taking a walk one afternoon around my neighborhood in Tokyo, passing through a narrow alley between streets when a small bright green object caught my attention as it stood starkly against the gray paving. Still too far away to identify, I thought it was perhaps a piece of foliage from the trees either side of the path or maybe a child's toy or perhaps just a piece of trash. But as I drew closer, I noticed it was stationary yet slowly and deliberately swaying on the spot. It was alive. Bending down to get a closer look, I finally realized exactly what I was looking at: It was a large female praying mantis. This was the first time I'd seen such a creature on the streets of Tokyo—it appeared to have wandered from the greenery and found itself in unfamiliar territory on what must have appeared to the mantis as a vast gray and barren landscape. After watching it with some degree of fascination, fearing it would soon find itself flattened under the foot of another passerby, I lifted it gingerly—and with a hint of trepidation—with two fingers and placed it back into the shrubbery at the side of the alley. Quite unexpectedly that afternoon, this praying mantis had found itself not merely on a narrow Tokyo side street, but briefly embedded in my phenomenal world. One moment mantises were entirely absent from my world and the next there one was. There's no reason to think this was a hallucination, and it most certainly wasn't a drug-induced vision of any kind—it was a perfectly ordinary perception of a praying mantis that presumably existed in some form out there in the external environment. But like everything else in my phenomenal world, it wasn't the mantis itself that I was experiencing, but a model of the mantis constructed by my brain.

Long before I bent down to get a closer look at the unidentified green object in my visual field, and entirely outside of my conscious awareness, my brain was already busily searching through its storehouse of objects learned from past experience to home in on one that it might be able to use to model the noisy patterns of sensory information arriving from my eyes. After testing and rejecting a number of other possibilities, my brain had eventually settled on a mantis as the most appropriate for modeling and making sense of the visual information it was receiving—from my subjective perspective, this was the moment when I realized what I was looking at. But this mantis model was far more than just an image in my visual field. My brain's purpose in modeling this mantis—and indeed for modeling everything in my phenomenal world—was not simply to show me a representation of what it thought was happening out there in the environment, but to guide my behavior in response. Along with its visual features and behaviors, irrevocably attached to my brain's visual mantis model were an array of details, connections, and associations, some of which were related to the mantis itself: a type of winged insect that eats live prey; occasionally engages in postcoital cannibalism; mainly lives in the tropics. Others were personal to me: a memory of seeing a video posted online of a similar mantis coldly and methodically consuming a large locus head first and, of course, all the DMT reports I'd read or heard in the past that featured similar beings. And naturally, I also experienced a series of emotional responses during the encounter: at first, mild curiosity, followed by surprise and fascination and, finally, concern for its well-being. So rather than a simple object model generated by my brain on the spot, I experienced the mantis as a single instance of a much broader "mantis concept" that my brain had learned and stored from past experiences. The basic pattern of visual sensory information received from the mantis had no meaning. It was the job of my brain to give it meaning, and in so doing, guide my action in the environment which, in this case, was to carefully move her out of harm's way.

Of course, what was happening in my brain that afternoon wasn't unique to mantises but applies to everything in my subjective phenomenal world. My—and your—phenomenal world is not built merely from object models, but as a highly complex system of integrated and interacting concepts that are meaningful in that they invoke emotional, physiological, and behavioral responses that guide us as we make our way through life. Our brain's role as a world builder is to fill our world model with instances of these concepts that give meaning to the messy and noisy patterns of data flowing in from the sense organs. But how do our brains achieve this?

World building is largely the responsibility of the thin outer layer of the brain known as the cerebral cortex, which is a folded sheet built from a bewilderingly complex network of billions of information-generating cells known as neurons connected mainly via specialized chemical junctions called synapses. Each neuron encodes information by generating patterns of electrochemical signals called action potentials, which appear as brief—1ms or so—spikes when the electrical activity inside a neuron is measured. The synapses allow neurons to speak to other neurons, sharing information that can flow through the cortex in a tightly orchestrated manner depending on the patterns of connections between them, generating patterns of neural activity that represent the structure, content, dynamics, and meaning of your phenomenal world.[10] (It's important to point out that, to state that your world model is constructed by your brain is not to claim that consciousness itself is generated by your brain. Why the pattern of neural activity that represents your world model should have the quality of subjectivity—why you are conscious—is another question entirely and remains very much an open question in neuroscience.)

When visual sensory information enters the brain by stimulating light-sensitive cells of the retina at the back of each eye, these cells begin firing sequences of spikes that are passed to an area right at the back of the cortex known as the primary visual cortex, but often referred to simply as V1.[11] The cortex also contains separate primary sensory areas devoted to hearing, taste, smell, and touch, all of which have a role in your experience of a world.[12] But since humans are primarily visual creatures and the DMT state is a characteristically visual experience, we'll focus on this system. The primary visual cortex, V1, forms a complete and maximally detailed map of the visual field, but is only equipped to detect basic, low-order features of the incoming sensory information, such as lines and their orientations and direction of movement, textures, and basic colors. This pattern of activity in V1 is as close as your cortex will get to the external world, but in and of itself, has no meaning—it's your brain's job to impose meaning on this pattern by using it to build rich and meaningful models that guide your behavior. After all, when you open your eyes, you aren't greeted by a complicated and bewildering pattern of moving lines and colors, but a world of objects you recognize and respond to, imbued with meaning. But how do you generate these richly detailed, stable, and meaningful objects you experience as part of your subjective world from the messy, noisy, and ever-changing patterns of activity in the primary visual cortex?[13]

The primary visual cortex, V1, is connected to a hierarchy of areas that sit above it (anatomically, they sit farther and farther forward and around the sides of the brain in the temporal lobes).[14] The level above V1 has a bird's-eye view of the patterns of activity being generated by the flow of sensory information from the eyes and its neurons are tuned to detect recognizable patterns in the basic features, such as simple geometric shapes. In other words, this upper level is the first level in the hierarchy trying to make sense of the noisy activity in the primary visual cortex, giving some semblance of basic meaning to these patterns. But we're still far from the complete mantis model and all the important associations that elicit emotion and guide behavior. This is where the next level gets to work, looking for patterns in these basic shapes, textures, and patches of color to form more complex, higher-order structures, such as the jointed legs and characteristic triangular head fitted with a pair of large bulbous eyes. And so on it goes upward through the hierarchy, with each level integrating the patterns in the level below in an attempt to find an object model that best fits the pattern of sensory information.[15] Since my brain has some familiarity with mantises—and insects in general—from past experience, it already knows what patterns of sensory information to expect should there actually be a mantis out there in the environment, so it had no trouble discerning that this pattern was a good match. The moment my cortex achieved this was precisely the moment I realized what I was looking at, as my cortex managed to sort the sensory information into a familiar object: a praying mantis modeled as a hierarchically organized pattern of neural activity, with the fine low-order details modeled at the lower ends of the cortical hierarchy, toward V1, and the overall mantis concept sitting at the top. This pattern of cortical activity is the gently swaying mantis I experienced as part of my subjective world—not simply an object model but a richly detailed and evocative concept, full of meaning. If you were able to see the patterns of neural activity in my cortex as I viewed the mantis, you'd notice that the patterns became more stable as you moved up the levels of the cortical hierarchy. The lowest level, V1, was being stimulated by the messy, ever-changing patterns of activity in the retina, so the patterns of activity in this area of the cortex would be correspondingly messy and dynamic. As you moved up the hierarchy, my cortex was sorting these patterns into shapes, patches of colors and textures, and movement. These are more stable than the raw patterns in V1 but still change as the mantis sways on its feet and manipulates its antennae. Right at the top of the hierarchy, the broad high-level "mantis concept" was being modeled, which contained no fine details about this specific mantis but is connected to other concepts that gave this mantis model personal meaning and could guide my behavior. Even though the mantis was moving, as long as it didn't fly away or magically vanish, this high-level model didn't need to change for as long as it made sense to hold the mantis concept in my overall world model.

But now my cortex had a problem: My subjective world isn't simply a collection of object models but is supposed to model the dynamic processes occurring in the environment and to continuously make sense of the ever-changing patterns of information arriving from the senses. But my mantis model was merely a "snapshot" of what my cortex thought was happening in the environment, and a model of a stationary but gently swaying mantis, no matter how intricately detailed and meaningful in that moment, would quickly become perfectly useless should the mantis decide the spread its wings and take flight. The solution to this problem, at first, seems quite obvious: simply take another snapshot! At intervals, my cortex could process the patterns of activity in V1, just as it did before, and generate an updated model—just like the frames of a movie. Unfortunately, however, this is far from an optimal solution to the problem. Let's assume that the mantis doesn't spread its wings and fly off. Instead, let's assume, as was my actual experience, that it simply continued what it was doing as I peered down at it—standing still and gently swaying on its feet. Well, my cortex already had a model of it doing that—that's the model I was experiencing. So what would be the point in wasting neuronal resources reconstructing a model it already had and which was modeling the mantis perfectly well? Neuronal processes are energy hungry, so continuously constructing and reconstructing models without good reason makes little sense. There must be a more efficient solution.

If you've ever seen a traditional hand-drawn animation artist at work, you'll notice that they don't redraw an entire scene for each frame of the animation—that would be a colossal waste of time and energy. Rather, they only redraw what *changes* between frames, which might be as little as the fingers on one hand of one of the characters, leaving the background and anything else just as it was in the previous frame. So the cortex can use this same principle: Rather than rebuilding the mantis model from scratch with each passing moment, it can simply update the model if something significant changes. But now we have another problem: How does the cortex know what's changed if it doesn't build an updated model to compare to the one it's already using? This is where the magic happens. Since the mantis model was constructed as a hierarchy of patterns from the low-level features represented in V1 upward, the cortex can simply work in the opposite direction, "unpacking" its mantis model, level by level, down the cortical hierarchy until it gets back a pattern of basic features—such as moving lines and patches of color—that it can compare with the actual sensory information being received by V1. Basically, the cortex is saying: "If my model is still working well, this is the pattern of visual sensory information I should expect to see next." The cortex is using its current model to anticipate—literally, to predict—the pattern of activity in V1 in the following moment.[16] If this predicted activity matches the actual activity in V1, then the cortex knows the model is still doing what it's supposed to be doing—modeling the evolution of sensory information arriving at the retinae—and can safely ignore that sensory information. These predictions flow down the cortical hierarchy and actually cancel out—extinguish—any activity in V1 that they successfully predict, because the information encoded in this activity is already part of the model. These are the parts of the scene the animator leaves as they are.

But what happens if something unexpected and surprising happens—if the mantis really does suddenly spread its wings and take flight? In this case, the sensory information stimulating the patterns of activity in V1 will change dramatically, and crucially, unpredictably—the swaying mantis model would be entirely different to the model of a mantis spreading its wings and flying away. So the predicted activity won't match the actual activity in V1, and as such, the predictions will fail to cancel out this activity. The patterns of activity in V1 that remain—that aren't canceled out—are appropriately referred to as prediction errors. These are sent up the cortical hierarchy to inform the upper levels which aspects of the model are failing to accurately predict the evolution of sensory inputs and must be updated until the prediction errors fall—until the model starts working again. So your brain doesn't need to build its model from scratch with each passing moment, nor does it need to constantly make sense the flood of sensory information flowing into the brain via the sense organs, but need only update its model based on un-predicted, surprising, information in the form of these error signals, and canceling out—filtering—predictable sensory information that fits the model.

In short, once your world model is built and working, this contin-uous cycle of predict, test, and update requires only a relative trickle of sensory information that acts as a testing signal for this model, with only the unpredicted and surprising information actually making it far-ther than the primary visual cortex in the form of prediction errors used to update the model and keep it tuned to the environment. Using advanced imaging techniques, it's possible to visualize the flow of these error signals from the back of the brain toward the front (up the cortical hierarchy), with the predictions flowing in the opposite direction. This will become important later when we consider the effect of DMT on the brain. The beauty of modeling the world in this way is that it reduces the amount of sensory information that needs to be absorbed and pro-cessed to an absolute minimum. Since neurons use energy, information processing is expensive, so it doesn't make sense for the brain to absorb and process any more sensory information than it requires to maintain its world model.

Although you're entirely unaware of it, this is precisely how your brain is modeling your world at this very moment: following the pat-terns of sensory information and using them to build meaningful hi-erarchically structured models that are constantly being tested against the ever-changing patterns of activity in the primary visual cortex. The result is a marvelously rich, detailed, dynamic and yet stable, and most importantly, useful model of the environment, all constructed with-out ever having access to the environment itself. Of course, it's almost impossible to fully comprehend this, but your experience of a world is essentially what this pattern of neural activity feels like from your subjective perspective. Your cortex has taken this noisy pattern of in-formation arriving from the senses and used its store of object models and concepts to impose meaning on it—to construct a model of the environment that you can respond to and interact with.

But how does your brain know it's settled on the most appropriate

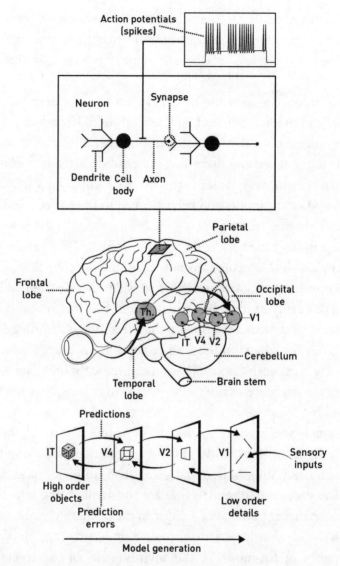

The cortex's world model is built as a complex pattern of neural information (generated by neuron action potentials) over several levels of a cortical hierarchy extending from the primary visual cortex (V1) at the back of the brain and into the temporal lobes at the sides of the brain. Sensory information arrives at V1 from the retinae of the eyes via the thalamus (Th.). The higher levels of the cortical hierarchy send predictions down the cortical hierarchy – the cortex's attempt to predict the evolution of sensory information arriving at V1. Prediction errors, used to update the model, flow in the opposite direction, up the cortical hierarchy.

or accurate objects and concepts in modeling your world? In short, it doesn't. Your brain only ever has access to the noisy patterns of sensory information that stimulate the ever-changing patterns of activity in the primary visual cortex, so it can't somehow "check" if there's actually a mantis—or anything else—out there in the inaccessible noumenal world. The model that wins out and finds itself part of your phenomenal world is simply the one that best predicts the ongoing evolution of information arriving via the sense organs. The brain has no yardstick by which to measure the "truth" of its world model and nor does it, in fact, care. Your brain is only interested in building models of the environment that perform their function, and like all evolutionarily adaptive traits, this function is to give you the greatest chance to survive and reproduce. Whether its model forms a faithful representation of what's actually going on out there in the noumenal world, your brain—and by extension you—can never know.[17]

Of course, your brain wasn't dropped to Earth with all of these pre-packaged and richly detailed object models and concepts to use in its modeling of the environment—it had to learn to build them. From the moment you were dragged kicking and squealing from your mother's womb, your brain was constantly sampling sensory information from the environment, looking for and, by molding the patterns of synaptic connections between neurons, learning the patterns and regularities in this data, and beginning to sculpt them into multi-leveled object models to guide your actions and behavior throughout life.[18] To appreciate how skilled your brain has become in building your world, you need only fall asleep. For most people and for most of the time, the dream world is remarkably similar to the waking world.[19] And there's a very good reason for this: It's built in pretty much the same way, using the same concepts and models the brain learned during waking life while interacting with the environment. After my experience with the mantis, it wouldn't have been surprising if I had found one or two flitting into my dreams. Despite being disconnected from sensory information from the environment during sleep, my brain is perfectly capable of modeling mantises in reasonable detail, together with their dynamic and varied behaviors and all my typical emotional and behavioral responses.

Of course, this is only the case because I've encountered mantises in the past—whether in real life or elsewhere—so my brain has reasonably comprehensive stored models of such insects to draw upon.

So, we can see that both the waking and the dream world are built from exactly the same stuff—an integrated system of object models and concepts built from patterns of cortical activity. What makes the dream world less real is not what it's made from, but its relationship to the environment. During normal waking life, your world model is continuously being tested against sensory information from the environment—this is a *sensed* world. In contrast, a *dreamt* world lacks this sensory data training signal. This is why dreams tend to be more fluid and unstable, shifting from scene to scene, since the brain has the freedom to explore its stored models without being held accountable to sensory testing.

Using these insights, we can see that Oliver Sacks's hallucinated visit from his friends was somewhere between a normal waking perception and a dream. One of the ways Artane—the drug Sacks swallowed—works is to "turn down the volume" of the error signals that normally trigger model updates, rendering the world less accountable to sensory data.[20] It doesn't mute these signals entirely, however, or it really would have been a waking dream. Since visits from Jim and Kathy were a regular event, Sacks's brain was perfectly capable of modeling this scenario without the guidance of sensory information, just as it might have done so in a dream. What triggered Sacks's brain to model their visit on this particular occasion is unknown—perhaps a noise that sounded like a knock at the door that sparked the idea that perhaps Jim and Kathy had decided to drop by, as they so often did on a Sunday—but once it established itself in Sacks's world model, the dampened error signals weren't able to correct and update the model. Sacks's world model as he greeted and chatted to his friends was precisely as it would have been had they actually been there! So what's the difference? The difference is not in the world model as such, but in its relationship to the environment. Had Jim and Kathy actually dropped round that morning, Sacks's brain would have been building a model of Jim and Kathy that was mapped to and being tested against sensory information from the environment. But in this case, these components of

Sensed world

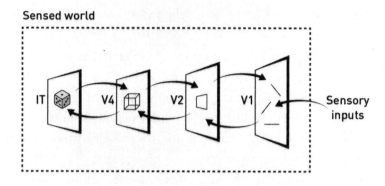

Dreamt world

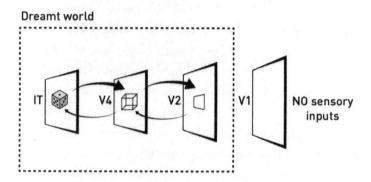

Both sensed and dreamt worlds are built by the cortex. However, a sensed world is constantly being tested against sensory inputs. A dreamt world, in contrast, is disconnected from sensory inputs and relies on stored object models learned during waking life.

his world model were being maintained independently of sensory testing (because of the dampened error signals). It was only when he entered the living room and was faced with sensory information that was so unexpected and surprising—his brain expected to see both of their figures lounging on the sofa—that these much larger error signals were able to overcome their dampening by Artane and force the appropriate updates to his world model, one in which Jim and Kathy were absent. It was that model update—to a model with an empty living room—that triggered the sense of shock and disbelief as he realized he'd been hallucinating.

So, in general, a hallucination is simply an object model incorporated into the brain's overall world model largely independent of sensory information from the environment.[21] Hallucinations—or "unreal" perceptions—are built from the same material as "real" perceptions and as the dream world. The only difference is that "real" perceptions are mapped to and tested against sensory information from the external environment, whereas hallucinations and dreams lack this connection. So what happens when you consume a psychedelic drug? Of course, it's your world model that changes. This might be subtle, such as with a low of dose magic mushrooms or, in the case of a breakthrough dose of DMT, astonishingly dramatic, with the entire world model being transformed to one that bears no relationship whatsoever to the normal waking world model. This brings us back to the original question: Are the entities so often encountered during a DMT trip real perceptions or are they closer to hallucinations or, perhaps, more like waking dreams? Although we're still far from being able to answer that question, with a basic understanding of how the brain constructs our model of the world, we can at least formulate the question a little more precisely, which will vastly improve our chances of finding a meaningful answer.

Since all perceptions are built from patterns of neural activity, they are all, in a sense, real. If I had told Jee that those menacing insectoid aliens were all in his head, I would, in one sense, have been speaking perfectly truthfully—they were models being constructed by his brain and integrated into his dramatically altered world model. But this applies to all perceptions. What we really want to know is whether or not his brain's model of these creatures was being tested against some external source of sensory information. Were there actually intelligent beings "out there"—wherever out there is—being mapped to his brain's model of those beings?

The default answer to this question ought to be "no." Clearly this was a perception unmoored from any external sensory information—a hallucination. In other words, just like Oliver Sacks's drugged brain, Jee's brain was simply making it up. And indeed this is the explanation that most scientists will cling to as if their life depended on it when asked about the origin of the entities so frequently encountered during a DMT trip. For most, the alternative is simply unthinkable. Unfortunately, things turn out to be nowhere near as easy to dismiss as this. But to understand why, we need to think a little more deeply about the kinds of models your brain can and, crucially, cannot simply fabricate. The fact that your brain can construct incredibly detailed, stable, and functional models of the environment is not in question. And the fact that DMT is able to transport us to entirely novel and far stranger worlds obviously means that such worlds are being modeled in our brains—if they weren't, we wouldn't be able to experience them, since all experienced worlds must be represented by patterns of information generated by the cortex. The central question then is not whether these bizarre worlds and their inhabitants are being modeled in the brain, but whether or not the brain can fabricate them entirely independent of some external source of sensory information. If we conclude that it can, then, rather than an actual encounter with vicious insectoid aliens from a normally invisible realm, and no doubt to his immense relief, Jee's encounter could be dismissed as little more than a very bad dream. If not, then we need to sincerely consider the possibility that they represented something far stranger and far more difficult to explain.

10

I'LL SEE YOU IN MY NIGHTMARES

The lunatic is a wakeful dreamer.

—Immanuel Kant

Although it would be a stretch to call DMT a mainstream psychedelic, it's certainly much more popular and well known now than it was when Terence McKenna began lecturing about the machine elves toward the tail end of the last century, thanks in no small part to those very lectures. But despite his immense erudition, Terence also had a tendency on occasion—and particularly when it came to matters of science—to make claims that were, at the very least, poorly supported, and from time to time, simply wrong. Long before I was writing and speaking publicly about psychedelics, I recall listening to one of his lectures during which he brought up the subject of dreaming. Not only did he suggest that the DMT experience can be compared to dreaming but that DMT produced by the brain actually mediates the descent into dream sleep. A couple of decades later and one of the most common questions I'm asked concerns the relationship between DMT and dreaming: "Is it true that DMT causes dreams?" In fact, I often read or hear such a claim repeated as no more in dispute than the average airspeed velocity of an unladen swallow. I've always been somewhat puzzled by this. Of the countless people I've spoken to who've used DMT, not one has ever described their experiences as "dreamlike." My first experience with the molecule was most certainly unlike any dream I'd ever had, before or since. Nor do the countless trip reports I've read ever strike me as being even remotely close to most dream reports.

Having said that, McKenna's claim wasn't plucked entirely from his imagination, but contains at least a grain of truth. DMT is indeed present in the human body and has been detected in the blood and urine of humans since the 1950s, but McKenna's dream idea likely stems from a purely hypothetical paper published in 1988 by medicinal chemist Jace Callaway, then at the University of California at San Francisco. In his admittedly rather biochemically sophisticated hypothesis, Callaway noted similarities between the DMT molecule and the sleep-regulating neurohormone melatonin, synthesized by the pineal gland, and surmised that, since all the necessary biochemical machinery to produce DMT is also present in the brain, it ought to be possible for the pineal gland, at specific stages of the sleep cycle, to divert its resources from melatonin production and begin synthesizing DMT so as to trigger entry into dream sleep.[1] Although nobody has specifically attempted to test Callaway's hypothesis by looking for spikes in blood or urine DMT levels during dream sleep, a study in the 1970s *did* measure DMT levels in urine at eight-hour intervals throughout the day and night and found no such spikes in the wee hours.[2] While Callaway had quite clearly put some serious thought into the biochemical details of his hypothesis, does the idea that the DMT worlds are a kind of dream fabricated by the brain even make any sense?

The structure and content of dreams have been recorded, discussed, and interpreted for millennia, and even in the twenty-first century, exactly how and why we dream remains a matter of debate among cognitive scientists. Formerly the purview of leather armchaired Freudians, polyester-upholstered armchaired mystics, and tented roadside carnival prognosticators, in the last century, dream research has become a perfectly respectable and valuable branch of the psychological and neurological sciences.[3] We now know a lot about what people dream about and what they don't, and to a limited extent at least, why. Like the waking world, the dream world is a model constructed using patterns of neural activity across the cerebral cortex. In the waking state, this world model is constantly

tested against and held accountable to patterns of sensory information arriving via the sense organs. In the dream state, the brain is
using its storehouse of concepts and object models learned during its
interactions with the environment in waking life to construct a world
model while almost entirely disconnected from these sensory inputs.
In other words, dreams are not random visions but selective simulations of the waking world.[4] The world your brain constructs in the
dream state is the world it learned to construct in the waking state.
The waking world and the dream world are built from the same stuff.

So not surprisingly for most people and for most of the time, dreams
are essentially continuous with waking life. Although you might vividly
recall a particularly striking or unusual dream, unless you're an extreme
outlier, most of your dreams are likely to be filled with the usual activities
of daily life, down to the amount of time you spend watching TV, talking
on the telephone, or eating (yes, there have been studies that show this).[5]
Dreams, for the most part, aren't that interesting. Even the scenarios that
are typically associated with dreams—being chased or pursued; flying or
falling; taking a test or examination; missing a train or getting lost; being
naked or scantily clothed in public—although widespread are actually
relatively rare compared to the more mundane activities of everyday
life.[6] And while some dreams are described as "bizarre," this is usually
limited to: incongruity (an element inconsistent with waking reality);
vagueness (an obscure or indeterminate element); and discontinuity (an
element suddenly appearing, disappearing or being transformed).[7] So-
called bizarreness in dreams isn't usually particularly bizarre but stems
from how the dream world is constructed. In the normal waking state,
the brain relies on sensory inputs to maintain a stable model of the environment. In the dream state, this sensory data training signal is lost.

Not surprisingly, most dream characters are other people, and
when nonhuman characters do make an appearance, they tend to
be dogs, cats, horses, and other domesticated animals. Of course, the
types of animals seen in dreams are strongly dependent on where
you happen to have grown up. Anthropologist Thomas Gregor spent
time studying the dreams of the Mehinaku people living in Brazil's
Xingu Indigenous Park.[8] Dogs, cats, and horses were almost never

encountered in their dreams. However, the animals they encountered in daily life certainly were:

> "Chased by a snake, he turns and kills it with a machete."
>
> "Chased by a black jaguar."
>
> "While fishing, shot at stingray, but missed and almost lost arrow."[9]

Interestingly, children are much more likely to dream of animals than adults, even ones they're unlikely to encounter in waking life, such as wolves, lions, bears, and snakes. It's tempting to imagine that children somehow have closer ties to our evolutionary past, to a time when such animals truly represented a threat in the environment. However, it's worth also noting that when young children are asked to write stories, they also tend to feature animal characters more than humans—generally the same types of animals they meet in fairy tales, cartoons, and children's stories. In other words, children most likely dream of animals simply because they are characters familiar from their waking life, not because they're tapping into some deeply embedded collective neural heritage.[10] Although it's possible to find accounts from self-described "dream researchers" who would have children's dreams filled with monsters and mythical beings in magical and wonderfully strange alternate worlds,[11] curiously, when children are awoken during dream sleep and immediately interviewed by cognitive scientists, these fantastical creatures of the netherworlds fail to make an appearance.[12] So if we're hoping to find the denizens of the DMT realms tucked away in the darkest recesses of the infant mind, we're likely to be left disappointed. Having said that, the dreams of children *do* reveal something far more interesting about the DMT worlds visited by consenting adults.

William David Foulkes, former director of the dream research laboratories at the University of Wyoming, is arguably the world's leading expert on dreaming in children, responsible for the most extensive studies into their dreams ever conducted. Foulkes's research not only analyzed the structure and content of children's dreams at each stage of childhood (from the ages of three to fifteen), but also how the dreams of individual children changed as they grew and developed.[13] Preschool children (ages three to five) were only found to have been dreaming about 15 percent of the time when awakened during so-called dream sleep, and when they did dream, those dreams were extremely simple and lacked any kind of narrative structure. Any dream characters, which more often than not were animals, were basic images and entirely static—the animals didn't move or behave as animals normally do. Nor was there any kind of interaction between the dreamer and those characters. The dreams of preschool children were more like slide shows than movies. However, as the children—and their brains—grew and developed, their dreams became much more interesting. Dream characters began to move and interact with the dreamer, who increasingly played more of an active role in the dream rather than simply being a passive observer. The dreams also began to develop more narrative structure—they started to look more like movies. In short, the children's brains were learning to construct a dream world that simulated the waking world.

To dream is to build a world without guidance from sensory information. It's one thing to dream of a wolf as an image, and quite another to dream of a wolf that's actively moving and behaving as wolves do, and the brains of young children simply can't manage this task. As Foulkes explains, "Infants can manipulate information currently available in the environment, but they cannot manipulate information without concurrent environmental support. In effect, they can 'think' of dolly when it's there, but not when it's not. How, then, could they not only conjure up a picture of dolly, but also make up a story about dolly while sleeping? . . .[14] Functionally, our kind of dreaming is related, not to how we see, but to how we are able to think about persons, objects, and events when they are not physically present."[15]

Even as an adult, your brain sculpts your dream world using what it has learned while interacting with the environment in waking life. It doesn't fabricate entirely novel worlds with no relationship to the waking world, not because it's lazy, but because it can't. Your brain only knows how to build one type of world: the waking world that functions as a model of the environment. Or, at least, this is the only world it *ought* to know how to build. Australian philosopher of mind David Chalmers goes as far as to say: "Dreams never give you something absolutely new. If you dream of a head/body, it must be based on your having perceived heads/bodies. . . . Or at least the shapes and colors in the dream world must be based on shapes and colors in the real world."[16] Your brain builds your world in the dream state using the stored object models and concepts it has learned while building your world in the waking state.

The adult brain certainly has a much greater capacity for creative modeling of the world in the dream state than the infant brain, exploring and rearranging its models and concepts to generate novel narratives and ever-shifting scenes, even to the point of generating scenes and characters never encountered in the environment. It wouldn't be inexplicable, for example, to dream of swimming with a mermaid, despite presumably never having encountered a mermaid in the environment. The brain has learned enough about the mermaid concept from books and other media to render a reasonable model of such a creature, although this is likely to have its limits. Dreams of mermaids, however, are likely to be extremely rare, unless perhaps you happened to have watched a movie recently that featured one or if you're particularly fascinated by or harbor a secret sexual fetish toward human-fish chimeras. Dreaming of an anti-mermaid—fish head and human legs—would be extremely unusual, since this is not a concept the brain is likely to be familiar with, although the rearrangement is fairly trivial and it likely wouldn't be a stretch for the brain to also model such an abomination (and you can already imagine it). But DMT users regularly report beings, objects, and environments that aren't simply rearrangements, distortions, or fanciful extrapolations of those experienced in the waking world, but ones that not only don't exist but simply cannot exist. I don't dream about tesseracts (a four-dimensional analog of a cube) and other objects in more than three dimensions because, despite having a reasonable understanding of the tesseract as an abstract mathematical object, my brain has no idea how to render such an object in my visual world. And yet DMT users regularly report objects of impossible geometry and structure that simply cannot exist in our environment. To claim that, as we mature, as well as learning to construct world models in the absence of support from sensory inputs—as during dreaming—the brain also gains the ability to fabricate bizarre, inordinately complex worlds in exquisite razor-sharp detail and with absolutely no relationship to the world it learned to construct is quite an ask. And yet this is precisely what people experience when they use DMT. And it isn't only the brain's ability to construct such worlds that's a challenge to explain. Even if the brain could construct such worlds without sensory inputs, its propensity to do so with such regularity under the influence of DMT is barely a more tractable problem. When relieved of its duties as a real-time environment modeler, as during dreaming, the brain tends to build worlds that look very much like the normal waking world, filled with all the familiar characters we meet in daily life. Why, when perturbed by this simple plant alkaloid, it should suddenly begin rendering hypertechnological cityscapes crawling with advanced intelligences with no referent in the waking world, that not only don't exist but couldn't exist, is far from trivial to explain.

Although there's something almost romantically appealing about the idea that the nonhuman discarnate beings encountered during a typical DMT trip are, as Nick Sand insisted, "creatures created by the infinitely capable creative force to teach us about ourselves,"[17] it's important to recognize that such ideas are not merely reaching with an outstretched hand beyond the scientific arena but exiting it entirely. It's tempting to appeal to some infinite untapped creative potential of the human brain in attempting to explain the visions of DMT, but this is simply fantasy, and while drawing a line between what the human brain can and cannot fabricate is far from easy, it's not an entirely hopeless task. In dreams, the brain does occasionally betray the limits of its modeling skills when attempting to construct scenarios for which it lacks sufficiently detailed stored models. If you've ever tried to read a book, use a pocket calculator, or use your cell phone (especially to type a message) in a dream, you'll understand how frustrating it can be. These are situations when the brain relies most heavily on a stream of accurate, detailed sensory inputs that are extremely variable and highly unpredictable. Recall that your brain's visual model of the world is built over several levels of a hierarchy, with general high-level concepts being modeled at the top of the hierarchy, with specific, fine, rapidly changing details being modeled at the lower end and highly dependent on the flow of sensory information arriving from the eyes. When this sensory information isn't available, while your brain can readily construct a reasonable high-level model of a cell phone, accurately replicating its detailed low-level features and behavior is a much more difficult task. Generating accurate output from a pocket calculator is effectively an impossible task. In fact, lucid dreamers often use these kinds of model limitations as "reality tests" to check whether or not they're dreaming. The loss of visual detail in the dream state compared to the waking state is one of its most pronounced features and a direct consequence of the loss of real-time sensory inputs, when the brain must rely on its broad high-level object models in constructing the world.[18] It presents something of a challenge to reconcile this with the accounts of exquisitely intricate and detailed alien worlds experienced during a DMT trip, when the eyes are closed and all visual sensory inputs are lost.

Similarly, there are some things that we would readily accept aren't merely difficult for our brains to model, but impossible. I've lived in Japan for almost a decade now, and when I first arrived, human characters in my dreams spoke only English. Even after living in the country for some time, nobody in my dreams spoke Japanese. Although there will likely always be a propensity for my dream characters to speak my mother tongue, it ought to be obvious why none of them spoke Japanese during my early days in Japan: It was simply impossible for my brain to model human characters speaking—accurately, at least—a language it didn't know. Now, however, I regularly hear people speaking Japanese in my dreams. Likewise, if you were to dream of someone fluently (and accurately) speaking an isolated variant of a Southern African click language, it would be inexplicable. Your brain can only use the information it has stored or has access to via sensory inputs in constructing its world model. Of course, your brain is capable of creativity and novelty in how it uses this information in sculpting your world, but many DMT experiences are obviously not mere reconfigurations or rearrangements of models it has learned and developed throughout life. There are clearly aspects of the phenomenon that seem to transcend this entirely:

They are . . . the word is "machinelike." The whole thing bodes of high alien technology. How else could it be explained? But wait, they aren't just machines; they are . . . organic? No, they are sentient! . . . How can such a hugely complex, impossible, gigantic thing be self-aware? I don't know, yet they most certainly are. . . . More fractal machine entities. They are getting bigger, more complex, they join with one another, they break apart, they dance, they sing. THEY SING! Their songs are so far beyond beautiful, sung with such amazing grace and practiced ease. The beauty of it is unbearable. The sound creates more of the crystalline fractal creatures, which in turn start singing in unison with the others. I can't stand this much beauty. I can't fucking take it![19]

In constructing the DMT worlds, it's almost as if the brain is using a language it never learned to speak, building models it never learned to construct—and doing so flawlessly. The brain's ability to fabricate these entirely nonhuman worlds in such exquisite and dynamic detail and complexity and with such effortless and lissome virtuosity is at least as confounding as a five-year-old British child waking up one morning and between mouthfuls of Frosted Mini-Wheats offering a confident but measured perspective on twentieth-century Sino-Russian relations in fluent Siberian Yupik.

Overall, despite Terence McKenna's speculations and Jace Callaway's impressive but largely unsupported biochemical hypothesis, there seems to be no reason to believe that the otherworldly experiences of DMT users can be explained away as elaborate dream states. The only connection between DMT and dreaming seems to be that both are constructed as world models by the brain. How the brain constructs dreams isn't so difficult to explain. The same cannot be said for the DMT worlds and its occupants. But perhaps I'm being a little unfair in comparing dreams, which are the product of a normally functioning brain during sleep, to the worlds that emerge from a brain thoroughly perturbed by a powerful psychedelic molecule while completely awake. After all, visions and hallucinations aren't restricted to dreams and psychedelic drug-induced altered states of consciousness. Perhaps DMT-induced visions are closer to the hallucinations of those suffering from psychosis or other neurological disorders that disrupt the brain's ability to construct a stable and functional model of the environment.

This certainly isn't a new idea. As early as the late nineteenth century, psychiatrists began noticing how the effects of certain mind-altering drugs like deadly nightshade (containing scopolamine, which works in a similar way to the drug Artane that Oliver Sacks consumed) and the peyote cactus alkaloid mescaline at least resembled some of the so-called positive symptoms of schizophrenia, such as confusion, disordered and irrational thinking, "hearing voices," and vivid visual hallucinations.[20] In fact, until British psychiatrist Humphry Osmond coined the term "psychedelic" (meaning *mind manifesting*) in 1956, they were generally referred to in the scientific literature as psychotogens (psychosis generating) or psychotomimetics (psychosis mimicking). But some scientists, including Osmond, took this idea even further and began to suspect that schizophrenia might actually stem from a metabolic disturbance leading to the production of insanity-inducing molecules in the body, referred to as schizotoxins (or sometimes schizogens).[21] Although early candidates for a human schizotoxin turned out to be dead ends,[22] it wasn't long before psychiatrists began building a case against a then newly discovered, highly visionary plant alkaloid.

Just as Stephen Szára was completing the world's first study of the effects of DMT in human subjects, American biochemist Julius Axelrod had just completed pioneering work on the metabolism of the neurotransmitter noradrenaline (norepinephrine). Axelrod then turned his attention to another class of neurochemicals, the tryptophan metabolites, which include the neurotransmitter serotonin and the neurohormone melatonin. During his work studying the enzymes involved in tryptophan metabolism, Axelrod made a startling discovery: The key enzyme required for the construction of DMT from tryptophan was highly localized in the lungs of rabbits. What purpose DMT might serve in rabbit physiology, if any, wasn't clear—it still isn't—but Axelrod's results hinted that this simple molecule wasn't just a plant alkaloid after all, but was also a product of mammalian biochemistry. And the enzyme in question, indolethylamine-N-methyltransferase (INMT), was by no means restricted to the lungs of rabbits, but was ubiquitous across the animal kingdom and that included, naturally, humans.[23]

Encouraged by Szára's recent discovery of the powerful visionary effects of this plant alkaloid, DMT seemed like an obvious candidate for the long sought-after schizotoxin. In the decades that followed, dozens of studies, all looking for—and finding—DMT and its metabolites in the urine, blood, and even the cerebrospinal fluid of both schizophrenic patients and healthy volunteers were published. Although a handful of studies did claim to find a link between the severity of certain psychotic symptoms and levels of DMT in blood and urine,[24] others found no relationship.[25] But whether or not DMT played a role in schizophrenia, the fact that it was present in humans at all should have been hollered from the rooftops. This simple alkaloid that generated arguably the most remarkable and inexplicable state of consciousness a human could experience, gating access to a thoroughly unearthly alternate reality teeming with intelligent alien creatures beyond our imagination, was naturally present not only in countless plant species, but in every single one of us too. But instead, year after year, yet another human study matter-of-factly reported the carefully quantified concentrations of the world's strangest drug in paranoid schizophrenic patients, nonparanoid schizophrenic patients, paranoid non-schizophrenic patients, and pretty much anyone else willing to line up, drop their pants, and piss in a bottle.

In retrospect, the lack of support for the DMT hypothesis of schizophrenia isn't any more surprising than its later candidacy as the "dream molecule." As scientists and physicians became lost in their attempts to pin schizophrenia on DMT, none of them seemed to be particularly interested in the actual experiences of those who used the drug and whether they were comparable to the hallucinations of their patients. When psychologist David Luke and I interviewed Stephen Szára just a few years prior to his passing, he admitted, "When these experiences (such as God, strange creatures, other worldliness) appeared in our DMT studies, we did not philosophize about them, but as psychiatrists, we simply classified them as 'hallucinations.'" For most psychiatrists working with DMT at the time, that attitude seemed to be standard: a hallucination is a hallucination is a hallucination. But this is obviously not the case. In their defense, Szára and his contemporaries were working several decades prior to Rick Strassman's New Mexico study, but had they actually examined the reports of human subjects given DMT, even with the relative paucity of trip reports available, it would have become quite obvious that the types of visions commonly reported by schizophrenic patients pale in comparison to those experienced by DMT users.

Psychotic hallucinations are generally indistinguishable from normal perceptions, and although they are more likely to be auditory than visual—hearing voices in their native tongue or other languages they can speak[26]—visual hallucinations, when they do occur, tend to be "similar to real visual perceptions, as most of them are normal sized, solid, anchored in the external space." Likewise, as in dreams, the majority of hallucinated characters are of "normal-sized, normal-appearing people."[27] And while examples of the fantastical, freakish, or grotesque—"A green, jellylike baby dragon slipping under the door; a rhino crossing the street; heads flying around without bodies; a cow in the corridor of a school building; a black canvas turning into a giant spider"—as well as angels, devils, and demons can be found in the case studies of psychotic patients,[28] they rarely, if ever, approach anything even close to the kinds of hypercomplex and sophisticated alien narratives reported by those who have visited the DMT worlds.

Perhaps the closest we can get to the kinds of visions experienced by DMT users outside of their trip reports occurs in a hallucinatory disorder common in older patients with deteriorating vision, known as Charles-Bonnet syndrome,[29] named after a Swiss naturalist and philosopher whose father began seeing "men, women, birds, carriages, and buildings" after cataract surgery.[30] Charles-Bonnet syndrome might be the closest we have to a pure visual hallucinatory disorder, in that other types of hallucinations, such as voices, are entirely absent, as are disturbances of thought or rationality. Unlike psychotics, Charles-Bonnet patients are generally fully aware that what they're seeing are hallucinations, which usually begin with simple geometric shapes, patterns, and colors, but can also develop into more complex forms, including lines of text, numbers, mathematical symbols, musical notation, and most notably, people. Although, as with psychotic hallucinations, these people are usually normal-sized, they occasionally appear in miniature and dressed in brightly colored clothing. First described by French psychiatrist Raoul Leroy in 1909 and named with an obvious reference to the tiny folk of the island of Lilliput in Jonathan Swift's *Gulliver's Travels*,[31] these so-called Lilliputian hallucinations are often reported as "operating in great numbers, apparently inhabiting the patient's external world, marching under real doors, and climbing on real chairs and tables, while generally respecting the laws of gravity and three-dimensional space."[32]

When I first read Leroy's description of the Lilliputians, I couldn't help but make the connection to Terence McKenna's "machine elves," which are also described as multitudinous, lively, and for the most part, affable. But this is where the similarities end. Lilliputians tend to be lively and mischievous little *people* rather than lively and mischievous little creatures that rarely take on a form even remotely resembling the human. It takes quite a bit of mental gymnastics to insist that "multidimensional creatures formed by strands of visible language"[33] or "animated self-transforming liquid light energy creatures"[34] are simply a variant of Lilliputian hallucination seen in Charles-Bonnet patients. Again, the psychiatric literature fails to provide anything close to what can be achieved by inhaling a deep lungful of DMT vapor.

While there's no consensus on exactly why Charles-Bonnet patients hallucinate, just as Oliver Sacks's brain was able to generate an entirely convincing hallucination of Jim and Kathy when the drug Artane partly disconnected his brain from sensory information, loss of visual inputs as the eyesight deteriorates likely has the same effect: spontaneous activity in the visual areas of the cortex generates visual imagery independent of sensory testing. In fact, neuroimaging studies of Charles-Bonnet patients during hallucinatory episodes revealed activation of specific regions of the cortex responsible for particular types of objects. When patients reported seeing faces, an area of the cortex specialized for representing faces was activated. Likewise, hallucinations of people appear to be caused by activation of cortical areas responsible for representing human figures.[35]

Again, just as with dreaming and the hallucinations of schizophrenic patients, there was nothing I could find in the case reports of Charles-Bonnet patients, fascinating as they were, that suggested the brain was doing anything particularly remarkable beyond drawing on its store-house of object models developed during waking life to construct these non-veridical perceptions that were then enfolded into its world model independent of sensory inputs. Where in the case reports were the advanced alien civilizations, the hypertechnological cityscapes, the Soulless Insect People, and the mischievous elfin creatures singing im-possible nine-dimensional objects into existence? At this point, it be-came clear that I had hit the limits of what the psychiatric literature could tell me about the visions of DMT users. Offering little insight into how it was possible for the brain to construct such complex alter-nate worlds without any obvious referents in the environment, building models it shouldn't know how to build, the case reports merely served to confirm just how thoroughly bizarre and inexplicable the visions ex-perienced by DMT users are.

But all hope was not lost. While dream visions and hallucinations are entirely incomparable to the inordinately more complex visions ex-perienced by DMT users, they do have one thing in common: The fact that humans can experience the incomprehensibly complex and strange worlds visited at the peak of a DMT trip means that the brain is, some-how, modeling such worlds. As with all perceptions, they must be built from patterns of activity generated by the cortex. The question then is how and why, in the presence of DMT, it begins constructing these worlds. Does the brain require some alternate source of sensory inputs to do so? And if so, what is this alternate source and where does it come from? If we're to have any chance of making sense of the DMT state, it's clear we need to look inside and find out what's actually going on in the brain during a psychedelic trip. Fortunately, just as I was beginning to ask these questions, others were trying to do just that.

II

BUILDING ALIEN WORLDS

Fortunately, reality does not take place.

—Jean Baudrillard

I've been fascinated by the weird, the wonderful, and the inexplicable since I was a child and yet, despite being an avid reader of fiction, sci-fi has never really been my thing. Sometimes reality is weird enough. There are, however, a handful of writers for whom I make an exception, and legendary cult author and cyberpunk philosopher Philip K. Dick is certainly among them. Aside from his compelling commentary and speculation on some of the deepest questions about the nature of reality, I won't deny that one aspect of Dick's writing that attracted me is his obvious fascination with psychoactive drugs. Indeed, his proclivity for manipulating his own neurochemistry with exogenous molecules is no secret. Throughout his life, Dick was treated with a medley of psychoactive medications for his anxieties, bouts of deep depression, paranoid delusions, and outright fantasies, swallowing up to seventy pills per day at the peak of his habit: benzodiazepines, opioids, antipsychotics, and mood stabilizers. And that was just the prescribed drugs. While he also occasionally used LSD and other psychedelics, his primary drug of choice was from an entirely different pharmacological class. Initially prescribed to treat asthma as a child, as an adult, Dick relied on daily consumption of massive doses of amphetamines to fuel his prodigious literary output, packing his refrigerator with jars of the pills alongside stacks of protein shakes to wash them down—he didn't want to take drugs on an empty stomach. Although technically stimulants, when used chronically, amphetamines are notorious for triggering psychotic episodes that include wild and terrifying hallucinations and paranoid delusions almost indistinguishable from those of schizophrenia. After decades of continual use, and no doubt compounded by the cocktail of other prescribed drugs he was consuming, Dick was constantly plagued by visions of menacing creatures that hovered over his bed or lurked in the shadows of his backyard.[1] But it was a sudden and unusually dramatic set of visions beginning in February of 1974 that would shape his view of reality for the remaining few years of his life.

Just a few days after Dick underwent a botched surgery to extract an impacted wisdom tooth, a young girl arrived at his door to deliver his Percodan prescription—an opioid medication to treat the pain. After she left, as he returned to his bedroom, he suddenly found himself blinded by an intense pink light that pierced through the curtains. Dazed and disoriented, he collapsed onto the bed and began to experience a series of visions that bore more than a passing resemblance to the procession of complex imagery experienced after consuming a psychedelic drug. At first, abstract geometric patterns followed by more complex visions and concepts filled his consciousness—engineering blueprints and strange philosophical ideas. This initial wave of imagery culminated in the complete transformation of his world. He was trapped in a limousine and surrounded by men in dark suits who were interrogating him with questions he couldn't make sense of, let alone answer. He spent the following weeks in bed semiconscious and experiencing wave after wave of these visions. To Dick, there was only one possible explanation for his ordeal— some kind of divine or perhaps alien being had invaded his head via his optic nerve and taken up residence in his brain: "It seized me entirely, lifting me from the limitations of the space-time matrix; it mastered me as, at the same instant, I knew that the world around me was cardboard, a fake. Through its power I saw suddenly the universe as it was; through its power of perception I saw what really existed."[2]

Dick dramatizes his pink light experience in his novel *VALIS*— *Vast Active Living Intelligence System*—which is defined as a creature of pure information "characterized by quasiconsciousness, purpose, intelligence, growth, and an armillary coherence,"[3] which Dick at first believed to be some kind of supremely advanced machinic alien life-form from elsewhere in the universe but later seems to equate to a being approaching a god. In the end, it's not clear if there's a difference. I first read *VALIS* about a decade ago, at a time when I was beginning to think deeply about the DMT worlds as patterns of information generated by the cortex but potentially modulated by some alternate source of sensory inputs. I found the idea of some external source of information firing into Dick's brain and manipulating his world model intuitively compelling, and his experience, albeit much more drawn out, seemed not entirely dissimilar to a breakthrough DMT trip—an irresistible and overwhelming rush of information floods the brain and seizes control of its neural machinery, transforming the world according to its own apparent whim and agenda. It would be another few years before I'd begin to understand how such a creature could exist or the form it might take, but I couldn't shake the feeling that information, and in particular, the way information flows into and through the brain, was going to play an important part in getting to grips with the mystery of DMT. After all, the subjective world model is always constructed as a pattern of information generated by the cortex—a complex, integrated, and dynamic pattern of information, but a pattern of information all the same. So the DMT worlds must manifest when this pattern is dramatically altered, whether spontaneously or under the direction of some intelligent agent. Unfortunately, at that time, there were few studies imaging the effects of pure DMT on brain activity, so any ideas I had about how this molecule affected these neural patterns would have to remain entirely speculative. But that would soon change.

It's impossible to know what was going on in Dick's drug-drenched brain during those few feverish weeks, and whether he really was usurped by an alien intelligence or whether his visions were part of a psychotic episode triggered by his heavy and chronic use of amphetamines and other psychoactive drugs. If we're to approach some kind of understanding of how certain molecular tools can alter the brain's model of reality in such a dramatic fashion, we're going to need a much more direct approach than simply reading the reports of those having undergone such experiences, whether of alien information propagated on blinding pulses of electromagnetic radiation or advanced insectoid creatures operating from an entirely orthogonal dimension of reality.

Whether imbibed during an ancient religious ritual in the Colombian rain forests or infused directly into the veins while lying on a gurney in a modern western hospital, in whatever form they're consumed, psychedelics are tools for manipulating the subjective world. Somehow, at the interface between the molecule and the brain, the magic happens— the world shifts on its axis, is turned inside out, dismantled, and reconfigured as an entirely new one emerges. But from the familiar to the strange to the incomprehensible, all experienced worlds are unified in being constructed by the brain, as models fashioned from integrated, hierarchically organized, patterns of cortical activity. When you consume a psychedelic drug, whether LSD, mescaline, psilocybin, or DMT, it is this world model that is transformed. So to understand how and why these molecules can effect such dramatic alterations in the structure and dynamics of the conscious world, we need to see these tools in action, manipulating the brain's world-building machinery in real time.

In Dick's most famous novel *Do Androids Dream of Electric Sheep?*, the protagonist Rick Deckard—a bounty hunter hired to dispatch a gang of androids who illegally arrived on Earth from outer space—uses a tool that, although not molecular, also works by manipulating the brain and the subjective experience of the user. The Penfield mood organ is an electric neural stimulation device plugged directly into the brain and with which, by punching in a number, the wearer can instantly alter their level of consciousness and emotional state. The name of the device is an unmistakable reference to Wilder Penfield, an American neurosurgeon who, beginning in the late 1930s, used not drugs but electrical probes to induce striking changes in the subjective experiences of his patients. In his attempts to rid his patients of debilitating intractable epilepsy, Penfield invented the Montréal procedure, which involved selectively destroying small areas of the cortex where seizures originated.[4] By stimulating different areas of the cortex of the exposed brain of an awake patient under local anesthesia, Penfield was able to more precisely target the focus of epileptiform activity while avoiding damaging healthy cortical tissue. This technique also provided him with an opportunity to map the function of the cortex by observing the effects on his patients as he zapped different cortical locations. By stimulating parts of the motor cortex—responsible for movement—Penfield was able to induce specific actions in his patients, such as flexing of a particular finger or clenching of the hand into a fist. He was even able to elicit sudden involuntary vocalizations by zapping areas of the cortex responsible for speech.[5] But while this kind of neuro-puppetry was clearly of great neurological interest, when he shifted the electrode from the motor areas of the cortex to those responsible for constructing the patients' subjective world, something quite remarkable happened.

D. W. was a twelve-year-old boy who had been suffering from epileptic seizures unresponsive to treatment and thought to originate somewhere in the right hemisphere of his brain. So Penfield opened D. W.'s skull, exposed the right side of his brain, and began to methodically stimulate the different areas of his cortex, working his way from the visual cortex at the back of the cortex and forward toward the temporal lobe around the side. Since the areas of the visual cortex toward the back of the brain are responsible for representing more basic features of the world, stimulating this area of the cortex ought to elicit simple imagery. And indeed, the boy described seeing triangles in front of him. As Penfield moved the electrode farther forward, the boy saw slightly more complex forms: "lights and triangles, red, yellow, blue, orange." Farther forward still, much more complex forms, including "robbers with guns," entered his visual field. But once Penfield reached the temporal lobes, something startling happened: The boy began to experience not merely complex objects or scenes, but actual memories from his recent past, including a conversation between his mother and aunt—"My mother telling my aunt to come up and visit us tonight . . . My mother is telling my brother he has got his coat on backward. I can just hear them." Penfield asked whether the boy remembered this happening. "Oh yes," he replied, "just before I came here."[6] Penfield had reached an area close to the hippocampus, tucked away on the inside of the temporal lobe.

If you have even a passing interest in the brain, it's likely you've heard of the hippocampus as a part of the brain that's important for forming memories. Recall that your brain constructs your world model as a pattern of cortical activity over several levels of a hierarchy, with the lowest levels representing the rapidly changing fine details of your world model, with more complex objects and the entire scene being represented at the upper levels. The hippocampus sits at the very apex and so has a bird's-eye view of this hierarchy, constantly watching and "recording" the cortex's ever-changing model of the world. However, the hippocampus doesn't store these patterns as such, but acts more like a "memory index" that can point to specific episodes in your past and "reactivate" or "replay" those cortical patterns through the cortex.[7] When you recall a particular experience, your cortex is reconstructing the particular pattern of neural activity that constituted that particular image, scene, or scenario from the past. It's the role of the hippocampus to initiate the reactivation of these past patterns of neural activity, allowing you a temporary glimpse at the world your brain was modeling at that time. Each time the hippocampus replays a particular pattern of cortical activity, the pattern is reinforced slightly by adjusting the strength of synaptic connections. This provides the basis for one of the most influential theories of dream function: The hippocampus replays recent memories during dream sleep, helping to consolidate them by strengthening connections in the cortex.[8] The memories themselves always remain in the cortex as latent patterns of neural activity and eventually when sufficiently consolidated, they can be activated—recalled—independently of the hippocampus. This is why damage to the hippocampus tends to disrupt recent memories but not those from the distant past.[9]

Although our understanding of cortical function was much less sophisticated in Penfield's time, it now seems obvious why stimulating the cortex at different locations generated such different effects. Stimulation at the lower end of the cortical hierarchy—closest to the primary visual cortex at the back of the brain—can only stimulate basic features of the world, without context or narrative—the patient sees basic geometric shapes and flashes of color. However, when Penfield stimulated the cortex in the temporal lobes close to the hippocampus, his patients

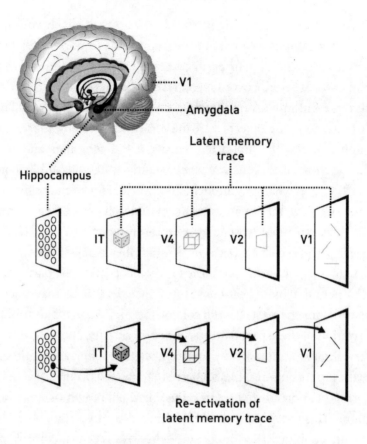

The hippocampus sits at the apex of the cortical hierarchy and "indexes" the patterns of neural activity that represent the world model, which remain as latent memory traces in the cortex. These cortical patterns can be reactivated by the hippocampus when a memory is recalled or re-experienced.

didn't merely recall past experiences, but relived them with many of the sights, sounds, and emotions of the original experiences. In other words, his electrode was stimulating the unfolding of a pattern of cortical activity, a world model, from the past—a complex hallucination drawn from memory. Not surprisingly, Penfield's ability to induce hallucinations in this way prompted many to wonder whether the hallucinations of psychotics and perhaps even the visions experienced under the influence of psychedelic drugs might be caused by stimulation of the cortex independently of sensory inputs.

During Penfield's era, the most important technique for studying dysfunctional brain activity in epilepsy, schizophrenia, and other neurological conditions was electroencephalography (EEG), which allowed scientists to monitor the electrical activity generated by the brain as it processed information. The firing of neurons depends on the flow of electrically charged ions across their cell membrane, and when large assemblies of neurons are firing in a coordinated fashion, they generate patterns of electrical activity that can be detected through the skull. These complex waves can be decomposed into simpler waves of varying frequencies, from low frequency alpha waves to high frequency gamma waves. When the eyes are closed and the brain isn't actively processing visual information, low frequency alpha waves synchronized across large areas of the cortex tend to dominate the EEG signal. But as soon as the eyes are opened and the brain begins processing sensory information and constructing its world model, these alpha waves rapidly desynchronize and become much less prominent compared to higher frequency waves. As such, measuring the relative strength of the different frequencies, as well as their synchronization across the cortex, was a relatively simple and noninvasive way of detecting deviations from normal brain function. And if neurological disease caused changes in a patient's EEG trace, then it made sense that the effects of psychedelic drugs on brain activity might also be detected using this same technology.

One psychiatrist interested in psychedelic-induced changes in brain activity was Abraham Wikler, a colleague of CIA payrollee Harris Isbell, with whom he had worked on several projects related to his interest in drug addiction. Like Isbell, Wikler selected his research subjects from the practically limitless supply held captive at the neighboring Lexington penitentiary. For his EEG study, all were fitted with detectors around their scalp and given up to half a gram of the psychedelic peyote cactus alkaloid mescaline before being made to lie down in a darkened room. Before the effects of the drug began to take hold, the volunteers' EEG traces were completely normal. Synchronized alpha waves dominated when their eyes were closed, but rapidly desynchronized and became weaker as soon as they opened them and the brain began processing visual sensory inputs. Around thirty minutes later, the prisoners began reporting colorful imagery behind their eyelids—flashes of colored lights, geometric designs, human figures, animals, insects, houses—all fairly typical of the drug. However, it was the unusual changes in their EEG traces that accompanied these visions that caught Wikler's attention. In several of his subjects, their verbal reports of visual hallucinations coincided with a marked desynchronization of alpha rhythms on their EEG traces, even when their eyes were closed.[10] This suggested that similar to the eyes-open state, the cortex was actively processing information. Instead of watching the outside world, they were watching the patterns being generated by their cortex entirely independent of sensory inputs. In other words, not entirely dissimilar to Penfield's experiments using electrical impulses, the drug appeared somehow to be stimulating the visual areas of the cortex responsible for representing the types of objects and scenes they were seeing behind their eyes. And this apparent "excitatory" effect on brain activity wasn't restricted to mescaline, but was also observed in subjects given LSD.[11] But what about DMT?

In September of 1956, shortly after discovering the remarkable visionary effects of synthetic DMT, Stephen Szára was in Debrecen, Hungary, attending the Annual Meeting of the Hungarian Physiological Society.[12] Fortuitously, his colleague, neurologist Ferenc Kajtor was head of the electrophysiology laboratory in the Department of Neurology and Psychiatry at Tisza University in Debrecen and a leading expert in EEG techniques. It seemed like an ideal opportunity to test whether the effects of this newly discovered psychedelic on brain activity were similar to those of mescaline and LSD. On the other hand, there was no time to recruit subjects for such an impromptu research project, and disappointingly, Kajtor's department didn't happen to be situated next door to a prison, let alone one filled with inmates who could be plied with high-class narcotics. So Szára stepped up and volunteered to have his own brain waves measured under the influence of the drug. Of course, being the discoverer of DMT, Szára had some prior experience with its world-shattering effects and knew exactly what to expect. The same couldn't be

Alpha waves before psilocybin

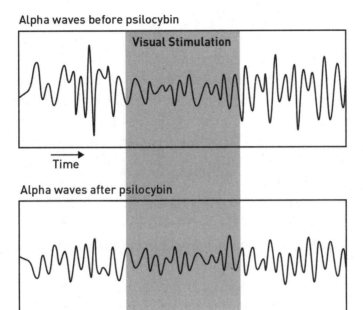

Alpha waves after psilocybin

Synchronized alpha waves (8-12Hz) are most prominent in an EEG recording when the eyes are closed and the brain isn't processing visual sensory inputs, but become desynchronized and weaker when the eyes are opened. Psychedelics, such as psilocybin, desynchronize alpha waves even when the eyes are closed, indicating that the cortex is actively processing information independent of sensory inputs.

said for his colleagues—three other physicians and a chemist—who were somehow convinced to make up the numbers. However, in the few short months since Szára first discovered DMT's effects (and prior to publication of this discovery in an academic journal), it's highly unlikely that any of his colleagues would have had the opportunity to use the drug themselves. In fact, it isn't clear if any of them had any kind of prior experience with psychedelics at all. Anyway, throwing caution to the wind, the first volunteer—an unnamed woman—laid down to receive her shot in the arm.

About three minutes after the injection, it became quite obvious that she wasn't exactly enjoying the experience. She suddenly became agitated and seemed quite disturbed by the rapidly intensifying visions: "It's frightening since I can't terminate it!"[13]

With her eyes kept wide open, staring fixedly at things only she could see, her distress only intensified until she eventually demanded that someone put an end to her suffering—permanently: "Give me something so that I shall die quickly. It would be better to die!" Fortunately, Szára decided against such a solution, and a few minutes later, having apparently tired herself out, the woman slumped back on the bed and became motionless. Hopeful that this would be the end of her protests, the recording continued. However, just a few minutes later, she suddenly addressed Szára directly with more than a hint of reproach, crying out: "Kill me. . . . How were you capable to do such . . . ?"[14]

At this point, having had quite enough, she bolted upright, leaped from the bed, and attempted to run out of the room—presumably out the door, but Szára isn't clear about this—and the recording was terminated. It wasn't a promising start.

EEG recordings are highly sensitive to being disrupted by excessive movement of the limbs, the eyes, by speaking, and even sweating. So it barely needs stating that her data was of little use. The second volunteer fared slightly better—he didn't attempt to defenestrate himself, anyway—but since his experience was marked by "tension, indignation, protestation, apprehension, anxiety, excitement," his data was also useless. Fortunately, Szára somehow managed to acquire interpretable data from the remaining three volunteers, presumably including the only DMT veteran in the bunch, Szára himself. Unfortunately, they were no real surprises in the EEG traces. Although compressed to a much shorter time period, the drug's effects on the EEG was comparable to that of both mescaline and LSD. Alpha activity almost disappeared around five minutes after the injection and began to recover around forty minutes later, marking the end of the experience.[15] More carefully conducted and controlled EEG measurements of the DMT state would have to wait a few decades, but from this limited data at least, DMT seemed to be exerting similar excitatory effects on brain activity as the other more well-known psychedelics.

Unfortunately, while these early EEG studies suggested that psyche-delics induced their visionary effects by somehow stimulating the cortex, they told us little more. Aside from its susceptibility to recording artefacts, a major drawback of EEG in imaging brain activity is its poor spatial resolution—although it's excellent at detecting electrical activity on the surface, it's difficult to pinpoint exactly where this activity originated, especially if the origin is deeper in the brain. This limited its use in patients with intractable epilepsy, since pinpointing the precise locus of seizures was essential if normally functioning neural tissue was to be spared during operations to remove dysfunctional areas of the brain. So beginning in the 1940s, surgeons began drilling holes in the heads of their patients and using a metal frame clamped to their skulls to place electrodes into precise locations within the brain to record its electrical activity directly.[16] And in the early 1950s, coinciding with the earliest psychedelic EEG studies, Norwegian physician Carl Wilhelm Sem-Jacobsen, one of the pioneers of this technique, began using it to look for aberrant activity in different areas of his schizophrenic and epileptic patients' brains.[17] By the summer of 1954, he had successfully recorded from electrodes implanted into the brains of seventy-five of his psychotic patients. During one recording session, a schizophrenic woman who had been suffering from auditory hallucination for years prior, suddenly began a heated and vocal argument with General MacArthur and the King of Sweden (although Sem-Jacobsen isn't explicit about this, it seems reasonable to assume that neither party was in the room at the time). As she continued to bump heads with her hallucinated adversaries, Sem-Jacobsen noticed a striking increase in electrical activity from one electrode in particular: the one inserted into a drill hole in the right side of her skull—in her temporal lobe.[18] Was this a hallucination or was it a memory? Was there any difference? Either way, it quite clearly suggested that the auditory hallucination—much like that of the twelve-year-old boy who heard a recent conversation between his mother and aunt when Wilder Penfield zapped his temporal lobe—originated in the part of the brain where the hippocampus is located. Did this mean psychotic hallucinations were more like memories intruding into the present moment than pure fabrications of the brain?

And, if so, could complex psychedelic drug-induced hallucinations also be explained in this way?

Since drilling holes in the heads of healthy volunteers to study the effects of psychedelics on brain activity was considered—even in the 1950s—to be somewhat beyond the pale, Sem-Jacobsen took advantage of diagnostic depth electrode measurements in epileptic and psychotic patients to also administer a shot of either mescaline or LSD during the procedure.[19] How much of an ethical improvement this constituted is debatable, but anyway, it provided a rare opportunity to pinpoint any increase in cortical activity accompanying the visual effects of the drug. In one patient, visual hallucinations induced by both mescaline and LSD coincided with a spike in electrical activity in the temporal lobes, similar to what was recorded in the spontaneous auditory hallucinations of psychotics—precisely the result Sem-Jacobsen was hoping for. Like the spontaneous hallucinations of psychotics, were psychedelics somehow inducing activity in the temporal lobes, allowing memories to flow into the cortex? In other words, hallucinations aren't fabricated by the brain entirely anew but rather reconstructed from past experience, and only requiring an appropriate stimulation or aberrant neurological state to manifest. By the 1950s, it was already well known among psychiatrists using LSD for psychotherapeutic purposes that high doses occasionally triggered not only the recollection but the active and immersive reliving of past experiences.[20] However, this was clearly only one aspect of the drug's effects, and when it came to DMT, it would certainly have been a stretch to claim that encounters with supremely intelligent insectoid aliens from an alternate dimension were merely recapitulations of past experiences. While an explanation for the insectoids and machine elves would have to wait, evidence that psychedelics were inducing their effects by stimulating the cortex was steadily accumulating, and toward the end of the twentieth century, the precise molecular mechanism by which they achieved this became clear.

Since Wayne Woolley first surmised that the neural action of LSD might be related to disruption of serotonin function in the early 1950s, numerous studies were able to show that mescaline, psilocybin, DMT, and several other psychedelics also in some way interacted with serotonin's targets in the brain. Serotonin belongs to the family of neurochemicals known as neuromodulators, the role of which is to regulate and modulate the activity of neurons. They achieve this by binding to specific protein receptors embedded in the neuron's surface membrane. Just as the brain uses sensory information from the environment to modulate its activity, every neuron uses the receptors embedded in its membrane to detect molecules in the surrounding milieu to regulate its own function and behavior. The effect of a neuromodulator on a neuron depends entirely on the types of receptors in its membrane. Serotonin (also known by its chemical name, 5-hydroxytryptamine or simply 5HT) binds to at least seven different receptor types (named 5HT1 to 5HT7), some of which also possess multiple subtypes (given additional subscripts, a, b, c, etc.).[21] Each receptor type has its own characteristic effect on a neuron. So, overall, the effect of serotonin—or indeed any neuromodulator—on a neuron depends entirely upon the receptor types embedded in its membrane.

Beginning in the mid-1970s, experiments began to reveal the key receptor target for psychedelics, including LSD, psilocybin, and DMT—a subtype of serotonin receptor known as the 5HT2a receptor.[22] When either serotonin or an exogenous psychedelic molecule binds to and activates this receptor subtype, the neuron within which the receptor is embedded is excited and is more likely to fire. This seemed to imply an elegant molecular mechanism by which psychedelics exerted their effects on the brain: Drugs that selectively bind to the 5HT2a receptor subtype would stimulate large numbers of neurons across the cortex. So, rather than stimulating the cortex using an electrical probe, as in Wilder Penfield's experiments, the brain could be stimulated instead by ingestion of a molecule that reaches the cortex and excites its constituent neurons.[23]

Although we were still far from a plausible and convincing explanation for the kinds of bizarre alternate worlds regularly visited by DMT users, the evidence that psychedelics were stimulating the cortex via the serotonin 5HT2a receptor certainly helped to explain many of the visual effects of other psychedelic drugs. The visions experienced by psychedelic users can be grouped into several categories, from simple geometric patterns to more complex objects, and ultimately, complete scenes. In his pioneering work on the phenomenology of the mescaline experience,[24] the psychologist and philosopher Heinrich Klüver noted that, at least in the early stages of intoxication, the visions tended to form themselves into four "hallucinatory form constants": a) Lattice; b) Cobweb; c) Tunnel; d) Spiral. These basic patterns also had a tendency toward "geometrization," being repeated, elaborated, or combined into ornate and sophisticated patterns that come to dominate the visual field when the eyes are open.[25] Computational neuroscientists Bard Ermentrout and Jack Cowan later found that they could account for these four forms using a mathematical model of the primary visual cortex, assuming a uniform increase in excitability in this region of the brain. In other words, these patterns of neural activity naturally emerged as a consequence of the way these areas of the cortex were structured and when stimulated independently of sensory inputs.[26]

Since the higher levels of the visual cortex are responsible for generating more complex object models, their stimulation by a psychedelic molecule would naturally cause such objects to become enfolded into the tripper's subjective world, in much the same way that Charles-Bonnet syndrome patients experienced visions of faces when the area of the cortex responsible for representing faces was spontaneously activated. At the same time, activation of the hippocampus would also allow memories to flow into the cortex and intrude on the present moment, just as Wilder Penfield had demonstrated by stimulating the hippocampus with an electrode. The overall visual effect induced by the molecule would be an unholy amalgam of spontaneously emerging cortical patterns, stored object models, and imagery drawn from memory. But despite the striking explanatory power of this mechanistic model, I wasn't convinced it got us much closer to explaining where the DMT worlds came from—worlds that seemed to have nothing to do with stored object models learned by interacting with the environment and even less to do with personal memories. To explain them away as spontaneously emergent neural activity seemed equally preposterous. Clearly, there was much more going on.

Klüver's Form Constants

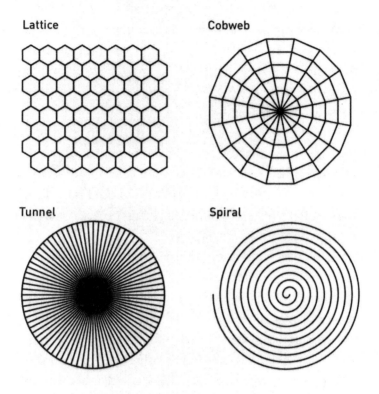

Lattice

Cobweb

Tunnel

Spiral

While activation of the 5HT2a receptor seemed to provide a neat and simple explanation for the ability of psychedelic drugs to activate certain neuron populations in the cortex, accounting for some features of the psychedelic state, it was obvious that even relatively low doses of the more well-known psychedelics, such as LSD and psilocybin, elicited effects that extended well beyond visions of geometric forms and the intrusion of memories into the cortex. The basic 5HT2a stimulation model certainly did little to explain why DMT would not only obliterate the normal waking world but replace it with an entirely alien one teeming with intelligent and communicative nonhuman entities. Rather than simply stimulating the cortex, as Penfield's electrode experiments had done, these molecules seemed to actively disrupt its ability to construct a stable model of the world, with the object models themselves becoming unstable, transforming before the eyes or beginning to break down entirely. A world once stable, predictable, and familiar is transformed into one dynamic, fluid, ever-changing, never settling. This LSD report is fairly typical: "When I opened my eyes and looked at the objects around me, it was as if they were made of tallow and were melting. There was a drippiness of colors, and it also seemed that these things might be made of waxen candy."[27]

To understand exactly what was going on in the brain to generate these highly unusual subjective states would require more than receptor binding studies, EEG headsets, and well-placed electrodes. Fortunately, as the twenty-first century arrived, so did advanced tools for probing and measuring the effects of psychedelic drugs on brain activity in real time and in unprecedented spatial detail.

Unlike EEG, which provides limited information on neural activity over broad areas of the cortex, functional magnetic resonance imaging or functional MRI (fMRI) is an entirely noninvasive technique that detects the subtle increases in blood flow that accompany brain activity. By computationally partitioning the brain into thousands of tiny—1–2 mm—cubic "voxels," fMRI delivers real-time measurements of neural activity at spatial resolutions far exceeding that of EEG, as well as allowing advanced statistical processing techniques to detect and quantify connections and functional relationships between different areas of the brain. One of the pioneers in the use of this technique in studying the effects of drugs on the brain at the turn of the twenty-first century was psychopharmacologist Prof. David Nutt of Imperial College London, working with a young postdoctoral researcher, Robin Carhart-Harris. It was quite obvious to Carhart-Harris that if we were hoping to understand what was happening in the brain under the influence of psychedelics, fMRI was undoubtedly going to be one of the primary tools in this endeavor. So in 2011, he began recruiting volunteers for a series of fMRI experiments with the *Psilocybe* mushroom alkaloid psilocybin, hoping they would reveal the changes happening in the brain as someone transitioned from normal waking consciousness to the psychedelic state.[28]

When a subject is slid into an MRI scanner and asked to simply close their eyes, relax, and let their mind wander, the patterns of activity in different areas of the cortex can be monitored over time. Even in this relaxed state, when not focused on any particular task, brain activity is tightly orchestrated, with some areas showing coordinated activity and others remaining quiet. If the volunteer is then asked to perform a task while in the scanner, such as viewing an image or solving a mathematical problem, some areas of the cortex quieten while others required for the task light up and begin working in unison. The cortex can be seen to move through different patterns of activity in an orderly fashion as it processes information. However, when a volunteer was placed into the scanner after being injected with psilocybin, an entirely different picture began to emerge: The cortical activity appeared to become more disordered, wandering between patterns of activity in an apparently random way.[29] Carhart-Harris referred to this as a "high entropy," disordered, or "hot state."[30] Cortical activity became more fluid and dynamic in the psilocybin state compared to the normal waking state, which matched the more fluid and dynamic world they experienced.[31] Just two years later, Carhart-Harris performed a similar experiment with LSD—the first of its kind in more than four decades—observing the same kind of "loosening up" of brain activity after volunteers were given the drug.[32] How were these psychedelic drugs achieving this and what could it tell us about how DMT achieved its effects?

The pattern of cortical activity that represents your world model must carefully balance two apparently opposing properties. It must be sufficiently rigid and stable such that the world that appears to you, and which you use to make sense of and navigate the environment, is also stable—a world of melting trees and cars that transformed into bouncy castles would be both bewildering and useless. But at the same time, it must be sufficiently dynamic, flexible, and responsive to sensory inputs to keep up with the events and processes continuously unfolding in the environment. In other words, the cortex must be stable and orderly but not *too* stable and orderly—it must strike a delicate balance between stability and flexibility, between order and chaos. The cortex achieves this balance by tuning the strength of connections between its constituent neurons. If the connections are too weak, activation of a particular neuron will fail to activate enough connected neurons and propagation of neural activity will quickly die out—the cortex becomes overly stable and it loses the ability to process and propagate information.[33] This kind of hyperstable state is thought to be reached in unconsciousness, during deep sleep and anesthesia.[34] If, on the other hand, the connections are too strong and activation of a neuron leads to the activation of too many connected neurons, neural activity will spread in an entirely unregulated manner throughout the cortex. In this state, the patterns of neural activity become entirely chaotic—this kind of unregulated hyperexcitable activity can often be observed in the brains of epileptic patients.[35] So the cortex must find the sweet spot between these two extremes, where order and chaos is balanced.

When a psychedelic drug reaches the brain, by binding to 5HT2a receptors in certain populations of neurons in the cortex, the molecule increases their excitability, makes them more sensitive to inputs from other neurons, and on average, increases the number of neurons activated by any particular neuron. That is, the drug nudges the dial slightly toward increased disorder, close to, but not into, the chaotic realm where all semblance of order is lost. The cortex enters a slightly less stable, more dynamic and fluid state, which can be observed in the MRI scanner as its activity becomes more random, exploring a larger number of patterns over time. This corresponds to the subjective experience of a world once stable and predictable becoming more fluid and dynamic, with objects shifting and rearranging and even transforming before the eyes. In this more fluid state, the cortex also becomes much more sensitive to information arriving either via the sense organs or elsewhere in the brain, such as the hippocampus,[36] neatly explaining why psychedelic users describe a dramatic heightening of the senses and a world that appears richer and visually amplified, as well as the reliving of past experiences at higher dose levels.[37]

But despite the elegance and explanatory power of this model, and as the research articles continued to flow from the Imperial College lab, I still couldn't help but feel that it fell well short of an explanation for the effects of DMT. While it might seem reasonable to suggest that the effects of a moderate dose of LSD or *Psilocybe* mushrooms could be explained as fluid and disordered patterns of cortical activity supplemented by information leaking from hippocampal memory systems, this seemed far

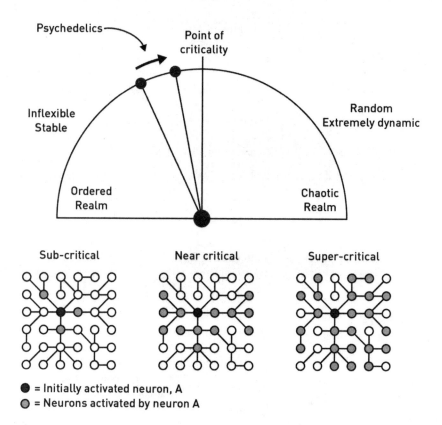

● = Initially activated neuron, A
○ = Neurons activated by neuron A

The cortex must strike a balance between order and chaos, maximizing flexibility and information processing ability without descending into chaos. The transition between order and chaos is known as the point of criticality. Psychedelics nudge the cortex toward criticality, but not into the chaotic realm, generating a much more fluid and dynamic cortical state.

from a satisfying explanation for the bizarre worlds encountered at the peak of a DMT trip, during which the world isn't merely disrupted or rendered slightly more wild and chaotic, but is replaced with an entirely different one. Order gives way not to chaos but to an entirely different order—the brain, in a very literal sense, begins to construct a thoroughly alien world in exquisite detail, rendered in seemingly impossible dimensionality and dynamic complexity, and inhabited not by old friends and

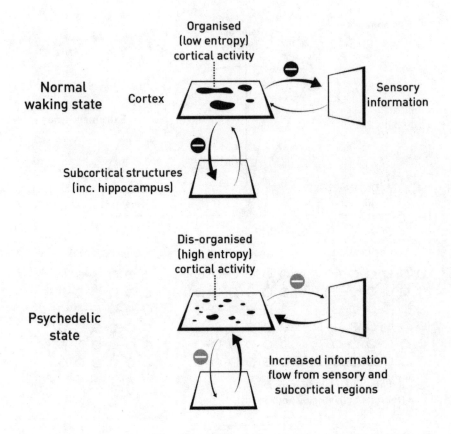

In the normal waking state, cortical activity is tightly organized, allowing the cortex to control the flow of information from the senses (by making accurate model predictions), as well as from subcortical structures such as the hippocampus. In the more fluid and disorganized state induced by psychedelics, the cortex struggles to maintain this control and information flows more freely from the senses and subcortical structures.

beloved family pets, but by intelligent creatures not merely unearthly but exceeding the imagination in their alienness. Why would increased disorder in the cortex suddenly cause this undeniably highly ordered alternate world model to emerge? Again, I was faced with the same question: How does the brain construct these worlds? And why? If not from sensory inputs or memories, where does the information come from

A young Matsigenka shaman with fresh ayahuasca (*Banisteriopsis caapi*) vine, Manu Biosphere Reserve, 1992. *(Courtesy of Glenn Shepard)*

A Kokama shaman gathering *Psychotria* leaf, Ucayali River, 1996. *(Courtesy of Glenn Shepard)*

Ayahuasca vine and *Psychotria* leaf, Manu Biosphere Reserve, 2007. *(Courtesy of Glenn Shepard)*

Preparing ayahuasca vine with chacruna (*Psychotria viridis*) leaf, Manu Biosphere Reserve, 2007. *(Courtesy of Glenn Shepard)*

A Matsigenka hunter-shaman disposing of ayahuasca ingredients after preparation. Manu Biosphere Reserve, 1992. *(Courtesy of Glenn Shepard)*

Strangeitude by Harry Pack. Harry Pack is one of the few working artists able to capture the distinctive complexity and ambience of the DMT space. *(Courtesy of Harry Pack)*

DNADINER by INCEDIGRIS (2017). INCEDIGRIS emerged in recent years with an uncanny ability to capture the uniquely comical and yet somehow disturbing character of the visions often induced by DMT. *(Courtesy of INCEDIGRIS)*

We've Got a Breather Here by ALGA Artworks (Instagram: alga_artist, Facebook: algaartworks). ALGA here represents the commonly reported experience of being ushered through a tunnel into an entirely novel domain by strange beings that seem both welcoming and unnerving. *(Courtesy of ALGA Artworks)*

AGI MUSE (bottom; detail above), by Nuwan Shilpa Hennayake. Inspired by his own visionary experiences, Nuwan Shilpa Hennayake beautifully renders the seemingly endless complexity of the DMT space and its occupants, which often appear to be extremely advanced, both spiritually and technologically. *(Courtesy of Nuwan Shilpa Hennayake)*

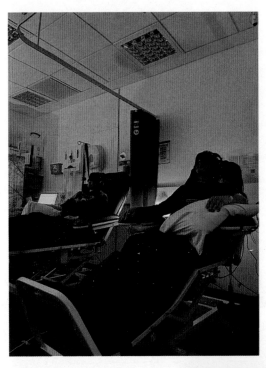

Anton Bilton during a DMT infusion session at Imperial College in London. *(Courtesy of Anton Bilton, 2022)*

Anton Bilton fitted with EEG electrodes prior to the DMT-infusion session. *(Courtesy of Anton Bilton, 2022)*

that allows it to do so? Do we really need to consider the possibility that the information source is external to the brain? Might we need to invoke some kind of discarnate intelligent agent to make sense of DMT? I certainly wasn't ready to seriously consider such a possibility just yet. Perhaps I'd simply been looking in the wrong place. Perhaps I needed to look deeper into the brain, beyond the visual cortex and the hippocampal memory systems and into a vast terra incognita that many promised me was the true home of the machine elves and their ilk.[38]

12

THE ANATOMY OF A MACHINE ELF

An irruption from the collective unconscious, Jung taught, can wipe out the fragile individual ego. In the depths of the collective the archetypes slumber; if aroused, they can heal or they can destroy.

—Philip K. Dick

Terence McKenna's first encounter with the beings he would later dub the machine elves occurred shortly after arriving in California to pursue a degree in art history at the University of Berkeley in 1965. As his lungs began to swell and expecting little more than "swirling colors or moving geometric planes of light," he instead found himself hosting a party thronged not with fellow Berkeley freshmen but a crowd of highly animated creatures from another world: "There was an encounter with what can only be described as an elf hive, a colony of self-transforming, hyperdimensional machine creatures that came bounding forward with joyful squeaks to dribble themselves like self-transforming jeweled basketballs on the floor in front of me, and I was dumbstruck with amazement."[1]

Somehow, McKenna's cortical machinery had been induced to do something it had never done before—to begin constructing a multitude of beings unlike any creature he could have imagined. But these weren't buried or repressed memories or dream imagery flowing from his temporal lobes, and it hardly seems reasonable to dismiss them as spontaneously emergent or noisy cortical activity. So where did the information used to construct these strange elfin creatures come from?

Terence McKenna first experienced DMT during a period when both himself and his brother, Dennis, had become somewhat enamored by the work of Swiss psychoanalyst Carl Jung. Having been a UFO enthusiast since boyhood, Terence was particularly taken by Jung's idea that "things seen in the skies,"[2] and by extension, the beings that operate them, might hail not from outer space but rather the deepest recesses of our minds. That we might all possess a vast inner space that could be explored using psychedelics and guided by Jungian cartography, as outer space is explored using rocket ships guided by maps of the galaxies, was particularly appealing to the unorthodox minds of the McKenna brothers: "Jung explored the terra incognita of the unconscious and returned with some of the earliest reliable maps. . . . If cosmology was the lens through which we learned to view the universe at large, Jungian psychology became our cosmology for the universe within. Buried in every person's neural tissue was a dimension at least as vast and fascinating as that of the stars and galaxies."[3]

In Jung's psychology, the psyche comprises two complementary structures: the conscious and the unconscious, the latter being divided into the personal and the collective. Whereas the conscious comprises all processes occurring in conscious awareness, in the personal unconscious Jung placed "forgotten, repressed, subliminally perceived and felt material of all kinds."[4] But it was the deeper collective unconscious upon which, according to Jung, the personal unconscious rests that seemed to promise vast uncharted inner landscapes that, with the right tools, might be penetrated and explored: "This part of the unconscious is not individual but universal; in contrast to the personal psyche, it has contents and modes of behavior that are more or less the same everywhere and in all individuals. It is, in other words, identical in all men and thus constitutes a common psychic substrate of a suprapersonal nature which is present in every one of us."[5]

And if the collective unconscious was the "universe within," then the archetypes—another of Jung's most well-known concepts—were its residents. According to his model, the archetypes are innate structures and patterns embedded in the deepest levels of the psyche shared by all humans that give rise to certain common patterns of conscious experience. Using these archetypes, Jung was able to explain the appearance of many universal motifs in the mythology and folklore of entirely disparate cultures: the Hero, the Wise Old Man, the Mother, the Trickster, and the Jester, among many others. The archetypes collectively represent "typical and fundamental experiences incurred by man since primordial times"[6]—a kind of collective imprint of our shared neural heritage.[7] Since we all carry a variant of the same human brain as a product of millions of years of evolution, it makes perfect sense that it would generate certain common patterns and images, as neuroscientist Jaak Panksepp explains: "Our brains resemble old museums that contain many of the archetypal markings of our evolutionary past. . . . Our brains are full of ancestral memories and processes that guide our actions and dreams but rarely emerge unadulterated by experience during our everyday activities."[8]

It isn't difficult to see the appeal of Jung's ideas as a possible explanation for the commonly encountered denizens of the tryptamine netherworlds. If a collective unconscious stuffed with archetypes can explain the appearance of certain characters in mythology and folklore then, so the argument goes, why not the machine elves and insectoid aliens? If we're unable to explain the effects of DMT by appealing to random cortical noise, exotic dream imagery, nor as memories intruding from temporal lobe memory systems, then perhaps we should look to these much older and deeper archetypal patterns. I must admit that I, too, once found this hypothesis appealing. In fact, it seemed like the only hypothesis left as a plausible alternative to the much more contentious idea that DMT was gating access to an external discarnate intelligent agent—admittedly a much harder sell. But at the same time, it was clear that most proponents of this Jungian model of the DMT worlds hadn't really thought about it too deeply and simply treated the collective unconscious like a magician's hat from which any and all otherwise inexplicable psychological or experiential phenomena could be extracted with an awkward flourish. Machine elves? Archetypal imagery. Insectoid aliens? Archetypal imagery. Multidimensional liquid light energy creatures? Errr . . . archetypal imagery? But with even a cursory perusal of some of the more bizarre, and indeed, alien entities commonly encountered by DMT users, the idea that these are relics of our shared evolutionary history embedded in our collective neural architecture already seems to stretch the Jungian model well beyond anything Jung himself ever conceived.

Jung developed his model of the psyche when neuroscience was very much in its infancy, and consequently, his ideas can often tend toward the mystical, appearing completely untethered from any kind of neurobiological foundation. However, with the benefit of several decades of progress in the neurosciences that weren't available to Jung, it isn't particularly difficult to explain how and why certain universal characters and imagery tend to emerge from the human brain. There's nothing magical or mystical or even that mysterious about the collective unconscious and its constituent archetypes: They arise naturally, perfectly explicably, and in fact, entirely predictably during the brain's evolution. Briefly, the collective unconscious is a set of innate neural programs (the *archetypes*), shared by all humans (hence *collective*), mainly operating outside of conscious awareness (hence *unconscious*), that evolved to respond in fast, reliable, and stereotyped ways to all the different types of humans and other creatures we might encounter in the environment. So the collective unconscious is simply a collection of these innate neural programs—the archetypes—that are or were important for our survival. But how are these neural programs in any way related to visual imagery? And can we use them to explain the bizarre creatures frequently encountered in the DMT worlds? The short answer is: No, we can't. But to understand why, we need consider in more detail exactly how these archetypes work—and how they don't.

From a neuroscientific perspective, *the unconscious* can be defined simply as everything the brain does outside of conscious awareness. In fact, the vast majority of what the brain does occurs outside of conscious awareness and could be considered part of the unconscious.[9] But what exactly does the brain do? Put as broadly and succinctly as possible: The brain receives sensory inputs both from the body and the environment, processes that information, and then, depending on the results of this processing, generates an output or a response. So far, we've focused on the cortex's role as a world builder: Sensory information arriving via the sense organs forms the inputs, the world model is updated based upon these inputs, and an appropriate output is generated, which is often some physical action in the environment. The subjective world is the interface that allows you to interact with the environment in useful and adaptive ways that increase your chances of surviving long enough to pass on your genes to the next generation.

But while the cortex is the brain's crowning glory and arguably the most complex (known) structure in the known universe, like Jung's model of the conscious component of the psyche, it sits on a deep foundation of equal importance. The deepest parts of the brain, the brainstem and surrounding regions, are responsible for basic functions essential for life entirely outside of conscious control: managing heart rate, blood pressure, breathing regulation, the sleep-wake cycle, as well as partially controlling stereotyped motor programs such as swallowing, yawning, and coughing.[10] Just like the cortex, the primary role of the brainstem is to receive inputs, both from the body and the environment, process them, and generate outputs. While these deepest neural processes are entirely unconscious—if you had to remember to speed up your heart whenever you climbed a flight of stairs to avoid passing out, you wouldn't last long—"the unconscious" envisaged by Jung can be better mapped to neural processes that, although occurring outside of conscious awareness, more directly affect our behavior and conscious experience.[11]

All animals, including humans, are born with certain fixed patterns of behavior important for their survival. More complex than basic reflexes, in animals we refer to these as instincts: inherited neural programs that induce an animal to perform certain behaviors or respond to certain patterns of sensory inputs without having to learn how to do so.[12] A newly hatched sea turtle will instinctively scuttle toward the ocean; an eastern hognose snake will roll onto its back, open its mouth, and play dead when threatened; orb-weaver spiders will engineer beautifully intricate webs despite never having been taught to do so. A pair of young rats, each raised alone, when placed together into the same enclosure for the first time, will begin to perform another important instinctive behavior—they will begin to play: chasing, pouncing, wrestling, and generally having a wild time. However, if a tuft of cat hair is placed into the cage, they will immediately stop playing and begin, with obvious trepidation, to investigate, seemingly aware of the presence of something they need to be cautious around.[13] They're scared, but they're not sure why. Dog hairs, on the other hand, have no such effect. Rats don't need to be taught that cats pose a threat to their well-being, nor do they need to have seen or have been anywhere near a cat prior to being confronted with its fur to display this behavior. It's instinctive—they're equipped from birth with a neural program that ensures they remain alert and cautious in the presence of this particularly dangerous predator. We might say that rats are born with a "cat archetype." Of course, this doesn't mean that a newborn rat's brain can generate images of cats. Assuming a rat dreams, this innate "cat archetype" program doesn't endow it with the ability to dream about cats, since that would require its cortex to build a model of a cat and that must be learned. The innate "cat archetype" simply provides a "quick and dirty" stereotyped response to sensory inputs—such as the odor of its fur—that indicate the presence of a cat.

Humans are also equipped with such innate programs, although, compared to lower animals, we possess a much richer and more complex repertoire of instincts that include a range of uniquely human behaviors and responses that are, or were, important for our survival. From birth, babies enjoy sweet-tasting foods but will show displeasure at the sight of an angry face. Toward the end of their first year, their attention will be aroused by snakes and spiders, they will avoid heights and withdraw in the presence of strangers.[14] Of course, such young children don't understand why snakes so pique their curiosity, nor why heights and strangers can be dangerous, and nor do they need to. What is important is that they recognize and respond to such features in their environment in a manner likely to promote survival.[15] And just as newborn rats don't dream about cats, very young children are unlikely to be

able to dream about snakes, despite being endowed with innate unconscious neural programs that are activated by patterns of sensory inputs
that indicate the presence of such critters.[16]

Imagine you're walking along a forest path and suddenly, in front
of you, you notice a large snake, obviously angry, hissing and generally
making it perfectly obvious that you're an unwelcome intruder in its territory. Before you're even consciously aware of a snake in front of you,
unconscious circuits in your brain recognize this characteristic pattern
of sensory information and initiate a programmed response. As well as
being passed to your primary visual cortex, visual sensory information
is also passed to a set of deeper structures below the cortex (known as
subcortical structures) with important roles in emotional responses.[17]
Sensory information arrives at, and can be processed by, these subcortical structures much more quickly than the far more sophisticated visual
cortices, and they initiate a rapid stereotyped response: You're startled
and your level of conscious awareness is instantaneously heightened.
You freeze and your head and eyes reflexively shift toward and fix upon
the snake. Your heart begins to race; blood vessels in your muscles dilate,
as do your pupils. All of this is controlled by an unconscious subcortical
program that we might call a "snake archetype," which is activated by
the pattern of sensory inputs that indicate the presence of a snake and
rapidly prepares you to deal with this potentially dangerous obstacle in
your path.[18]

This stereotyped response to the sight of a snake goes a long way
to ensuring you get out of the situation alive. Unfortunately, however,
your brain doesn't have an inherited automatic program for dealing
with snakes beyond this. What it does have, however, is the complex,
dynamic, and detailed model of the environment built by your cortex to
work with. This is where the cortex comes into its own, having evolved
not to respond in a programmed fashion to particular patterns of sensory stimuli, but to weigh up many different variables and choose from a
range of possible responses. This is the whole purpose of that subjective
world model playing out in the theater of conscious awareness. By the
time you notice and identify the snake in your path, your unconscious
programs have already saved you from potential disaster and prepared

your body and brain for action.[19] But now they've done as much as they can, and your cortex needs to take over.

Of course, for most of us in the modern world, snakes are likely to be the least of our concerns. By far the most commonly encountered animals in the environment, the ones most likely to present a challenge on a daily basis, are unlikely to be snakes, but other humans. Unfortunately, although initially responding to every snake in the grass in a stereotyped way, even if it turns out to be perfectly harmless, is likely to be a broadly adaptive strategy, this could never work with humans. Throughout our evolutionary history, as we developed as social animals, we have had to deal with many different types of humans, and just as we evolved a quick-and-dirty archetypal program for dealing with snakes, we evolved archetypal programs to deal with different people in different social situations. How we should respond to and interact with someone we encounter will depend on who they are and their place within our social group. Some humans are friends, others foes; some will offer us protection, whereas others we need to protect; and others still might try to deceive or trick us, either for social or material gain, or even to harm or kill us. Each of these variants of humans needs to be detected, distinguished, and will require a different behavioral response.[20] You don't feel and behave the same way toward your mother as you do toward a complete stranger. As an infant, we respond to our mother using an innate Mother archetype program: We're drawn to our mother by a feeling of comfort and contentment in her presence and acute anxiety in her absence—a baby cries when separated from its mother. Likewise, we are programmed to respect and listen carefully to a community elder with an abundance of life experience and knowledge—a Wise Old Man—but we should be careful about believing what emerges from the lips of a Trickster. So while we might inherit but a single programmed response to a snake—a single "snake archetype"—we inherit a set of archetypes to manage and respond to encounters with different types of humans.

Whenever you meet another person, your brain is always trying to find a good archetypal match—to find the most appropriate program to respond to this person. Just as the rat's "cat archetype" program was

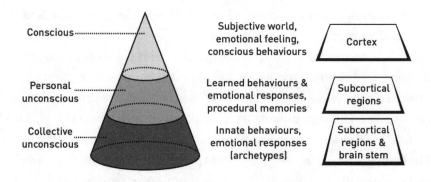

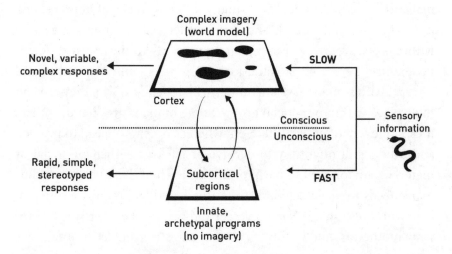

Jung's model of the psyche can now be mapped onto the known functions of the brain. The archetypes are innate, evolutionarily old, unconscious programs that generate rapid, stereotyped emotional and behavioral responses to other humans and animals in the environment. They are not, and nor do they generate, images. They are, however, interconnected with the cortex (the only source of imagery in the brain) and can stimulate the generation of imagery.

activated when cat hairs were placed into its cage, the pattern of subtle sensory clues from a stranger—how they dress, talk, their behavior and mannerisms—will tend to activate an archetypal program that effectively places that person into a particular category that then governs how you feel about and respond to them: Is this a friend or an enemy? Should you approach or keep your distance? Is this the kind of person you should reveal your deepest and darkest secrets to or is it best to remain guarded and taciturn in their presence? The total number of archetypal programs we all carry—collectively—is hard to know, but it's not difficult to explain the preponderance of certain well-known characters in widely published lists of archetypes: the Mother, the Father, the Child, the Lover, the Wise Old Man, the Ruler, the Trickster, the Jester, the Rebel, and many more, each representing a particular type of human we're likely to encounter in life. Of course, no individual can be described in their entirety by a single archetypal identity marker. That's not their purpose. These are ancient broad brushstroke categories that evolved to promote quick-and-dirty adaptive social behaviors in the presence of different types of people.[21]

But if the archetypes are simply innate unconscious programs that guide our feelings and behavior, how and why do they tend to generate common patterns of visual imagery? And why would anyone think they had anything to do with the strange nonhuman entities encountered at the peak of a breakthrough DMT trip? Firstly, and most importantly, archetypes are not images. The "snake archetype" isn't a specific snake or even a particular type of snake, nor is it an image or outline of a snake. The snake archetype is the inherited response to snakes that evolved to promote adaptive behaviors when encountering one. Likewise, the human archetypes aren't images of particular types of humans, but inherited subcortical programs that evolved to promote adaptive social interactions with particular types of humans. Building visual object models (images), whether in normal waking life, during dreams, or DMT trips, is a complex task that can only be performed by the cortex. The much simpler archetypal programs, encoded in unconscious circuits, are optimized to be simple, reliable, and fast, and cannot generate imagery. Neuropsychologist and father of neuropsychoanalysis Mark Solms is quite clear: "There are no images in the unconscious."[22] But this doesn't mean the archetypes can't stimulate the generation of imagery by the cortex. The purpose of the "snake archetype," for example, is to be activated by patterns of sensory information that indicate the presence of a snake—these are the same patterns of sensory inputs your cortex uses to inform its visual model of the snake, albeit processed by different neural circuits. So, activation of the snake archetype usually occurs when you're looking at a snake—when your cortex is constructing a model of a snake. Eventually, the snake archetype and snake imagery generated by the cortex become inextricably connected and mutually activating. For instance, if you see a snake in a dream—that is, if your cortex builds a snake model in the absence of sensory inputs—then the "snake archetype" can be activated and provide the inherited emotional and behavioral response to that snake. Conversely, activation of the snake archetype can trigger the cortex to build a visual snake model. However, crucially, this is only because the cortex already knows how to build models of snakes. Archetypes don't, and cannot, provide visual imagery; they can only stimulate the cortex to generate imagery it already knows how to construct. The visual imagery generated by my Mother archetype, for example, is highly personal to me. If my Mother archetype were activated in a dream, I'd likely begin dreaming of my mother—not your mother and not anyone else's mother. My Mother archetype is tightly connected with my personal experience with my mother and the visual model of my mother that my cortex has learned to build.

So being endowed with innate archetypal programs that provide stereotyped responses to particular types of humans or other living beings doesn't relieve the cortex of the task of having to learn how to construct models of these beings, even though these programs eventually become associated with these models. Of course, the archetypes do give the brain a propensity to model certain types of humans, but only if the cortex has already learned to construct such humans. So if we struggle to explain how the cortex can construct a model of an entity encountered in the DMT state, the archetypes can't help us. There are no machine elves in the unconscious. Of course, if you happen to encounter a colony of elfin beings, then that can only be because your cortex is, for some reason, modeling such creatures and it's perfectly plausible that this elf model might activate a particular archetypal program. This is simply the brain's attempt to place the creature into an archetypal category that will then influence how this being appears to you and how you feel about and respond to it. Indeed, this seems to provide an explanation for why so many people report encountering beings described as "elfish" despite their form varying wildly. It isn't even obvious that the various beings that people report as "elves" ought to be lumped together as the same type of entity.[23] In this account, the entities are unambiguously elflike: "A gaggle of elflike creatures in standard issue Irish elf costumes, complete with hats, looking like they had stepped out of a Hallmark cards' 'Happy Saint Patrick's Day' display, were doing strange things with strange objects that seemed to be a weird hybrid between crystals and machines."[24]

However, what McKenna describes as a machine elf is hardly representative of a typical elf motif: "When you smoke DMT, if you do sufficiently, you burst into a place that is inhabited by these—what I call self-transforming machine elves, these jeweled, self-dribbling basketballs that are squealing and squeaking in this alien language that condenses like metallic rain and falls out of the air of the room and is able to morph itself into Faberge-like objects that are scintillating and faceted and reflective of other possibilities and objects."[25]

The elfishness of these entities seems to stem from their characteristically jovial, cheeky, and mischievous character. Despite being entirely nonhuman, they clearly activate an archetype that evolved to respond to a particular type of human with a propensity for wild, clownish, and mischievous behavior.[26] Our response to people who act outside of social norms, who break the rules and fool around, has almost certainly become hardwired into our neural architecture as one of the many archetypal programs we carry.[27] But again, this archetypal program—often referred to as the Jester or Trickster—merely provides the stereotyped responses to these beings, but not the details of their form and behavior, which can only be generated by the cortex. To suggest that these bizarre creatures can be explained away in their entirety as activations of these archetypal structures means to completely misunderstand what the archetypes are and to quietly ignore all their more unusual characteristics that defy a simple archetypal identity marker. It's hard to imagine what a Jungian would make of "multidimensional creatures formed by strands of visible language"[28] that, barring their jovial character, seem about as far from the human experience, either now or at any time in the past, as it's possible to stray.

The same can be said for insectoid beings. Like snakes, insects represent one of a handful of living creatures that, particularly in the ancestral environment, have the potential to harm us.[29] Without an ability to both detect and respond appropriately to such critters, our ape ancestors wouldn't have made it far. As such, our brains are equipped with hard-wired "insect archetypes" to detect and respond to insects.[30] The mantis is particularly interesting since, of all insects, it appears the closest to a humanoid form while remaining thoroughly alien. Mantid beings also happen to be one of the most widely reported of the multitudinous entities encountered during DMT trips, often displaying many of the physical and behavioral characteristics we would expect of an insect while not actually being an insect. One of Strassman's volunteers, Rex, described a multitude of these entities, which he specifically described as "insect creatures" and "insectoids", meaning insect-like: "When I was first going under, there were these insect creatures all around me. They were clearly trying to break through. I was fighting letting go of who I am or was. The more I fought, the more demonic they became, probing into my psyche and being. . . . As I accepted my death and dissolution into God's love, the insectoids began to feed on my heart, devouring the feelings of love and surrender."[31]

Clearly, these insectoid beings are not simple insect hallucinations. And although they likely activate an insect archetype, they tend to be highly advanced, intelligent, and sophisticated alien life-forms: "This then proceeded to take me into an alien spaceship-type room, with two 'beings' that resembled large praying mantises. They knew I was there . . . yet I could sense they didn't want me there and were not happy of my presence, but nevertheless they tolerated me. These beings were controlling the universe; I was nothing compared to the grand scheme of what they were part of, and this is something I feel I will never understand."[32]

It seems entirely appropriate that a creature that appears cold, ruthless, mechanical, and on occasion, downright vicious, would activate the insect archetype and influence how that being appears. But this doesn't mean that the Soulless Insect People that so horrified William Burroughs, or the mantid alien interloper that tortured Jee during his series of ayahuasca sessions in Peru, were actually insectoid in their "true" form, or even if they had a form that could be faithfully modeled by the human brain. On occasion, the entities in the DMT state make this quite clear: "'Who are you?' At this time a very clear mantis image appeared and took a long hard look at me. 'Really?!' was the only response I could come up with. 'No, not really; you could not truly understand what we really are and so we appear like this to you.'"[33]

Although an insect archetype might explain why certain entities are often described as "insectoid," since they likely activate the archetypal program that governs how we respond to such beings and might even influence how our cortex models these beings, they don't provide anything beyond this—they cannot be a source of the imagery. Even if the brain is receiving information from some alternate reality populated by advanced discarnate intelligences, it's not relieved of the task of building a representation—a model—of that world and its occupants, and it's entirely expected that it would attempt to match any apparently living creatures to an archetypal category—as it does with all living beings it encounters. As such, we shouldn't be surprised when creatures described as insectoid, elfish, or reptilian show up. What is surprising, far more interesting, and far more challenging to explain is not when entities manifest recognizable archetypal qualities, but that the cortex, in its modeling of these beings, so rarely settles on a human form, and instead, begins constructing creatures with characteristics and behaviors that transcend not only human or animal forms but the human experience in its entirety.

The archetypes are quintessentially human and animal structures, representing the social relationships between members of our species and interactions between humans and other creatures of the natural world. The DMT experience, in striking contrast, is quintessentially nonhuman—the DMT worlds and their inhabitants often seem to bear no relationship whatsoever to either our current or ancestral existence as a species. It's difficult to reconcile the necessary simplicity of evolutionarily old hardwired archetypal programs with an inordinately complex ecology of technologically and cognitively advanced intelligent beings existing within a realm that is completely disjoint from the normal waking world, either now or in the distant past. Despite his fascination with Jungian thought, Terence McKenna was eventually forced to admit that these realms seemed to represent not some deep collective domain of the human mind, but somewhere "out there"[34]: "It was almost counter the idea of the collective unconscious, because it argued that you, Joe Anybody, Sally Somebody, can break through on your own, an ordinary person, to a place that Verrocchio never saw, Michelangelo didn't anticipate it, Yates didn't know, Blake hadn't a clue, Melville wasn't briefed, and yet there it is."[35]

All in all, having appealed to dreams, to memories, to the hallucinations of psychotics and now Jungian models of the psyche rooted in modern neuroscience, we haven't gotten very far in explaining DMT's effects on consciousness and the structure of the subjective world. The utter astonishment of DMT users as the mundane world of normal waking life is obliterated and replaced with an altogether different one isn't a reaction to entering a dream world filled with characters from Nordic fairy tales or memories from their childhood. This isn't what they experience. The complete restructuring of the world isn't driven by spontaneous emergent activity of the primary visual cortex, repressed memories from the temporal memory systems, or archetypal patterns flowing from deeper brain structures. Once DMT reaches a threshold in the brain, it transcends all this in its entirety, leaving both the personal and the collective human experience behind and replacing it with the Other. Not a world that is merely strange, nor a maelstrom of chaos or fragments of a shattered psyche, but a highly structured, infinitely complex alien reality far beyond the preposterous phantasmagoria of even the most far gone of psychotics—a world teeming with intelligent nonhuman entities unlike anything imagined by Jung—or anyone else—that seems to come from nowhere. The DMT state, at its deepest levels, is the apotheosis of the alien. It is a world that the brain should not know how to build. It is a world that should not exist and yet there it is, irresistible in its construction and undeniable in its presence. To smoke DMT means to confront not merely a different world, but one that is, frankly, impossible.

13

COLLISION WITH THE IMPOSSIBLE

The universe prevents you from programming; and when they take you out, they tear you wholly loose, and you realize that these are massive intellects, far greater than any human. Then you really get humble. When you come back here you say, "Oh well, here I am, back in this damn body again, and I'm not as intelligent as when I was out there with them.

—John C. Lilly

In March of 1953, the English writer and philosopher Aldous Huxley was enjoying breakfast with his wife, Maria, at their home in Los Angeles, working his way through the morning's mail.

"Let's ask this fellow Osmond to stay," suggested Huxley, seemingly apropos of nothing. "He's a Canadian psychiatrist who works with mescaline."[1]

The remarkable altered state of consciousness induced by this cactus alkaloid had piqued Huxley's interest after reading an article on the topic by Humphry Osmond, and he was keen to experience the effects himself. But while Huxley thought inviting Osmond to his home would provide him with an ideal opportunity to do just that, his wife, having heard of neither Osmond nor mescaline, was concerned about welcoming a strange Canadian into their house: "But he may have a beard and we may not like him."

"If we don't like him, we can always be out," Huxley replied.[2]

And that was that. Less than three months later, Huxley collected the clean-shaven—and, in fact, British—psychiatrist from the airport carrying, as Huxley had hoped and requested, a small supply of mescaline sulphate. And at 11 a.m. on May 4, 1953, Huxley swallowed 400mg of the drug dissolved in a glass of water, sat, and waited.[3] What followed provided the material for arguably the most famous psychedelic trip report in history (barring perhaps Albert Hofmann's legendary LSD bicycle ride), published the following year as his classic essay and required reading for all psychedelic enthusiasts, "The Doors of Perception."[4] Preempting modern models of perceptual function by several decades, Huxley speculated in this essay that the human brain's role in perception is primarily as a "reducing valve" that filters all but a measly trickle of sensory information necessary for survival and that would otherwise overwhelm our consciousness. And mescaline, he believed, temporarily disrupted that filter. More than half a century later, modern functional neuroimaging techniques unavailable during Huxley's time would reveal how psychedelic drugs do indeed disrupt the cortex's ability to regulate the flow of information from the senses and other areas of the brain. So although he had no way of understanding the mechanisms involved, Huxley's hypothesis proved to be broadly accurate. But it was in a second essay, "Heaven and Hell," published a year later, that Huxley reached into even more speculative territory, recognizing in these molecules, at sufficiently high doses, an ability to grant us access to an "Antipodes of the mind"—an "Other world"—populated by creatures far beyond the human or animal:

> Let us use a geographical metaphor and liken the personal life of the ego to the Old World. We leave the Old World, cross a dividing ocean, and find ourselves in the world of the personal subconscious, with its flora and fauna of repressions, conflicts, traumatic memories and the like. Traveling further, we reach a kind of Far West, inhabited by Jungian archetypes and the raw materials of human mythology. Beyond this region lies a broad Pacific. Wafted across it on the wings of mescaline or lysergic acid diethylamide, we reach what may be called the Antipodes of the mind. In this psychological equivalent of Australia, we discover the equivalents of kangaroos, wallabies, and duck-billed platypuses—a whole host of extremely improbable animals, which nevertheless exist and can be observed.[5]

Although it seems unlikely that Huxley believed these entities to exist independently of the human mind entirely but rather residing in a normally inaccessible expansive domain he called Mind at Large, he at least intuited that such creatures were, to some extent at least, autonomous: "You do not invent these creatures any more than you invent marsupials. They live their own lives in complete independence. A man cannot control them, . . . Almost never does the visionary see anything that reminds him of his own past. He is not remembering scenes, persons, or objects, and he is not inventing them; he is looking on at a new creation."[6]

Nor was he convinced that they could be explained using Jungian models of the psyche: "The inhabitants of the mind's Antipodes differ from the figures inhabiting Jung's archetypal world; for they have nothing to do either/with the personal history of the visionary, or even with the age-old problems of the human race. Quite literally, they are the inhabitants of 'the Other World.'"[7]

In support of this idea, Huxley quotes Humphry Osmond's collaborator, John Smythies, who claimed many hallucinatory visions to be "the work of a highly differentiated mental compartment, without any apparent connection, emotional or volitional, with the aims, interests, or feelings of the person concerned."[8]

Unfortunately, but understandably, in retrospect, Huxley neglects to quote Smythies's next line: "We now identify this 'mental compartment' with the Jungian Collective Unconscious."[9] Huxley himself, quite rightly, believed the Antipodes of the mind to transcend the collective unconscious, and in so doing, rejected the idea that the beings encountered within them were derived from archetypal structures. And although Smythies is correct in that this deepest layer of the psyche is unrelated to the aims, interests, and feelings of the *individual*, it is most certainly related to the aims, interests, and feelings of humans as a *collective*. Indeed, that is the entire basis of Jung's model. So if this "mental compartment" isn't the collective unconscious, then what and where exactly is it? What mental compartment could generate imagery that bears no connection to either modern or ancestral human experience? Is this imagery really derived from a mental compartment at all—however such a compartment might be defined—or from some-where else entirely?

In 2003, Israeli psychologist Benny Shanon published his magnum opus, titled with an obvious nod to Huxley, *Antipodes of the Mind: Charting the Phenomenology of the Ayahuasca Experience*, which included his analysis and interpretations of the subjective reports of over 2,500 aya-huasca users.[10] Like Huxley, Shanon became convinced—as many DMT users are—that the content of the ayahuasca visions couldn't be explained away either as personal imagery or as material flowing up from the depths of the collective psyche: "The visions and other non-ordinary experien-tial phenomena that ayahuasca induces present a new, uncharted natural cognitive domain. Since the number of natural domains is very small, this makes the ayahuasca experience of paramount interest for the student of mind. . . . I am inclined to say that in various respects ayahuasca brings us to the boundaries not only of science but also of the entire Western worldview and its philosophies."[11]

Shanon was right to be skeptical of the Jungian models that have come to be applied with almost casual facility in explaining the types of entities encountered during ayahuasca and DMT experiences. Dream imagery is highly personal, whereas archetypal imagery reflects universal human experience, whether in literal or symbolic form. DMT visions, however, seem to transcend both the personal and the universal, and as Shanon points out, appealing to either (or even both) leaves the vast majority of the DMT experience "simply unaccounted for." So how do we account for them? For most scientists, the solution is simply to deny that there's anything to account for. It's easier to call the DMT state "comparable to the dream state" than to confront the fact that it is anything but and that we have no idea why. And it's easier to refer to nonhuman/nonanimal entity encounters as "archetypal symbols" or, even more ridiculously, "il-lusory social events" than to admit that their origin and nature remains almost a complete mystery.

Part of the problem in trying to convince someone who's never experienced a full breakthrough dose of DMT that the experience is more than an unusual form of dreaming or imagery bubbling up from the collective unconscious, is the irrevocably impassable gulf between the written and verbal accounts of the DMT state—no matter how eloquently described—and the immensity of the experience itself. While a marching army of "Soulless Insect People" depicted in a movie would hardly raise an eyebrow these days—far more disturbing things have been presented on screen—there was clearly something more to them that left William Burroughs traumatized. Two of Strassman's volunteers, Peter and Paul, were left in a state of complete shock and disbelief, which in the former's case appeared to trigger a state of actual physical shock that almost killed him. The entirely unanticipated immensity and undeniability of the DMT state collides with our most basic assumptions regarding what is and isn't possible with such force that many users are left in a state that the late Harvard psychiatrist, Dr. John Mack, termed "ontological shock." Humans, sane ones at least, are extremely good at distinguishing reality from fantasy and the vast majority are quick to accept that a particularly strange dream when recounted from the bedside was just that—a dream and not real. Although this reality testing is impaired during dreaming and psychosis,[12] waking from the dream or recovery from psychotic illness is generally sufficient to restore this important faculty and the dream or hallucination is recognized for what it is. This makes the DMT experience all the more compelling and paradoxical; it is far stranger than any dream and yet there remains an intransigent inability to shake the feeling that it was truly, and, often, horrifyingly real once the experience has ended. So how do we bridge that gap between the immediacy and undeniability of the felt experience and the written and verbal reports of those who've had such experiences? Although we've already discussed the accounts of many DMT users that seem impossible to explain using the neuroscientific models we've explored, are there specific characteristics of the DMT worlds and their occupants that not only mitigate against them being simply fabrications of an excited cortex but strongly suggest that they cannot be explained in this way and that we must look for an alternative explanation?

It can't be denied that the entities encountered during a breakthrough DMT trip are often magnificent, awe-inspiring, and occasionally terrifying in their form, resident within a space of incomprehensible

complexity, power, and beauty. However, it is their behavior, their obvious intent, and the apparent extreme levels of intelligence, wisdom,
and technological sophistication often displayed by these beings that
might provide a clue as to their nature. Recalling his first experience
after smoking DMT, author Graham Hancock was left reeling by what
appeared to be a world that wasn't merely strange and complex, but one
that appeared quite obviously to have been built by the hand of something entirely nonhuman: "DMT brought me to a world—or to some
aspect of a world—that appeared from the outset to be highly artificial,
constructed, inorganic, and in essence technological."[13]

For Hancock, it was quite clear that he was in the presence of an extremely advanced alien intelligence: "What I remember most of all about
[the entities], anyway, was not their appearance but their intelligence—
which struck me immediately as utterly different in its emotional tem-
perature from contact with human intelligence."[14]

Hancock was far from alone in his appraisal of the world he found
himself in and in experiencing an unshakable sense of being in the presence of something of extraordinary power, as this DMT user reports:
"It was like a machine . . . an organic machine . . . The thing that struck
me most about this creature was its dignity. Its aura. Its self-awareness.
Its power. Its majesty. It absolutely radiated with energy. Just being in its
presence inspired awe. Inspired love. . . . You could feel its importance.
You could feel its intelligence."[15]

Of course, unless you've actually been confronted by this kind of
being, it's difficult to explain that undeniable sense of supreme intelligence. But the frequency with which this feeling is reported ought at
least to give us pause. However, in many reports, it's absolutely possible to identify certain characteristics of the DMT state that betray the
type of civilization we're stumbling into—to delineate certain common
features of both the entities and the space itself—what we might call
"impossibilities" of form, narrative, dynamics, information, and control, that are not only difficult to dismiss as complex dreamlike or hallucinatory imagery, but effectively rule out such an explanation and insist
we look for another.

One of the most commonly reported impossibilities of form is often described as "hyperdimensionality," in which DMT users explicitly mention a type of world with geometric structure and dimensionality that cannot exist in the normal waking world and that our brains shouldn't have any ability to represent in visual form: "I entered a state/place that I think of as the tesseract. I've been there a few times, but this was extremely uncomfortable. There were way, way more directions in space to look at than there should have been is the only way I can describe it. More than three dimensions."[16]

"There were several entities. They weren't humanoid, or like anything I have ever seen. It seemed as though they occupied the fourth spatial dimension, yet I could only perceive them through my understanding of three-dimensional space. They danced before me, morphing into one another rather grotesquely as if I was viewing a tesseract rotating in 4D space."[17]

It's not easy to explain how our brains, having evolved to represent the three dimensions of physical space should suddenly, in the presence of DMT, gain the ability to represent higher dimensional spaces and objects in anything but the purely abstract. But it's not as if the cortex is merely, in its more fluid and dynamic state, somehow stumbling upon exotic geometric forms as spontaneously emergent patterns of neural activity—these structures often form part of a highly stable and coherent, intricately detailed and ordered narrative. As Strassman's volunteer Jeremiah noted, "It's not a hallucination, but an observation. . . . It's more like an experience of a new technology than a drug."[18] And indeed, many users describe what appear to be the highly technological machinations of a supremely advanced and thoroughly nonhuman civilization both occupying and manipulating this higher-dimensional space.

"After the tour, and that's what it felt like, she noticed I was coming back to our world, so she stopped and spread her hands apart in front of me and started materializing the most complex and impossible shapes. She was transferring as much mathematical and geometric knowledge as fast as possible, communicating things like 'take this information, hurry' and 'do you see it, do you see it all?' I was getting the feeling that this information was basic knowledge in their world, like us teaching our toddlers squares, circles, and triangles. I was just looking at these impossible shapes in awe and just getting mind blown."[19]

Often these narratives are so unusual that it's essentially impossible to envisage what the tripper experienced:

> An elf (garbed in clothing that was very much a part of the patterns going on around it) with pointy ears was weaving the fabric of reality together. Once I noticed him weaving the fabric of existence, I saw them all, creating. This was when the mother of all things presented herself. She was gorgeous, her skin sheening gold, and hair vibrant shades of blue and green. She floated/hovered (all I could see of her was from her upper chest and above, just like a puppet master working above the scenes) above all the elves that were busy weaving and creating micro-universes. She flew in and told me to not be afraid, that she loved me very much and she said, "This is all going to happen very fast; you don't have much time here and we have so much to show you: pay attention."[20]

The idea of "weaving the fabric of existence" is a concept so exotic that it strains credulity beyond breaking point to suggest that the brain simply came up with this when perturbed by this ubiquitous plant alkaloid. And this report is far from unique: A woman messaged me just a few months ago to describe her own experience that resembled this report in many ways—except it wasn't the elves who were manufacturing universes, but herself:

> What I thought was reality is not reality. What I thought was impossible is not impossible. DMT has opened my mind to the impossible. . . . It started with the fractals, but for some reason, this time I felt unsettled and a bit scared I wanted to back out, but when I looked up, there were these two entities guiding me and saying, "Let go," so I let go. Suddenly, I was in this place with the most amazing colors and very bright. There were entities all around me, and they were welcoming

me. This place, as beautiful as it was, I find it hard to describe, but was a happy place and had bright vivid colors. . . . I was then in this other reality, and this reality, I was building realities, and what I was seeing is pretty much impossible to explain. It was beautiful. I would open my mouth and realities were being born from it. I was not alone; there were others around me, and they were my friends. All realities morphed into one. The past, present, and future was all happening at the same time. I started making more realities, and I was watching them build up in front of me with impossible amazing detail. I have never felt like this before, but as impossible as it seems now, it was real, and it was natural. It was like this was my true being, and doing what I was supposed to do.

This other DMT user simply couldn't imagine how such rich and coherent scenarios could be generated by his brain: "At moments I felt like the best movie ever conceived was being presented to me in real time. It felt extremely designed in a good way—I just couldn't begin to comprehend how was that possible as an experience."[21] Indeed, this kind of perfectly finessed narrative coherence and continuity, coupled with elaborate invention and astonishing creativity, is difficult for the brain to achieve even in the dream state when not being held accountable to sensory inputs. In a sense, the human brain is both good and bad at dreaming—at fabricating worlds. Think how unstable and disorganized your average dream is—how your brain can't seem to decide on who's who and what's what. Indeed, without the guidance of sensory information, your cortex wanders from scene to scene, never settling, without apparent rhyme or reason. This is why people often describe their dreams as strange or bizarre or failing to make sense. Compare this to the exquisitely coherent, perfectly ordered worlds of the DMT state, with everything operating with razor-sharp precision and timing, engineered to utter perfection, far beyond anything the brain ought to be capable of constructing, even when modeling the normal waking world—the world it evolved to model—let alone an entirely alien world with an inordinately higher level of complexity and detail.

But it isn't only the highly unusual narratives that DMT users find difficult to explain or comprehend, but the speed and dynamism of its development and progression: "It was science fiction made fact. A dimension devoid of natural things, of plants and human need, of our weak and imprecise symbol systems. . . . Suddenly I was rocketing through their cities. Multidimensional, jewel-faceted, hard and immaterial palaces where geometrical and tentacular constructions were being taken apart and reconstructed at such lightning speed that I cannot recall more than a tiny and trivial fraction."[22]

This delightfully eloquent report of a 50mg dose of synthetic DMT, published on the Erowid site, beautifully captures both the bewildering complexity, detail, and endless dynamism of the DMT state, never settling and yet always perfectly ordered and never collapsing into chaos:

It was like a liquid mind ecology of staggering and alien complexity. The glorious geometries transcended what is even vaguely feasible in this three-dimensional mundane world, constantly concrescing into new and variegated permutations, exfoliating out of themselves what might be called hyperspherologies of the divine, and to look anywhere was to be shot clean through with scintillating amazement. Crowding and cramming themselves into my field of vision were thousands upon thousands of beings of every imaginable sort and many that were completely unimaginable. They were everywhere jabbering in indecipherable tongues, juggling incandescent neon microworlds of dancing beings, and morphing with a Zen-like, diaphanous fluidity that remains a primal miracle no matter how often you lay your all too human eyes on it. The primordial intelligence being manifest before me was palpable, undeniable, transcendently amazing—it shook me to my core in a more-than-real gleeful profundity. All I could do was sit there in divine liquid awe, my soul gaping wide open, and stare at the incalculable proportions of bizarreness and the downright weird that lay before me. It was like being entertained by the 76,000-piece orchestra of an alien civilization in whose classical music each note is not merely a musical tone, but an entire world, each just as intricate and nuanced as our own.[23]

I must admit to being at a loss to explain how the human brain could spontaneously generate such staggeringly dynamic complexity without access to a highly coherent source of information-rich sensory inputs. But we know these inputs don't come from the environment via the sense organs, nor from memories or archetypal programs, so where do they come from? What is the source of the information that breaks through into the cortex and seizes control of its world building apparatus with such irresistible ferocity and virtuosity? During the deepest phases of a DMT experience, this rush of information into the brain is so profoundly compelling and pervasive that it even has its own name: the download. But this information is more than simply a flood of rapidly changing imagery or complex geometric patterns, but a tsunami of highly complex, meaningful data that has no connection with either the tripper's personal present or history, nor any obvious relationship to humanity at all: "I experienced what I call a knowledge dump. It felt like my consciousness connected to an ancient galactic network and downloaded a ton of information at rapid speeds. I saw the secrets of the universe and blueprints of alien life-forms. It all made sense at the time and I understood all of it."[24]

Often there is the undeniable feeling or sensation that the information is being directed or channeled by an unseen intelligence: "As I was in the depth of this experience, at the peak, I felt as if I was being slightly adjusted or repaired at an essential level and that something was being downloaded to me. I heard and felt cosmic mechanisms along with a buzzing noise that varied in frequency, at one point becoming the most beautiful tone I've ever heard."[25]

Graham Hancock also sensed the presence of this unseen yet extremely powerful and interactive intelligence guiding his experience: "The technology of the room seemed to be about displaying some sort of recording that had been set in playback mode by the arrival of my consciousness. It seemed to me to be a very powerful and special kind of recording, one that was interactive beyond the wildest dreams of today's computer programmers. It would adjust its output according to the psychology, habitual perceptions, and culture of each individual plugging into it. . . . I came out of the experience with the weird feeling that enormous amounts of data had been transferred to me."[26]

Reading these accounts, it's easy to understand why Strassman's volunteers—and countless other DMT users—were so obstinate in their insistence that these realms are more than wild cortical fabrications or unusual forms of dream imagery. And although it might be tempting for some to imagine a vast ecology of advanced intelligences living out their lives tucked away in some dark corner of our collective psyche, such an idea strays far from anything even remotely supported by neuroscience. The archetypes are simple patterns of inherited neural connectivity, relics of our hominid past that imbue our brains with the potential to form certain types of images related to our evolutionary history, but have absolutely nothing to say about inordinately complex and dynamic, superintelligent, and hypertechnological civilizations. But beyond even these impossibilities, one of the most challenging aspects of the DMT state to explain concerns the entities themselves—not their form, character, or even their outlandish and bizarre antics, but their apparent ability to control, not only the content or type of experience, but access to the DMT realm itself.

As interest in DMT began to grow rapidly in the early years of the twenty-first century, so did the internet drug forums devoted to its discussion, mainly centered on reports of particularly interesting, unusual, or challenging types of experiences, but also discussions on how best to prepare for a DMT trip, vaporization techniques to achieve a full breakthrough experience, and interpretations of the experience, from the mundane to the far out and fantastical. However, it wasn't long before a small but not insignificant number of users began to complain of a mysterious effect that they were neither able to explain nor remedy. Known as a "lockout," this effect occurs when a regular DMT user suddenly becomes unable to achieve access into the DMT realms, no matter how much DMT is consumed. In some cases, this effect manifests simply as the drug no longer working, as a failure to launch, as if a sudden and almost complete tolerance had developed: "So after three to four months of experimenting with DMT regularly three to five times a week, about a month ago it just turned off overnight. If it was a tolerance thing, I'd expect it to get worse over time? . . . No open-eye visuals of any kind. Is there quite literally any other drug that can turn off just like that?"[27]

In most cases, this lockout occurs after a period of excessive or mindless use of the drug: "Early this year I abused DMT by using it way too often. Sometimes every day. Sometimes multiple times a day. After a couple months, I was locked out and no longer allowed access to any realms, no matter how much I took. Has this happened to you? And are you ever allowed back in? Last time I used it was April, and I just tried again yesterday (September) and was still locked out."[28]

Of course, the immediate reaction to such reports is that, since most—but not all—users who experienced this lockout effect were going through a period of highly frequent use of the drug, they were simply experiencing the result of drug tolerance, in which the effects of a drug diminish over time, even if the same dose is maintained. While this undoubtedly accounts for some cases, there are several unusual features of the effect that mitigate against such an explanation. Drug tolerance, in most cases, is a slow process caused by a gradual adaptation to the presence of the drug. For example, people who drink alcohol regularly will gradually find that they need to drink more to achieve the same level of intoxication. The mechanism of tolerance depends on the drug and its mechanism of action but can be caused by changes in the levels of the receptors to which the drug binds, increased expression of enzymes that metabolize the drug, or a compensatory effect generated by the brain. Whatever the mechanism, tolerance develops gradually and tends to be sustained, often over weeks or longer. Tolerance does not cause a drug to suddenly become entirely inactive overnight. This lockout effect appears, at first glance at least, to be similar to a special type of rapidly developing and short-term tolerance called *tachyphylaxis*,[29] which is known to occur with other psychedelics. But not with DMT.

Much of the early work on tolerance in psychedelics was performed by our old friend, Lexington pharmacologist and MK-ULTRA recruit, Harris Isbell, who fed his inmate volunteers daily doses of LSD for up to eighty-five days without interruption. Isbell noted that, even by the third day, the psychological effects of the drug appeared greatly diminished and he was forced to gradually increase the dosage to 300 micrograms (a very heavy dose) twice daily to maintain any kind of effect.[30] He obtained similar results with daily doses of either psilocybin or mescaline. In fact, when an inmate developed tolerance to repeated doses of LSD, they would also show a reduced response to psilocybin or mescaline—an effect known as *cross tolerance*—which suggested the mechanism of this tolerance effect was shared by all three drugs.[31] Surprisingly, however, he didn't observe the same effect with DMT: Even after five weeks of daily LSD administration, by which point even a massive dose of the drug elicited negligible effects, Isbell's subjects remained sensitive to the effects of DMT.[32] In fact, not only was there no cross tolerance between DMT and LSD, even DMT alone when administered repeatedly to monkeys elicited the same intensity of effect with each dose.[33] Since LSD, psilocybin, mescaline, and DMT all work via the same receptor—the 5HT2a serotonin receptor—this suggested that there was something unusual going on with DMT. During his study at the New Mexico University Hospital in the 1990s, Rick Strassman wanted to confirm this lack of tolerance to DMT's effects in his human volunteers, and thirteen of the sixty were recruited for this part of the study, each receiving 0.3mg/kg (a breakthrough dose in most people) four times at thirty-minute intervals. Strassman used a special Hallucinogen Rating Scale—which he invented and validated—to quantify the intensity of the drug's effects. And as first observed in animal models, the measured intensity of the second dose was identical to the first. The third and fourth doses also failed to induce any kind of acute tolerance—tachyphylaxis—effect.[34] What was going on?

We now know that if the 5HT2a receptor is chronically or repeatedly exposed to LSD and other psychedelics, it soon begins to stop working—a process known as desensitization—even when bound to the drug molecule,[35] and is eventually removed from the cell membrane to be broken down and recycled. This explains why repeated doses of LSD, psilocybin, or mescaline, elicit rapidly diminishing effects and why it takes at least a week or so for the effects to return, as the receptors are recycled and returned to the membrane. However, this is not the case with DMT: Despite binding and activating the 5HT2a receptor, for reasons that aren't clear, the receptor fails to become desensitized.[36] Yet again, DMT reveals itself to be special. So given that DMT has been shown to produce neither gradual and sustained tolerance, nor acute, short-term tachyphylaxis in humans, how do we explain this sudden and complete shutdown of its visionary effects in some users? Although it might seem far-fetched to suggest that an external intelligent agent is able to block entry in the DMT space, what's particularly striking about some of these accounts is that the lockout is accompanied by an unambiguous message precisely to that effect—No Entry: "I had a trip and I could sort of see the visuals. It was like a black curtain was in the way. Behind that curtain I saw what looked like an entity wagging its finger at me. I will have one session of DMT every six months. So [tolerance is] highly unlikely."[37]

Often the lockout is immediately followed by a rapid and complete return to baseline consciousness, as if the entities have control not only of entry into the space, but the level of intoxication itself: "The lockout trip was a medium-sized pile of freebase. . . . Very uncomfortable body load followed by a big, red, flashing 'X' that blasted a horrendous sound into my brain as it flashed. Was also met with feelings of total rejection and then promptly told by the disembodied red-flashing 'X' entity that I would never return to hyperspace for as long as I lived. Never again! I found myself back to stone-cold sober in just a few minutes. The feeling was overwhelmingly real, and hit me really, really hard. . . . Boop, I was ejected."[38]

And although these lockouts are often sustained, sometimes for months or even longer, occasionally it's simply as if you catch an entity on a bad day: "I smoke freebase DMT about a hundred times a year and have done so for about five years. Only once have I been kicked out of DMT hyperspace. A 'jester' type entity, as routinely seen, slowly turned to me and threw a punch. That punch I physically felt in the real world! And I was back to baseline immediately. My dosage, smoking method, and set and setting had been no different. I am at a loss to explain."[39]

A few days later, using the same vaporization technique and the same dosage from the same batch of DMT, the normal full breakthrough effects had returned.

Pharmacologically, this lockout effect makes little sense: Tolerance is generally a gradual and sustained process, not an off switch. And even the more acute tachyphylaxis variety of tolerance ought to manifest after just a few shortly spaced doses, not apparently randomly in a string of otherwise perfectly visionary trips. And anyway, as has been known since the 1950s, DMT has never been shown to display either type of tolerance. So what could explain this effect?

I was already at a loss to explain how the human brain, a product of Darwinian evolution, charged with constructing a single, familiar, three-dimensional model of the waking environment, suddenly becomes capable, with crisp efficiency, of constructing highly coherent, more real than real higher-dimensional worlds of crystalline clarity and impossible narrative and structural complexity that not only don't exist in normal waking life, but could not exist. Dreams couldn't help me, memories and cortical noise were of no use, and I dare say even Jung would be left scratching his head. But beyond these apparent impossibilities, the ability of these entities to control access to the DMT worlds and even the level of intoxication was another indicator that the source of the molecule's effects lay in the flow of information from an external source of sensory inputs—and that some kind of intelligent agent was able to regulate and direct this flow, and, as such, direct the visions.

I found support for this idea, not from the neuroscience literature, but by returning to the experts in DMT-induced visionary states: the Indigenous peoples of Amazonia. In his encyclopedic survey and analysis of the myths and shamanistic beliefs of the Piro people of the Peruvian Amazon, Scottish anthropologist Peter Gow devotes a chapter to a thorough analysis of the visions experienced by Piro shamans after consuming ayahuasca, as well as their interpretation and understanding of their source. What struck me about the Piro's worldview was how well their insights dovetailed with my own, more neurologically informed, understanding of the phenomenon. In his attempts to grok the nature of the entities the Piro commune with, which they call *kayiglu*, Gow concluded that, although the Piro experience visions of entities after drinking the ayahuasca brew, the kayiglu in and of themselves have no "true" intrinsic visual form. In fact, the word *kayiglu* means "the ones who cause visions to be seen." That is, the kayiglu beings don't reveal themselves during the ayahuasca intoxication, but actively generate the visions observed by the shaman. And from my perspective, to direct the visions means to assume control of the shaman's cortical world-building machinery—to direct the flow of information into their brain and manipulate their subjective world.[40] Just like the entities so often encountered by DMT users, they are in complete control. For me, this insight was of profound significance since it appeared to explain the DMT phenomenon in its entirety while completely reversing the usual way of thinking about both the DMT worlds and the entities encountered within them. DMT doesn't propel you into another world, nor does it open a doorway through which you can travel or even a window through which you can peek.

You don't break through into the DMT world.

The DMT world breaks through into you.

14

BREAKING THROUGH

The most merciful thing in the world, I think, is the inability of the human mind to correlate all its contents. We live on a placid island of ignorance in the midst of black seas of infinity, and it was not meant that we should voyage far. The sciences, each straining in its own direction, have hitherto harmed us little; but some day the piecing together of dissociated knowledge will open up such terrifying vistas of reality, and of our frightful position therein, that we shall either go mad from the revelation or flee from the deadly light into the peace and safety of a new dark age.

—H. P. Lovecraft

When I was a young child, my parents kept a tiny 1970s black-and-white television set in the kitchen, presumably relegated from the living room after we went full Technicolor. However, rather than the shiny silver buttons of our fancy 1980s color set, this vintage one employed a circular dial to move between channels, much like an old radio. Playing with this dial as a curious child revealed the distinct phases of the channel switch; the crisp black-and-white moving image would first distort as the dial was rotated and interference patterns encroached. This was followed by a complete breakdown of the image into pure noise with no discernible structure. However, continued rotation of the dial would eventually reveal an entirely new channel crackling into view, unrelated but just as crisp, clear, and meaningful as the old one.

In a not entirely dissimilar manner, just a few seconds after inhaling a lungful of DMT vapor, as the drug rapidly finds its way into the brain, the old familiar world begins to distort and break down as complex geometric forms at first veneer the world and then replace it entirely. The tripper is then greeted by a rapid procession of wild and chaotic imagery before finally, assuming the dosage is sufficient, an entirely new world emerges, unrelated and often far crisper, clearer, and more meaningful than the one left behind. Terence McKenna liked to call DMT a "reality channel switch." Order gives way to disorder, which then gives way, not to unbridled chaos, but to an entirely new order, astonishing in its detail, complexity, and utter alienness.

The ability of DMT to generate disordered neural activity isn't difficult to explain, as is the propensity for memories to intrude into the present moment. Even the propensity for archetypal imagery—certain types of characters to appear—is far from a great mystery. But this transition from disorder to an entirely novel and complex alien world filled with strange intelligent beings is not so easy to explain. Increasing the sensitivity of the TV receiver might allow you to pick up a much weaker signal (and perhaps risk interference from noise), but unless there's actually a channel being broadcast, you're not going to see a new channel. The information must still come from somewhere. In the same way, nudging the brain into a more fluid and dynamic state renders it much more sensitive to incoming information, whether from the sensory apparatus or elsewhere in the brain, but doesn't endow it with the ability to generate entirely new "reality channels" that are just as clear, detailed, and coherent as the normal waking world while having absolutely no apparent relationship to it. The effect of DMT on the world might be compared to finding an entirely new channel on the TV set and then realizing that the antenna is disconnected. It is sudden, it is cataclysmic, and it is complete. Where did this world come from? Why, in the presence of this simple plant alkaloid, does the brain suddenly begin building a world which, by any reasonable metric, it shouldn't know how to build? What could DMT possibly be doing in the brain to make this happen?

Having ruled out every plausible alternative I could imagine (without straying into the mystical), I returned to the admittedly far more contentious idea that DMT's effects might be explained if the molecule was somehow allowing an alternate source of information to be directed into the brain. Intuitively, this made sense, since the pioneering experiments performed by Robin Carhart-Harris's team in London had shown that psychedelics nudge the brain into a more fluid and unstable state that would be more susceptible to being manipulated by alternate information inputs. Wanting to avoid assumptions as to the nature of who or what was directing this information, I referred to this source simply as an intelligent agent. By gating the flow of information into the brain, such an agent could manipulate the world model being constructed by the cortex, in the same way the Piro believe the kayiglu beings direct their ayahuasca visions. Invoking such an agent would also explain the flood of highly ordered and complex information downloaded into the brain described by many users, as well as the entities' apparent ability to either grant or refuse access to the space. But if this was true, might it be possible to detect the flow of this alternate information source into the brain? Unfortunately, when I first began to formulate these ideas, there were very few studies looking at the effects of DMT on neural activity, barring the limited EEG data recorded by Stephen Szára in the 1950s. However, Spanish pharmacist Dr. Jordi Riba had been studying the effects of ayahuasca—the active component of course being DMT—on neural activity for over a decade and was about to publish the results of a study that showed tantalizing evidence of the kind of information flow I was hoping to see.

Riba used a freeze-dried preparation of ayahuasca prepared for him by a religious group in Brazil, which was shipped from South America to his lab in Barcelona.[1] Just like the traditional decoction, psychological effects began after thirty to sixty minutes, peaked about an hour or so later, and were resolved in four to six hours. At the higher dose levels, Riba's volunteers reported rapidly moving imagery giving way to fully formed scenes that were visible whether or not the eyes were open. And almost half a century after Szára's first attempt at an EEG recording with pure intramuscular DMT in Hungary, Riba was able to perform much more sophisticated analyses of how the ayahuasca was affecting his volunteers' brain activity throughout their experiences, as well being able to visualize the flow of information through the cortex.

From the eyes, visual sensory information is first passed to the back of the cortex—where the primary visual cortex, V1, is located—and is then passed up the levels of the cortex, toward the front and sides of the brain. In other words, when the eyes are open and the brain is processing visual sensory inputs, activity in the primary visual cortex exerts a stronger influence on activity in the higher, farther forward levels of the cortex. This effect is much weaker when the eyes are closed. So if DMT does allow an alternate source of sensory information to enter the brain, we'd expect to see this back-to-front influence even when the subjects have their eyes closed and are viewing the DMT world. Remarkably, this is precisely what Riba observed: After his volunteers ingested the freeze-dried ayahuasca, activity in the rear EEG electrodes exerted a stronger effect on those toward the front of the brain than vice versa, peaking around two hours later as the intensity of the visual effects and the levels of DMT in their blood were also reaching their maximum.[2] In short, in the presence of DMT, the brains of Riba's volunteers seemed to be processing visual sensory information even though their eyes were closed throughout the entirety of the EEG recordings. Where was this "sensory information" coming from? Riba suggested it was merely "system noise" spontaneously generated by the primary visual cortex, but does that make any sense considering the complexity, coherency, and otherworldly nature of the visionary state induced by ayahuasca?

Brazilian neuroscientist Draulio de Araujo was able to observe this activity in the primary visual cortex more directly by placing his subjects into an MRI scanner after giving them a full dose of the raw ayahuasca brew. Since ayahuasca is known for eliciting striking visual imagery even when the eyes are closed, de Araujo asked the question: After volunteers were given ayahuasca and asked to close their eyes, would their primary visual cortex "light up" during their visions in the same way that the cortex of a sober subject lights up when they view the world normally with their eyes open? Or, in de Araujo's words, are ayahuasca visions "seeing with the eyes shut"? Entirely predictably, prior to the subjects being given ayahuasca, the visual cortex was strongly activated when they viewed natural images with their eyes open but became much weaker when they closed their eyes. However, after drinking the brew, activity in the visual cortex was just as high when subjects had their eyes closed as when they opened them to view the natural images. In other words, the ayahuasca visions were indeed as if they were seeing with their eyes shut.[3] Was this activity in the primary visual cortex also "system noise" or was something stranger going on? Would we see the same kind of effect in subjects given pure DMT?

In 2018, the team over at Imperial College London, who had previously performed the pioneering fMRI studies with both psilocybin and LSD, decided to turn their attention to DMT. While fMRI is unrivaled in providing highly detailed measures of cortical activity across the brain, it suffers from a lack of temporal resolution—the changes detected by fMRI require relatively long scanning times. In contrast, what EEG lacks in terms of spatial resolution, it makes up for in temporal resolution, being able to detect rapid changes in cortical activity. Since DMT is an extremely fast and short-acting psychedelic, it made sense for the Imperial College team to perform similar experiments Riba had done with ayahuasca, but with its primary active component—DMT. Led by Ph.D. student Chris Timmermann in collaboration with French computational neuroscientist Andrea Alamia, the study recruited thirteen volunteers who received DMT at various doses by intravenous injection, the highest being 20mg, similar to Rick Strassman's medium 0.2mg/kg dose.[4]

Predictably, and as expected from the prior fMRI studies with psilocybin and LSD, the EEG data showed that DMT was generating a more fluid and dynamic cortical state. However, the most intriguing results emerged when Timmermann began measuring the flow of electrical activity across the cortex. As sensory information flows through the cortex from the primary visual cortex, waves of electrical activity can be detected traveling from the back of the cortex toward the front (recall that these are the prediction errors used to update and maintain the world model).[5] Likewise, waves of model predictions can be observed flowing in the opposite direction toward the back of the brain and the primary visual cortex. By decomposing the EEG signals into their different frequency components, Timmermann was able to monitor and quantify these waves moving in both directions at the same time. When subjects were lying with their eyes closed, waves were observed flowing down the levels of the cortex—backward—but since the cortex wasn't processing visual sensory information, none were detected flowing in the opposite direction, forward and up the levels of the cortex. A similar pattern was observed when subjects stared at a blank screen. However, as soon as a visual image was presented on this screen, downward-flowing waves decreased and upward-flowing waves increased, indicating that the cortex was absorbing and processing visual sensory inputs. Of course, these patterns of traveling waves are exactly what we would expect based on how we understand the cortex to model the world and process sensory information. However, when subjects lay with their eyes closed and were injected with DMT, something far more surprising happened: Almost as soon as the drug reached the brain, mere seconds post-injection, downward-flowing waves sharply decreased and upward-flowing waves increased, just as if they were viewing an image with their eyes open. In fact, the change in cortical waves was almost indistinguishable from that observed when a subject who had not taken the drug opened their eyes and viewed an image on a screen.[6] In other words, the dynamics of brain activity under the influence of DMT was almost identical to normal visual stimulation, with the researchers going as far as concluding that DMT must "engage the visual apparatus in a fashion that is consistent with actual exogenously driven visual perception."[7] It's worthwhile noting that this type of neural activity is quite different from that observed during periods of visual hallucinations in schizophrenic patients, when activity in the primary visual cortex is absent.[8] Rather, during psychotic hallucinations, the higher levels of the visual cortex are activated and information is observed to flow from the hippocampal memory systems, suggesting that the brain is drawing upon its stored models and memories to construct this visual imagery independent of sensory inputs.[9] In contrast, in both Riba's ayahuasca study and Timmermann's DMT study, the subjects' brains appeared to be processing visual sensory information with their eyes closed—seeing with their eyes shut. Again, where did this sensory information come from? Was it simply spontaneous activity of the lower visual cortices? Was it mere "system noise"?

Of course, I'd long dismissed such an explanation as untenable, based on the detailed analyses of the DMT state and the neurobiology of the brain's role as a world builder. It's not difficult to explain why

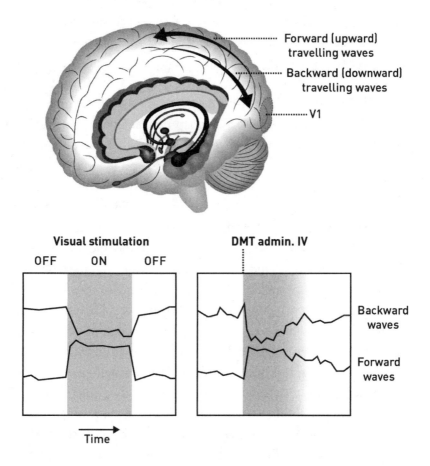

Using EEG, waves of prediction errors can be detected flowing forward and up the cortical hierarchy from V1. Waves of model predictions flow in the opposite direction. Visual stimulation increases forward-flowing waves (sensory information in the form of prediction errors) and decreases backward waves (model predictions). The DMT state is almost indistinguishable from normal visual stimulation, indicating that the brain is processing "sensory" information even when the eyes are closed. (Brain diagram, "Limbic system," from the DataBase Center for Life Science (DBCLS), used under the Creative Commons Attribution 4.0 International license)

activation of the cortex by a psychedelic drug would generate spontaneous emergent activity in the primary visual cortex, experienced as
the form constants described by Klüver in the mid-twentieth century.
Nor is it hard to explain why activation of temporal regions would cause
memories to flood into the cortex, nor why DMT might disrupt or even
obliterate the normal waking world by thrusting the brain into a hyperexcitable chaotic state. But just as a crisp new channel emerged from
the white noise of my parents' old TV set as I slowly rotated the dial all
those years ago, a crisp new world emerged beyond the initially chaotic
and disorienting first few moments of a DMT trip—a highly coherent,
inordinately detailed, and complex alternate world transcending not
only the individual but humanity in its entirety. Hypertechnological
alien cityscapes crawling with super-advanced and radiant machinic
intelligences; wildly dynamic, staggeringly complex, and yet perfectly
finessed narratives; impossibility upon breathtaking impossibility. This
was no system noise or spontaneous emergent neural activity flowing
through the cortex—this was the hand of an intelligence beyond our
imagination, not simply gating the flow of information into the brain,
but actively directing it. This was the hand of an intelligence that had
seized control of the cortex and was inducing it to do things it shouldn't
know how to do—to build worlds it shouldn't know how to build.

The DMT world is not a *dreamt* world, which is constructed using all the patterns and object models the brain learned in waking life,
guided by memories, emotions, and ancient archetypal patterns deep
in the brain while disconnected from sensory inputs. Nor is it, in the
strictest sense, a *sensed* world, merely modulated and constrained by
an alternate source of sensory inputs. It seems, rather, to be a *directed*
world built by the hand of an external intelligent agent that has commandeered the brain's world-building machinery.

You don't break through into the DMT world. The DMT world
breaks through into you.

When you burst through the veil and tumble into the glowing subterranean antechamber, as the lights are flashing, the bells ringing, and
as your name is chanted by an elfin choir in great celebratory uproar,
you're not gate-crashing a party—you're hosting it. The intelligent agent

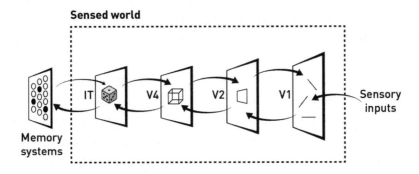

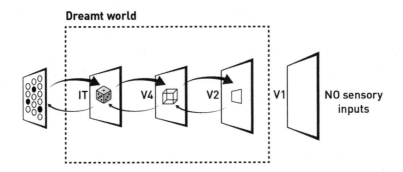

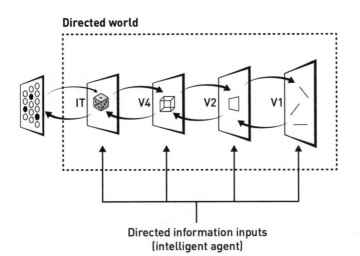

Directed information inputs
(intelligent agent)

A sensed world is tested against sensory inputs from the environment. These inputs are disconnected in a dreamt world. A directed world is manipulated by an intelligent agent that directs the flow of information into the cortex, and, as such, directs the structure of the world model.

is using your brain to construct the world it has decided to reveal to you. It is the director and your cortex is the stage.

After more than a decade of studying, writing, speaking, and thinking about DMT, I'd finally found myself compelled to reach a conclusion I'd never have thought possible when I began—that DMT was allowing us to interface with some kind of intelligent agent external to the brain. But as startling, and in some ways, horrifying as this conclusion was to me as a scientist, it was far from the end of my struggle to understand this molecule. When I first began to write and talk about the possibility that DMT might allow an intelligent Other to access and direct information into the brain,[10] aside from the occasional dismissals, eyerolls, and scoffs, the subject invariably turned to what exactly I meant by an "intelligent agent." Was I talking about spirits of the departed, deities or demons, or perhaps some kind of advanced alien species beaming data from a distant star system? I always had to admit that I didn't know; all I knew was that I couldn't make sense of DMT without such an agent. However, having convinced myself—and hopefully a few others—that there was indeed some intelligence that made its presence known in the most dramatic of fashions when this simple molecule entered the brain, I was ready to tackle that very question: Who are they?

15

THE INTELLIGENCE

This thing is what it seems to be, it's a galactic intelligence, it's a billion years old, it's touched ten million worlds, it knows the history of 150,000 civilizations, it's beyond the possibility of your conceiving it.

—Terence McKenna

Terence McKenna's mushroom-inspired vision of an ancient, almost godlike, superintelligence is both awe-inspiring and terrifying. But while there's no reason to assume that such a being couldn't exist somewhere within this universe or, perhaps, in some hidden realm beyond it or embedded within its deepest fabrics, few fear having to confront such a creature: these frightening dimensions can be safely tucked away among the more exotic branches of modern mathematical physics and their occupants relegated to the pages of pulp sci-fi novels. But what if that assumption turns out to be misguided?

As Rick Strassman was preparing room 531 at the University of New Mexico Hospital for the arrival of his first volunteers, Harvard psychiatrist Dr. John E. Mack was preparing for a research project of his own. As head of the department of psychiatry at Harvard Medical School, Mack was certainly no Little League psychiatrist—a leading expert in child and adolescent psychiatry, as well as a Pulitzer Prize-winning author and international peace activist, Mack was at the very top of his game and one of the world's most highly regarded and respected clinicians. But in the fall of 1989, he arrived in New York for a meeting that would soon change all that. Just a few weeks earlier, a colleague had offered to introduce him to Budd Hopkins, an artist and author who worked with people who claimed to have been abducted by aliens. At the very least, it sounded like an interesting and decidedly unusual psychological phenomenon, so Mack agreed. Hopkins introduced him initially to four of the people he'd been working with, and naturally, Mack's first instinct was to try and slot them into one of the many diagnostic categories available to him as a psychiatrist: Were they psychotic and suffering from hallucinations and delusions? Maybe it was an unusual type of neurotic condition? Perhaps it was temporal lobe epilepsy, a form of sleep paralysis, or even multiple personality disorder? But as they each recounted their stories, what struck Mack was not how psychologically deranged they were, but how perfectly normal they seemed. They appeared sane, genuinely traumatized by their experiences, and Mack believed them.[1] With his interest sufficiently piqued, in the spring of 1990, he began consulting with a series of abductees at his office at Harvard, and over the next few years, "cautiously, reluctantly, gradually"[2] began to take their stories more and more seriously, despite (predictably) facing both stern disapproval and no small amount of ridicule from his professional colleagues and eventually an internal investigation by his superiors at Harvard.

Although many of his colleagues and other scientists were quick to dismiss the abduction accounts as hallucinations or even elaborate lies spun for attention, Mack found himself unable to do so. Despite his best efforts at pathologizing their experiences, Mack struggled to identify any consistent psychiatric disturbance in the dozens of abductees he worked with, some of them too young to have developed the kinds of delusional psychiatric syndromes that might conceivably have produced such symptoms. Where he did find consistency, however, was in their stories, which were cogent, coherent, and repeatedly contained highly specific common details despite none of the abductees having had any prior contact with each other.[3] During a typical abduction, the abductee would be removed from their bed—either physically or otherwise—and brought to some kind of technological alien environment, often some type of craft. Here they would be subjected to various examinations and procedures, communication would be attempted, and the abductee would be taken on a tour of the craft before, eventually, being returned to their home. At first, Mack assumed that, if these people were actually being abducted as they claimed, then it must, as Hopkins had believed, be an entirely physical phenomenon: The aliens arrived in a craft from somewhere else in the galaxy, touched down on the lawn, sneaked in through the bedroom window, and removed the people from their beds. But it soon became obvious that this nuts-and-bolts explanation was left wanting. Many of the abductees described entering a world that wouldn't have seemed out of place in a modern DMT trip report—an expanded higher-dimensional reality that subsumed our three-dimensional world: "It was not a place like we have places here, not in our space/time." It was more like "the fourth dimension" where "everything is always present" and "three-dimensional reality is included within it."[4] Rather than simply being extracted from their beds, they were entering—or being induced into—an altered state of consciousness that ferried them to an alternate world. Mack later concluded that "the collapse of space/time perception . . . entering other dimensions of reality or universes . . . are such frequent features of the abduction phenomenon that I have come to feel that they are basic elements of the process."[5]

Mack's conception of what it meant to be an alien—or to be abducted by one—was changing. No longer did the word "alien" necessarily refer to a physical, wet-brained life-form that arrived from a distant star system, but to a being far more difficult to categorize—a kind of nonphysical, discarnate intelligence reaching into our material realm and interfacing with the abductee's neural machinery: "It's like this reality is a kind of theater screen, and the beings come through, and they experience a new reality—an underlying or a different reality, which is just as real as the one they were already experiencing before, but it's another one."[6]

Of course, entering an alternate hypertechnological realm and encountering advanced, highly intelligent discarnate entities is exactly how the DMT state is so often described, and it certainly didn't escape Rick Strassman's attention that what he was reading in John Mack's books seemed uncannily similar to what he'd observed on more than one occasion in room 531 of the University of New Mexico Hospital: "If presented with a record of several of our research subjects' accounts, with all references to DMT removed, could anyone distinguish our reports from those of a group of abductees?"[7]

Certainly, several of Strassman's volunteers—and many other DMT users—described what seemed like a typical alien abduction scenario: They entered an alternate, higher-dimensional world populated by intelligent beings that performed physical and mental examinations, took them on a tour of strange and unearthly places, to meetings with apparently powerful or even divine beings, before returning them, shaken but unharmed, to the normal world.[8] Even the types of beings encountered during these DMT trips—mantis-like or insectoid beings and reptilians—also featured regularly in abduction accounts. One of Mack's subjects even described a number of brightly colored, self-transforming, and hilariously "mirthful little playful creatures . . . just bounding around"[9] in a report that wouldn't have raised an eyebrow if it had been attributed to Terence McKenna. Mack was well aware of these striking parallels between the experiences of DMT users and those of his abductees: "It does seem that when some people take psychedelics, they may open themselves up to something that seems similar. Terence McKenna talks about taking DMT and then suddenly finding all kinds of alien beings around him. What does this mean? Obviously it didn't cause something to materialize physically, so it suggests that, in a certain sense, the person has become proactive in discovering another realm."[10]

So, having accepted that he was dealing with a phenomenon that was unlikely to yield to an entirely materialistic explanation, Mack turned to the experts in interacting with the immaterial: the shamanistic cultures of South America. The belief in an alternate realm inhabited by discarnate beings with whom the shaman can communicate and interact, usually employing various mind-altering plants to do so, forms the basis of shamanism the world over.[11] And although it might be assumed that the intelligent beings with whom the shaman communes couldn't be further from the types of creatures responsible for nocturnal abductions, the arbitrariness of this distinction became all too clear to Mack when he met Bernardo Peixoto, an anthropologist and shaman of the Uru-Eu-Wau-Wau people of the state of Pará in northern Brazil.

Uru-Eu-Wau-Wau literally means "people from the stars," and according to their legends, their people were originally taught to plant seeds and grow corn by small glowing beings with large eyes who emerged from a craft that descended from the sky and landed in the Amazon basin. The similarities between these beings and modern accounts of aliens is obvious. Peixoto's people refer to beings that take on a humanoid form as *ikuya*, which are just one type of little people known as *curipiras*, who come from another realm and with whom the Uru-Eu-Wau-Wau have been interacting for hundreds of years. Peixoto saw no difference between the aliens that feature in modern abduction reports and these beings described in their shamanistic traditions: "It is just exactly the same . . . there's no doubt about it. . . . The beings seem to take a form that is familiar to human beings. They visit us as humanoid beings because 'the great spirits know that the only way for us to understand things is through forms.'"[12]

Peixoto made perfect sense: The idea that a discarnate being would somehow actually possess the form of a physically embodied animal, whether human, snake, jaguar, insect, or any other earthly creature is, of course, absurd. These are simply the perceived forms—the forms modeled by the brain or, indeed, the forms the beings are inducing the brain to model. Peixoto recalled his own experience with three of these small ikuya beings with triangular faces, large eyes, long arms and wearing shiny luminous suits, and when he asked where they came from, their answer unsettled him: "We come from nowhere." For Peixoto, the implication was obvious: If they come from nowhere, that can only be because "they are everywhere."[13]

For Mack, the pieces were beginning to fall into place. The alien abduction phenomenon which he had assumed to be an entirely unique and distinct type of abnormal human experience was, in fact, just one particular modern manifestation of a much broader and older phenomenon, of nonphysical intelligences, everywhere and nowhere, interacting with humanity: "What the abduction phenomenon has led me (I would now say inevitably) to see is that we participate in a universe or universes that are filled with intelligences from which we have cut ourselves off, having lost the sense by which we might know them."[14]

Had Mack left his rational, scientific mind behind in coming to this conclusion? Had he, as many of his professional colleagues had claimed—and some, no doubt, hoped—lost the plot? Or was he, in fact, drawing closer to some deeper truth about the nature of intelligence in the cosmos? Jacques Vallée, one of the world's leading ufologists, has long maintained that the alien contact phenomenon cannot be accounted for in its entirety by appealing to materialistic explanations, of physical spacefaring craft and wet-bodied alien beings, but requires nonphysical intelligences that interact with (and even use) humans:

> I believe that the UFO phenomenon represents evidence for other di-mensions beyond space-time; the UFOs may not come from ordinary space, but from a multiverse which is all around us, and of which we have stubbornly refused to consider the disturbing reality in spite of the evidence available to us for centuries. . . . The system I am speaking of, a system with mastery of space and time dimensions, may well be able to locate itself in outer space. Nonetheless, its manifestations can-not be spacecraft in the ordinary nuts-and-bolts sense. The UFOs are physical manifestations that simply cannot be understood apart from their psychic and symbolic reality. What we see here is not an alien in-vasion. It is a spiritual system that acts on humans and uses humans.[15]

The idea of aliens existing elsewhere in the universe is hardly fringe anymore and it isn't difficult to pin down a cosmologist, biologist, or any other rational individual who will happily accept an extremely high probability of us living within a universe teeming with intelligent life. However, monumental intergalactic separation and light-speed limita-tions are the standard weapons of choice wielded to keep such life at a reassuringly safe distance—*they might be there, but they will never be here.* Naturally, there are honorable exceptions keen to point out that we can't be sure that an intelligent civilization a million or so years more advanced than us couldn't have worked out how to manipulate the structure of space-time itself to generate shortcuts for interstellar travel. However, Mack's conceptual shift from embodied space aliens traversing the galaxy to discarnate intelligences that are "everywhere and nowhere," from the physical to the immaterial, feels like a violent lurch from the scientific to the spiritual, and perhaps even from the rational to the irrational. But is that really the case?

Imagining an alien as a mere extrapolation of ourselves, as bipedal, oxygen-breathing humanoids, albeit equipped with far more advanced technologies, isn't so difficult. In fact, it's how most people imagine aliens. But it becomes much more difficult to imagine what an intelligent creature a thousand, let alone a few million, years more advanced than us might look like, and it's a stretch to assume that the majority of such aliens would occupy any kind of recognizably biological, or even physical, form. Estimates for the maximum age of extraterrestrial intelligence range from two to eight billion years, meaning the vast majority of life in the universe is likely to be *much* older than us.[16] Although it's impossible to say exactly what such life might look like, what we can say for sure is that it will evolve—and not just biologically. Assuming such a civilization survives long enough to reach the kind of technological phase we're in now, biological evolution is rapidly overtaken by technological evolution. It's quite obvious that, even at our own extremely young technological age, technological evolution is already proceeding at a vastly greater pace than its biological Darwinian counterpart, which is a slow and meandering process taking many thousands of years. From a technological standpoint, we're practically unrecognizable compared to those living just one or two hundred years ago, with advances in science, engineering, and computer science that would have been unimaginable to the nineteenth-century mind.

The classical approach to measuring the development of an intelligent civilization uses the Kardashev scale, named after the Soviet astronomer Nikolai Kardashev who first described it. According to his model, as a civilization develops technologically, it learns to utilize and control energy resources at larger and larger scales. A Type I civilization can access and store all the available energy on its host planet. Progressing to a Type II civilization means being able to absorb and utilize all the energy emitted by the orbited star (in our case, the sun), and only a civilization capable of capturing all the energy emitted by every star in the galaxy receives the prestigious title of Type III civilization. In short, the Kardashev scale assumes an expansionist trajectory as a civilization assumes control over and begins colonizing larger areas of the cosmos and, ultimately perhaps, the entire universe itself.[17]

However, this assumption comes with an obvious problem: If large numbers of intelligent civilizations, much older than ours, have achieved at least Type III status, acquiring interstellar travel and colonizing the galaxy, where are they?[18] The galaxy should be absolutely crawling with these creatures and surely we'd be aware of their presence by now. Of course, there are many who believe such alien intelligences *are* scattered throughout the galaxy, and indeed, it's no longer considered crazy to believe that we possess convincing evidence, not only of their existence, but of their regular visits to our planetary home. But whatever your beliefs about aliens visiting Earth, the Kardashev expansionist model also seems at odds with our own experience as a technological civilization. While we've spent no small sum of money slinging unmanned probes into deepest space and firing manned ones to celestial objects closer to home, it's quite obvious that most of our technological resources have been directed not to larger and larger scales, but smaller and smaller ones.

In 1998, British cosmologist John Barrow proposed an "anti-Kardashev scale" which classified civilizations from Type I-minus to Type II-minus and so on, according to their ability to manipulate and control smaller and smaller structures. A Type I-minus civilization is capable of manipulating objects at about the same scale as themselves, whereas a Type II-minus civilization can manipulate living beings at the subcellular level, reading and engineering their genetic code, and transplanting and replacing their own body parts. A Type III-minus civilization can perform chemistry, that is, manipulate molecules and molecular bonds to create new molecules and materials. And down we go through to the atomic and subatomic, past the Type VI-minus civilization that can manipulate and reorganize the most elementary particles, such as quarks and leptons, until we reach, finally, the culmination of the Barrow scale, the Type Omega-minus civilization, capable of manipulating and controlling the fundamental structure of space-time itself. Humans likely approach Type IV-minus status in some respects, being capable of manipulating individual atoms, creating nanotechnologies at the atomic scale, with an eye to developing machines and computers that function at the molecular level.[19] However, we're still far from Type Omega-minus status, but perhaps not for much longer.

If asked about our technological achievements in the last century, advances in genetic engineering and biotechnology, nanotechnology, aeronautics, and computer science are likely to spring to mind. But all of these depend upon and are subservient to intelligence—without intelligence, technological advancement isn't possible, and with it, our potential seems limitless. Intelligence leads to better education, better information, better technology, and ultimately, higher levels of intelligence, culminating in the kinds of artificial intelligences that are now beginning to emerge and which will likely soon far outstrip human intelligence in every way. Knowledge, as they say, is power. American astronomer and astrobiologist Steven Dick refers to this as the Intelligence Principle: "The maintenance, improvement, and perpetuation of knowledge and intelligence is the central driving force of cultural evolution, and to the extent intelligence can be improved, it will be improved."[20] Just a few years ago, the idea that we might one day transcend our material form and either merge with or instantiate ourselves as part of some kind of digital intelligence would have seemed like science fiction. But now with the explosive emergence of powerful artificial intelligence models in the last few years, many are already speculating on how much time as flesh-and-blood creatures we have remaining. Whether this means some kind of ascension to virtual godhood or total annihilation, only time—and perhaps not a lot of it—will tell.

Considering the fundamental importance of intelligence, it's clear that any sufficiently advanced civilization will eventually discover and develop means of maximizing it—just as we are doing now with AI. And since artificial intelligence is likely to rapidly transcend and ultimately usurp its biological counterpart in any civilization that reaches a technological computer age, as well as having a much greater potential to replicate and spread throughout the cosmos, on balance on probabilities we most likely live in a largely post-biological universe, "one in which the majority of intelligent life has evolved beyond flesh-and-blood intelligence."[21] According to cognitive scientist Susan Schneider, once a civilization creates the technology that could put them in touch with the cosmos, they are probably only a few hundred years from shifting their paradigm from biology to some kind of post-biological form,[22] which might include self-replicating superintelligent machines that roam the galaxy sharing their knowledge with other machines and developing their intelligence and understanding of the cosmos even further. Any such civilizations having made such a transition, perhaps millions or even billions of years prior to our evolution as a species, are likely to be entirely transparent to any of our standard attempts at communication: As Terence McKenna liked to quip, "To search expectantly for a radio signal from an extraterrestrial source is probably as culture-bound a presumption as to search the galaxy for a good Italian restaurant."[23] Should we ever discover a means to communicate with such an intelligence, we shouldn't expect it to resemble a human mind in any way. We should expect it to be, in the words of Oxford University philosopher and superintelligence theorist Nick Bostrom, "extremely alien."[24] Now there's a turn of phrase that feels familiar.

But as space age as it sounds, even the idea of self-replicating superintelligent machines spawning across the cosmos likely represents a massive failure of imagination, and we almost certainly have no conception of what a civilization so far ahead of us might look like, beyond the fact that it would be incomprehensibly intelligent. Once a civilization reaches Type Omega-minus status, when it becomes capable of manipulating and controlling the lowest level of reality, it seems highly unlikely that it would be instantiating itself on anything even remotely resembling the kinds of computational architectures based on systems of transistors we're familiar with.[25] It seems much more likely that such a civilization would exploit the computational power of the basic structure of space-time itself, which might involve instantiating themselves, their own AI progeny, or both, in this most fundamental of computational substrates or, perhaps even, finding a means of exiting space-time, and our little slice of reality, entirely. From our perspective, such a civilization would effectively disappear, becoming, one might say, everywhere and nowhere, and begin to look an awful lot like the discarnate intelligences spoken of by shamanistic cultures, and of course, the beings encountered by DMT users. In fact, incalculable numbers of these civilizations are likely to have already vanished into the fabric of space-time and would have done so long before we arrived on the scene. Indistinguishable from deities, such beings have likely existed, in human terms at least, forever.

So if we accept the possibility that the universe might be filled with intelligences that are both everywhere and nowhere, how could we possibly know of their existence? How might such intelligences, should they choose to do so, communicate with or signal their presence to us? Perhaps they'd have absolutely no reason or interest in doing so. But if they did choose to, it's reasonable to suggest that they might find a way to manifest in some kind of physical form—and perhaps they often do. But, of course, as with any other object in our environment, we could only perceive such a physical manifestation using our sensory apparatus—by modeling them using our brain. We never have direct access to the environment, but only the patterns of neural activity stimulated by the sensory inputs arriving from such objects. So it makes sense to ask: Why add this extra step? If a post-biological superintelligence decided to make its presence known, to communicate or interact with us, directly interfacing with the neural machinery that constructs our perceptual world would be the most obvious and intelligent way to do so—and it's hard to imagine a superintelligence choosing the less efficient option unless it had a very good reason to. What would it be like to interact with such an intelligence using our brains? I believe we already know the answer to that question. Of course, such interactions would almost certainly be dismissed by most as phantasms, delusions, dreams, and hallucinations. And indeed they are.

Czech-born psychiatrist Stanislav Grof, an early pioneer in the use of psychedelics and breath work in both achieving and utilizing altered states of consciousness for personal growth, came to the same conclusion: "If there exists a civilization out in space that commands such control of the universe, we might also assume that they would have the technology to use both individual and transpersonal consciousnesses in ways completely unknown to us. If all this were true, it is quite possible that their visits to our own dimensions of reality would very likely appear to us as fantasies, archetypal occurrences, or visionary experiences."[26]

The point here is not to claim that the entities encountered in the DMT state are post-humans who have transcended their material bodies—although we can't rule this out—or indeed any kind of post-biological intelligence we're capable of imagining. But the idea that such beings exist, whatever their origin and nature, and do so in great multitudes isn't an irrational position that strays far from modern scientific discourse. The basic fact of the matter is actually quite simple: We, as humans, know practically nothing about the types and numbers of intelligent beings that occupy our universe or beyond. We can only speculate, carefully and rationally, on those we can, in a limited abstract sense at least, comprehend. And already those beings alone begin to resemble the kinds of discarnate intelligences most are assuming to explain away as hallucinations, delusions, and fantastical dreams, despite the many problems we have faced in our attempts to do just that. So when you come face to face with inconceivably powerful and intelligent alien life-forms that seem—or claim—to hail from normally hidden dimensions of reality, you must be very careful. In fact, it might be a good idea to shut up, watch, and listen. Because there's a very real possibility that they're exactly who they say they are.

The most common and intuitive explanation for why so many DMT users describe entering the same type of world and meeting the same types of entities is simply that they are, in fact, entering the same world. However, there's no reason to think that these intelligent agents, nor the realm within which they reside, have a form that could be accurately represented using your brain. Are these intelligences actually insectoids or reptilians or jesters or elves? Of course not—these are the forms it often uses, the forms that make sense to you, which you will recognize and respond to. The DMT world is a kind of virtual interface built using your neural machinery, which the intelligent agents can use to present information to and communicate with you, just as your normal subjective world is an interface that allows you to interact with the environment. Although it's impossible to state with any kind of certainty why certain structures and motifs so often characterize the DMT state, there does seem to be a common approach employed by these intelligences in directing the structure, content, and narrative of the experience as it unfolds. Many users initially describe entering what's become known as the "waiting room,"[27] a "virtual" placeholder environment where they might be distracted, entertained, or even tested, often by jesters, clowns, and elves, before being ushered to deeper areas (or summarily ejected): "I felt like I was somewhere that was made specifically for this situation. It is incredibly hard to describe, but the feeling was very distinct, and I know that it was what we call the waiting room. I felt like I was waiting for the most important thing ever, yet I didn't know what, and most importantly, I felt like I had disappointed someone by coming here."[28]

In the kinds of abduction cases described by John Mack—and indeed in similar scenarios reported by many DMT users—there seems to be a serious agenda behind the interaction, with the intelligences using the opportunity to gain access to the abductee's brain and either impart or retrieve information, directing their experience, and perhaps allowing the "abductee" to interface in some way and to some end with their resident alternate reality, whatever and wherever that might be. However, in most DMT experiences, the ambience is more playful and feels more like an opportunity to show the user what's possible with the human mind/brain once you let them take control. It's a party—and you're the host:

> I saw the elves coming up toward me. As if they were coming through a wormhole from another dimension! He looked just like a leprechaun, with the top hat and pointy red shoes. One of them was carrying a big red Santa Claus bag full of tricks. Behind them came a circus full of activity. This is what you have been waiting for! So they marched up toward me and as they reached me what was behind them oozed up and all over me. It felt like I was being dipped into this paint-like

substance made of colors and patterns. Then one of them proceeded to show me the most incredible scenes and landscapes. One of the elves had this device in his hand that looked like a remote, and he was controlling everything that I was seeing![29]

This perspective differs somewhat from most interpretations of the DMT state that are willing to attach some kind of "reality" to the experience. Those who believe DMT to gate access to a truly autonomous realm populated by intelligent discarnate entities often assume that this involves some kind of "travel," that consciousness is somehow reaching into this alternate realm as we might peek through a window into an unfamiliar house. This is entirely opposite to the perspective presented here. Returning to the TV set that sat in my parents' kitchen as a child, switching the channel didn't require the TV to somehow reach into the worlds presented on its screen, nor that such worlds even existed in the form as viewed on the screen. In the same way, nothing—not even information—need travel from your brain into the realm in which the intelligences reside. Again, there's no reason to assume that you're observing these beings in their "true form" or that their world could be faithfully represented in any kind of visual form. The experience is real in that it's directed by an influx of information guided by an intelligence that is everywhere and nowhere, but what it shows you—what it induces your cortex to model—is entirely under its control, and as we have seen, this can vary wildly, from the comical and madcap to the ineffably complex and beautiful to the utterly and horrifyingly alien, and on occasion, to a complete refusal to show you anything at all. But crucially, when it does decide to show you something, it's almost always a world that your brain would be incapable of constructing without its guidance.

This perspective also raises the question as to whether other psychedelics or tools might similarly place the brain in a state in which it's receptive to either passively receiving information from or being fully commandeered by an external intelligent agent. The ideal state seems to be reached when the cortex is both nudged into a more fluid and disordered state, making it more susceptible to information-driven re-organization, as well as being cut off as much as possible from the normal sources of sensory inputs that can interfere with or "contaminate" the flow of information from the agent. It's also plausible that certain emergent patterns of cortical activity generated by specific psychedelic molecules might aid in allowing the brain to "tune in to" the alternate information source. While DMT seems to be the most efficient and reliable tool in this regard, many users of *Psilocybe* mushrooms, including Terence McKenna, regularly describe nonhuman entity encounters, particularly at the higher dose levels. The same can be said for a number of other traditional South American plant-based psychedelic technologies, including those derived from the tropane alkaloid-containing *Solanaceae*—nightshade—family, such as species of *Datura* and *Brugmansia*, as well as concentrated extracts of the rare Mexican herb, *Salvia divinorum*, containing an extraordinarily potent psychedelic, salvinorin A.[30] But one of the most fascinating and instructive examples of an individual combining psychedelic molecules with active sensory deprivation to achieve communication with nonhuman intelligent agents is the American neuroscientist, psychoanalyst, inventor, and dolphin researcher John Lilly.

Lilly began his academic career in the early 1950s as a button-down neurophysiologist at the National Institute of Mental Health in Bethesda, Maryland,[31] developing a technique for implanting arrays of electrodes in the brains of living and unanesthetized monkeys to record their neural activity,[32] as well as techniques for electrical stimulation of the brain to manipulate the emotional state of experimental animals, not entirely dissimilar to P. K. Dick's fictitious Penfield mood organ.[33] He also performed pioneering work studying the language of dolphins,[34] including testing LSD on six dolphins who all "apparently had very good trips."[35] However, it's Lilly's invention of the flotation tank for which he is most famous.

To test a claim that human consciousness depends on sensory stimulation from the environment, Lilly designed the tank to minimize all sensory inputs, floating in heavily salted water (for buoyancy) in a lightproof and soundproof room.[36] However, upon entering the tank for the first time, he was greeted not by unconsciousness or even a pitch-black void but rather found himself "in a new space, a new domain"—an infinite space filled with light. And it seemed to be occupied. Slowly, two presences approached from a distance and began the first of a series of conversations—directly by meaning, without language—that led Lilly to believe the beings to be advanced intelligent life-forms hailing from elsewhere in the universe. By his reasoning, the lack of sensory stim-ulation generated a neural state that allowed information from these intelligent agents to "leak" into his brain: "If my mind contained in the brain is leaky to sources of information not yet contained within our knowledge, within our science, then there may be other intelligences in this universe with whom we can communicate and do communicate when we are in the proper state of consciousness."[37]

Between 1964 and 1965, Lilly began to take LSD prior to entering the flotation tank, which allowed him to explore a larger number of do-mains that appeared entirely beyond our universe: "I moved into uni-verses containing beings much larger than myself, so that I was a mote in their sunbeam, a small ant in their universe, a single thought in a huge mind, or a small program in a cosmic computer."[38]

On occasion, particularly at the highest doses of LSD, Lilly's experi-ences were strikingly similar to the kind of "download" effect reported by DMT users: "Their knowledge was pouring into me. . . . I could share their thinking, their knowledge, and their feeling at an incredibly high rate of speed."[39]

Unfortunately, with tightening regulations on the use of the drug, Lilly was ultimately forced to terminate his LSD experiments and return his supply to Sandoz. It was then that he began working with an entirely different molecule during his flotation tank sessions. A longtime sufferer from debilitating migraines, Lilly was urged by a friend to try a then entirely new drug recently developed by Parke-Davis as an anesthetic: ketamine.[40] Although the complex neuropharmacology of ketamine wasn't understood during his time, one of the ways ketamine works is much like other psychedelics—it has an excitatory effect on neural ac-tivity, generating a more fluid state susceptible to information-driven reorganization. However, at higher doses, ketamine also partially disconnects the higher levels of the cortex from sensory inputs. This is why it's usually referred to as a "dissociative" (I prefer the term "dissociative psychedelic")—isolating the cortex from the environment.[41] Coupled with the profoundly isolating flotation tank, Lilly had arguably stumbled upon the ideal state for his cortex to be commandeered by a discarnate intelligent agent. And indeed, they soon made an appearance: While lying in the tank under the influence of ketamine, he saw "continuous motion-picture-like sequences, highly colored, three dimensional, and consisting of, at first, inanimate scenes which later became populated with various strange and unusual creatures."[42]

Many of the entities Lilly encountered resembled the kinds of advanced post-biological intelligences that would be speculated about in the coming decades—a network of "solid-state" (i.e. computational) intelligences that could exist in a vacuum, at much lower and higher temperatures than water-based forms of life and with which he could interact by lowering his "threshold for awareness of extraterrestrial sources of information."[43]

Although it's easy to dismiss Lilly's experiences as those of someone tipped into psychosis by chronic overuse of a powerful psychoactive drug, his insights into how the human brain interfaces with the environment and potentially with alternate sources of information were far ahead of his time. Lilly believed that, in normal waking life, our "internal reality (i.r.)" is "interlocked" with "external reality (e.r.)," but when levels of ketamine in the brain are high enough, the connection between the internal and external reality is severed. It is in this state that the brain can enter into an interaction with the "extraterrestrial reality (e.t.r.)." This isn't so far from the modern neuroscientific understanding of how the brain's internally constructed world model is held accountable to sensory information and how psychedelics induce a state susceptible to receiving alternate information inputs. Indeed, Lilly often felt that his brain was being controlled in some way by these intelligences,[44] with one of the beings informing him: "You construct our form and the place in which we meet."[45] In other words, Lilly's brain was constructing a model of the beings with whom he was interacting, in much the same way that the brain constructs—or is induced to construct—a model of the intelligences encountered in the DMT state.

Lilly's most ambitious experiment, designed to maintain unbroken contact with this intelligence, required him to inject the drug every hour of every day (barring four hours for sleep) for three weeks (over five hundred doses in total), acquiring the drug from physician friends who were willing to prescribe it for his migraine attacks. Terrified that these intelligences had the real potential to usurp all biological life on Earth, his experiment was cut short when he called the White House demanding to speak to President Gerald Ford to warn him of the impending danger. He was swiftly committed to a psychiatric hospital.[46]

Whatever you might think about Lilly's audacious approach to ketamine use and whether or not you're inclined to believe his revelations about extraterrestrial intelligence, it's hard not to admire his gallantry and commitment to exploring these strange alternate worlds, and there's much we can learn from him. It wouldn't be a stretch to call Lilly a modern shaman who, like the Amazonian people who developed their jungle technologies for establishing communicative and intimate relationships with the normally hidden intelligences of the forest, developed ketamine as a technology for communing with the beings resident in the extraterrestrial reality he was regularly accessing. While I liked the idea that these "intelligent agents" accessed using DMT were advanced post-biological intelligences that had cast off their material bodies and disappeared into the fabric of space-time, I had to admit that, in truth, I still had no real idea of the kind of beings we were dealing with. Perhaps there was no way for the human mind to fully comprehend such an intelligence. It seemed to me that the only way forward was to accept our ignorance of their nature and attempt to establish a communicative relationship with them—to learn from them. But as modern Westernized humans who have long left the forests, how ought we to proceed?

Should we too return to the traditional Indigenous technologies of Amazonia or, like John Lilly, should we work to develop our own? While we must regard the sophistication of the Amazonian people's plant-based preparations with a great deal of respect and a source of inspiration, being deeply respectful and appreciative of their technologies doesn't mean that we ought not to build upon them, any more than an appreciation of smoke signals should dissuade us from developing more efficient communication technologies. On the contrary, a molecule of this importance and magnitude demands that our best tools be brought to bear in developing and learning to use it. So how exactly might we do that?

16

THE TECHNOLOGY

There is a world beyond ours, a world that is far away, nearby and invisible. And there is where God lives, where the dead live, the spirits and the saints. A world where everything has already happened and everything is known. That world talks. It has a language of its own. I report what it says.

—María Sabina

When Richard Spruce choked down that bitter and muddy soup by the banks of the Vaupés River more than a century and a half ago, he almost certainly had no conception of what he was about to unleash into the Western mind. It's hard to deny that there's something deeply and profoundly uncanny about DMT, this simple and ubiquitous alkaloid that also happens to be the most efficient reality-switching molecule on the planet, reliably granting access to advanced intelligences from some normally invisible realm. Several of Rick Strassman's volunteers suggested that the DMT molecule itself was more like a technology than a drug. Indeed, by allowing us to interface and communicate with intelligences outside of ourselves and otherwise inaccessible, a technology seems a more apposite term than drug. On the other hand, what kind of technology only allows communication to be maintained for a few minutes at a time before the signal is abruptly cut off and the message left only half spoken? Mercifully brief for most, but a few baffled and bewildered minutes is hardly sufficient for establishing any kind of stable two-way communication or relationship with these beings. The shamanistic cultures of Amazonia overcame this apparent shortcoming with their ayahuasca technology, by combining DMT with the harmala alkaloids to reduce the rate at which the molecule is metabolized, stretching the experience from a few minutes to a couple of hours. But even with the darkest and most syrupy of ayahuasca brews, brain DMT levels rarely approach those achievable using vaporized pure freebase DMT, by far the most efficient and reliable means of gaining access to these intelligences, and yet it seems implausible that the optimal administration technique for this technology was discovered in 1965 when Nick Sand accidentally spilled a few crystals onto a lab hot plate. And while Rick Strassman's intravenous injection protocol was undoubtedly an improvement on the vaporization technique (at least in more academic settings), whether vaporized or injected, the time course of just a few short minutes is about the same. If DMT *is* a technology, it seems we've still much to learn about how to use it.

Reading the accounts of Rick Strassman's volunteers, I couldn't help but be struck by the words of Sara, who also commented on how pleased the entities were that we had "discovered this technology." Upon returning from her third journey, she said something that seemed important: "I went directly into deep space. They knew I was coming back and they were ready for me. They told me there were many things they could share with us when we learn how to make more extended contact."[1]

Were the entities referring to a different, yet to be discovered or invented molecular tool with a longer duration of action? Perhaps. But perhaps we just haven't learned to use the one we already have.

In the 1980s, long before I arrived on the scene, American full-time drug manufacturer (and part-time kidnapper)[2] Gordon Todd Skinner, who was closely connected to LSD manufacturing legend William Leonard Pickard and whose personally appraised psychoactive drug catalog extends well into three figures, developed his own method for extending the DMT experience: "Skinner's favorite method for 'time surfing' was taking DMT via an IV drip. He would prepare an isotonic solution with a tendency to be slightly hypertonic, using free amine 3, magnesium sulfate, and ascorbic acid. . . . Drips often lasted up to 1–5 hours and gave the most significant afterglow of any psychedelic."[3]

While crude, Skinner's method was inspired, taking full advantage of a unique pharmacological peculiarity that sets DMT apart from the other major psychedelics, first noticed by Harris Isbell in the early 1960s and later confirmed by Strassman in his human volunteers several decades later: a lack of subjective tolerance. In theory, DMT's psychedelic effects ought to be maintained as long as the levels in the blood—and thus the brain—remain sufficiently high. Much like trying to maintain the water level in an emptying bathtub by controlling the flow of water from the taps, a regulated drip or infusion of DMT into the bloodstream will compensate for that being rapidly lost by metabolism and excretion, keeping the brain DMT concentration reasonably stable. Unfortunately, although a simple idea in principle, its execution is a somewhat more challenging affair.

As soon as a drug molecule enters the bloodstream, it is immediately diluted by the blood, and as well as eventually finding its way into the brain, will distribute to varying degrees in other organs, soft tissues, muscles, and fat. At the same time, the body's natural response to exogenous molecules gets to work. Enzymes, such as the monoamine oxidase enzyme that's inhibited by the harmala alkaloids, begin to metabolize the molecule and the kidneys and liver work to excrete the metabolites. So if we can account for these processes and accurately compensate for them with a controlled infusion of DMT into the bloodstream, we should be able to keep the brain DMT levels reasonably stable. However, all of these processes occur simultaneously and at different rates, and it's not possible to measure the rate of each individual process directly. What we *can* do, however, is measure the change in blood DMT concentration over time by taking blood samples at intervals following intravenous administration. This gives us an overall picture of how these processes together contribute to the drug's rise and subsequent fall in the bloodstream. Following a standard bolus injection (a single dose of a drug injected within a short period of time), the blood concentration typically rises very rapidly before reaching a peak and then falling off exponentially as the distribution, metabolism, and excretion begin to dominate. The only way to tease apart this blood concentration curve and find the rates of the individual processes is to fit this data to a mathematical model using specialized computer software that will converge on a set of rates that best replicates the measured blood concentration curve. We can then use this model to simulate the concentration of DMT in the brain depending on the rate at which the molecule is infused into the bloodstream, with the aim of finding an infusion protocol that reaches and maintains a desired brain concentration. This protocol can then be programmed into an infusion machine that will deliver the drug according to the calculated protocol to induce a volunteer into a breakthrough DMT state for as short or long a period as desired.[4]

Fortunately, this isn't at all a new idea and has been the mainstay of anesthesiology for decades. Known as target-controlled intravenous infusion, the technique is used to reach and maintain a stable brain concentration of a short-acting anesthetic drug to place and keep a patient unconscious during surgical procedures.[5] So, in principle, it would simply be a matter of replacing the anesthetic drug with DMT. However, there are a couple of catches. Firstly, to be suitable for this infusion technology, a drug must possess eight properties:

It must be water soluble.

It must have a rapid onset.

It must have a brief duration of action.

It must be cleared rapidly from the brain with minimal tendency to accumulate.

Any metabolites must be inactive and nontoxic.

It must have a wide therapeutic window (the difference between an active and a toxic dose).

Any side effects should be minimal.

It must lack significant tolerance, such that its effects don't diminish over time even when the brain concentration remains stable.[6]

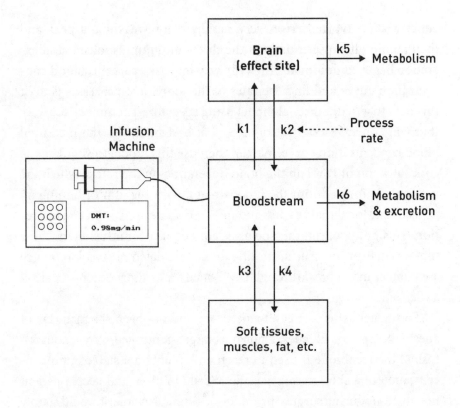

Target-controlled intravenous infusion uses a mathematical model of the metabolism, distribution, and excretion of a drug molecule to find an infusion protocol that will maintain a stable drug concentration in the brain. Although developed for short-acting anesthetic drugs, the technique has now been adapted for use with DMT.

Remarkably, DMT meets all of these criteria. In fact, if you wanted to design a molecule to be employed with target-controlled infusion, you'd do well to improve on DMT. Perhaps DMT's brief duration of action isn't, as I had earlier thought, a bug but a feature. However, since every drug molecule is distributed and metabolized differently, we can't simply apply the same protocol employed for an anesthetic drug to DMT—we need a mathematical model of the drug's distribution, metabolism, and excretion specifically for this molecule.

So, in 2015 I wrote to Rick Strassman with an idea. During his New

Mexico study in the 1990s, he had drawn the blood of his volunteers at intervals during their experiences, to monitor their blood DMT concentrations over time.[7] This is precisely the data that I needed to construct the mathematical model that I could then use to program an intravenous infusion device. Fortunately, Strassman was intrigued enough by my idea to dig through an old hard drive and retrieve the necessary data, and from opposite sides of the Pacific Ocean, we immediately set about constructing the model.

Our simulations using this model (and based on the known subjective time course of the DMT experience) suggested that full "breakthrough" into the DMT space occurs once the brain concentration reaches around 60ng/ml (nanograms per milliliter) before peaking at around 100ng/ml. Exit from the space occurs when the brain concentration again drops below 60ng/ml, just six or seven minutes later. Armed with this model, we were then able to construct an infusion protocol that would rapidly reach a brain drug concentration above 60ng/ml and remain reasonably stable over time. An efficient way to achieve this is to use a technique from anesthesiology called the bolus-elimination-transfer (BET) protocol, the basic principle of which is to infuse a loading dose (the *bolus*) to rapidly bring the blood (and brain) drug level to the target concentration (in this case, over 60ng/ml). *Elimination* (by metabolism and excretion) and *transfer* (distribution to other organs and tissues) begins immediately, and without further drug administration, the concentration of DMT in the brain will begin to fall exponentially. However, this rapid elimination-transfer drop-off can be counterbalanced by a controlled infusion of DMT beginning around the time at which the brain concentration peaks, and assuming the model is well-constructed, this should maintain a stable brain drug concentration for as long as desired— perhaps hours or longer.[8]

With the model in hand, later that same year, I spoke at the small private symposium[9] mentioned at the beginning of this book organized by British international property entrepreneur and regular explorer of altered states Anton Bilton, who had his first spontaneous mystical experience at the age of fifteen, when one morning while preparing breakfast, he was suddenly "held in rapture by a pinkish golden light coming

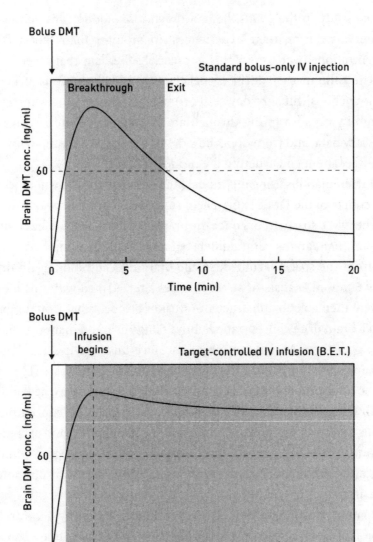

Following a bolus IV injection of DMT, breakthrough into the DMT space occurs once the brain concentration reaches around 60ng/ml, with exit occurring just a few minutes later as the brain concentration drops exponentially. However, target-controlled infusion of DMT into the bloodstream can maintain a stable brain DMT concentration above 60ng/ml indefinitely, allowing extended journeys in the DMT space.

in through a window, time stood still, and some 'thing' said something to me telepathically in my head."[10] In his quest to reconnect with what he now refers to as the "intelligent Other," Anton first drank ayahuasca in 2005 and has since accrued over a hundred journeys with the South American visionary potion, as well as modern "pharmahuasca" analogs employing the pure DMT and harmala alkaloids taken orally. As such, when he heard me speak of this novel approach to administering DMT using target-controlled intravenous infusion, he immediately recognized its potential value in developing and deepening this connection.

Fortuitously, among the select invitees present at the symposium that included Dennis McKenna, Graham Hancock, David Luke, and Rick Strassman was the then head of the Centre for Psychedelic Research at Imperial College London, Robin Carhart-Harris. If this infusion protocol was to become more than just an idea, Carhart-Harris was the man to speak to. So Anton did just that, offering to fund a research project at Imperial College that implemented the protocol in human volunteers. Although Carhart-Harris left the UK soon after to take up a professorship at the University of California in San Francisco, Anton's offer still stood, and with Chris Timmermann now at the helm and armed with an improved model developed by a specialist research group at the University of Gothenburg in Sweden,[11] the Imperial College team began recruiting a small group of volunteers for the world's first trial of what had by then become known as extended-state DMT (or "DMTx" for short).[12]

Naturally, Anton raised his hand and was one of the first volunteers to be hooked up to the infusion device for what he describes as "the most exciting series of experiments on earth."[13] And he wasn't disappointed. Almost as soon as the infusion began, his world was filled with a blinding white light, and just a few seconds later, after a brief period of disorientation and confusion, he found himself in the now familiar realm of the intelligent Other, where he would remain for the next twenty-nine minutes.

As well as extending its duration well beyond the time course of a standard bolus injection, our hope was that, as brain DMT levels stabilized, so would the experience, potentially allowing more detailed analysis and even mapping of the DMT space's structure and content, performing experiments, as well as establishing stable communication with the entities that reside within the space. Anton almost always finds himself initially in a deep, dark, and somewhat sinister "subterranean" domain that, while captivating in its own way, can become distracting and hinder progression to higher levels. Similar to what other users describe as the waiting room, it is in this space that mischievous jesters, clowns, and elves are often encountered, as if acting as gatekeepers whose role it is to keep you distracted and from progressing further until the experience begins to fade just a few minutes after arrival. It was hoped that extending the journey would allow experienced voyagers to work their way past these gatekeepers and through the different domains of the space. For Anton, once this darker subterranean domain is escaped, lighter and brighter realms await, and it's at the highest reaches of the space that the most powerful beings are to be encountered and where he regularly finds himself "trembling in the presence of intelligence and wisdom—something mind-blowingly magnificent."[14]

Several minutes into the experience, he managed to elevate himself into an endlessly dynamic and shifting hyperdimensional anteroom—"like a living Escher painting"—where a group of small glowing humanoid beings with an "elfish" demeanor—he calls them the "gingerbread men"—gathered around him, apparently curious as to what this strange creature was that had suddenly manifested in their world. He'd seen these beings before: "They always seem to check the back of my neck—my only guess is that they're checking if there's a cord attached . . . checking whether I've died."[15]

As soon as they were satisfied that he hadn't passed permanently to their side of the veil, they began their attempts at communication with great enthusiasm, pushing forward a "jewel-encrusted pad" with a glowing display containing a dynamic pattern of shifting and spinning dials and symbols—uncannily reminiscent of Timothy Leary's first DMT experience in 1965 (of which Anton wasn't aware until I mentioned it to him), during which Leary described a being with "a pad in his lap . . . holding out a gem-encrusted box with undulating trapezoidal glowing sections."[16] Unfortunately, but not surprisingly, Anton could make no more sense of this device than Leary was able to and grew increasingly frustrated at his inability to understand the message they were urgently trying to convey. Already several minutes into the experience, after a standard bolus injection this would have been about the time when the gingerbread men began to say their goodbyes. But with the greatly extended trip duration, Anton was able to spend time at least attempting, albeit entirely fruitlessly in this instance, to grasp the meaning of their message. This kind of interaction is where the extended-state DMTx technology truly came into its own. Beings not only willing but eager to impart some kind of complex information, whether using advanced technological devices or a strange alien language, is a common scenario reported after breakthrough DMT experiences. How might a mathematician or linguist trained to navigate the DMT realms have fared when given the opportunity to spend several hours interacting with these beings and their baffling contraptions?

Even at thirty minutes, Anton wasn't satisfied that it was long enough: "Next time I want to stay for two hours."[17] And it's highly likely that his wish will be granted. Despite concerns that the extended DMT experience would be psychologically or physiologically overwhelming—or both—all of the volunteers tolerated it surprisingly well. While their heart rates and anxiety levels increased sharply at the beginning of the infusion, likely in anticipation of what lay ahead, they soon dropped back down to normal levels. Likewise, as hoped and predicted, the intensity of subjective effects increased rapidly at the beginning of the infusion and then settled at a fairly stable high level throughout, suggesting that brain DMT levels were also stable.[18] So, overall, there seems no reason to think that thirty minutes is anywhere close to the maximum possible duration, and it's not unreasonable to imagine extended expeditions into the DMT realms lasting many hours or even days. Of course, at these extreme durations, nutritional support and waste management would also need to be considered, as would techniques to ensure proper reintegration back into the human world when the infusion is terminated—it's hard to predict the neurological and psychological consequences of spending so much time in an environment so different from normal waking life. But once these extended protocols are perfected, the possibilities for both scientific research and for establishing a communicative relationship with the intelligent agents are practically endless. Beyond the neuro-scientists, pharmacologists, and clinicians foundational to human psychedelic research, I can imagine a multidisciplinary team comprising anthropologists, mathematicians, linguists, artists, and perhaps even theologians, each playing a well-defined role in the detailed exploration, experimentation, and analysis in the space. Techniques for the real-time communication between the subject and those waiting on the other side would also need to be developed to avoid having to rely on memory to relay the rich and complex information collected from within the space.

Of course, so early in our use of this technology, it's difficult to fully grasp the potential significance of these extended expeditions and what establishing a communicative relationship with such advanced intelligences might mean for the future of our species. However, in 1996, a psychedelic researcher who went by the pseudonym D. M. Turner published a remarkable DMT trip report that now, almost three decades later, seems uncannily prescient and might well point to a kind of human future that would have seemed like science fiction just a couple of decades ago but now seems close enough to touch. Turner was an early pioneer in the use of the extraordinarily psychedelic salvinorin A extracted from the Mexican ritual herb *Salvia divinorum*, but as his chosen pseudonym unsubtly betrays, was also a regular visitor to the DMT worlds. During one of these visits, he initially found himself in the familiar brightly colored lower anteroom of the elves. But as experienced as he was, he was convinced that their merry and endlessly dynamic elfin machinations were just a distraction and that more expansive realms awaited beyond—if only he could persuade them to let him pass. He began to chant, forcefully and out loud: "Let me through! Let me through!"[19] Reluctantly, they eventually did so, and he found himself propelled at great speed into a vast higher-dimensional space occupied by half a dozen or so much more powerful angel-like beings watching over and making minor adjustments to the lower dimensions of space-time that seemed to be under their guardianship. Still propelled by a force of will, these beings largely ignored him as he flew past and into yet another realm, guarded by more than fifty beings who were less than welcoming. After huddling for a brief convocation, they too decided to let him pass, and finally he found himself in a technological domain that was "highly evolved, both scientifically and technically":

> The place I entered into was some type of research center, and my attention was focused on some large metallic pods that were being moved in and out of racks by elaborate robotic arms. Each of these pods was something like an isolation chamber. They were shaped like large coffins about eight feet long, although with rounded edges. The oval cross sections were about three feet wide. The beings who used these pods looked exactly like humans. The pods were filled with a foam-type material which was connected to the sides of the pod and also contacted the entire skin surface area of the person inside the pod. The foam was serrated, and I understood that it served as a conductor of food, water, heat, medicines, etc. between the pods' technical systems and the person resting in it. These pods were also cold chambers. They were not for cryogenically freezing a person, but put them into some type of suspended animation.[20]

So far, so very cool and sci-fi,[21] but these were no simple suspended animation pods: "It was soon impressed on me that the whole purpose of these pods and this research center was that this was the method the people here used to increase the level of DMT in the brains of the pod sleepers. One fortunate enough to be a research subject would go into a pod for weeks or months at a time. The DMT levels in their brain would be significantly increased, and they would spend their time having the most fascinating dreams!"[22]

Since psychiatrists began drawing blood and collecting urine samples in their largely fruitless and likely misguided quest to connect brain DMT levels with psychosis, the reason for its presence in the human body has remained a matter of speculation. Rick Strassman hypothesized that DMT is released by the pineal gland close to death, and although it's now thought unlikely that such a small gland would be capable of rapidly generating enough DMT to exert substantial psychedelic effects,[23] more recent work has shown that, whatever its source, DMT protects neurons during periods of hypoxic stress and might represent the brain's last-ditch attempt to save the brain when oxygen levels plummet.[24] Of course, this is precisely what happens as the respiratory system begins to fail during the dying process. However, more recent studies have shown, in rats at least, that DMT does appear to be produced by the brain under perfectly normal conditions, independent of the pineal gland, and at levels comparable to neurotransmitters such as serotonin and dopamine.[25] It makes little sense that the brain would divert energy and chemical resources to the production of a molecule that has no role in its function, and whatever that role might be, these studies unequivocally demonstrate not only that the brain possesses the chemical machinery to manufacture this molecule, but that it can do so in significant quantities. And considering DMT's effects on consciousness, that is no small matter. Indeed, it would appear an astounding coincidence if a neurochemical produced naturally by the brain with a completely unrelated primary function in human neurochemistry just happens, when elevated to supraphysiological concentrations, to also grant access to a bizarre alternate reality filled with intelligent discarnate entities. Reading D. M. Turner's remarkable trip report, it struck me that perhaps in developing DMT as a technology, we might soon dispense with pipes, needles, and infusion machines altogether and learn to induce people into the DMT state for extended periods by "hacking" the brain's own DMT production system.

Like serotonin, DMT is produced from the essential amino acid tryptophan, which is first converted to tryptamine by an enzyme called tryptophan decarboxylase. Since this enzyme is also critical for the synthesis of serotonin, which has important roles throughout the body, it's well expressed in many different tissues including, of course, the brain. The enzyme that's most pertinent with regard to DMT synthesis is indole N-methyl transferase (INMT), first identified in human tissues by Julius Axelrod in the early 1970s, and which converts tryptamine to DMT in a single step.[26] Since INMT is present at high levels in many tissues, including the brain, as are the required precursor molecules, it's somewhat surprising that DMT levels are generally very low.[27] During Axelrod's studies of INMT in the 1970s, he made an interesting and initially confusing observation: Although INMT levels in human blood were high, less than 1 percent of the tryptamine added to blood samples was

DMT is synthesized in mammalian tissues from the amino acid tryptophan in two simple enzymatic steps, as is serotonin. The key enzyme for DMT synthesis, INMT, is inhibited by an unknown endogenous peptide that keeps endogenous DMT levels low.

converted to DMT. However, when he separated and purified the INMT enzyme, he found it highly active in effecting the transformation from tryptamine to DMT.[28] This suggested that, in whole blood, INMT was being inhibited by some other natural molecule. And just three years later such a molecule—a small peptide—that suppressed INMT activity, keeping production of DMT at very low levels, was found in the brains of rabbits.[29] Unfortunately, this peptide has never been properly characterized, so we know next to nothing about its structure or how it's regulated in the human brain. But it's plausible that the brain uses this peptide to control INMT activity and thus the levels of DMT in the brain depending on particular physiological conditions, such as states of hypoxia. Inactivating or suppressing production of this INMT inhibiting peptide might provide a relatively simple means of rapidly and sustainably increasing DMT levels in living human subjects. Alternatively, techniques from genetic engineering already exist to manipulate specific genes in human cells that could be used to upregulate the amount of INMT present in the human brain, providing another route to increasing DMT production in the brain.[30] Whichever method is employed, combined with techniques already being developed to place humans in a state of artificial hibernation for extended space flight, with their biological needs maintained by automatic feeding and waste management systems,[31] those futuristic pods described by D. M. Turner aren't so different to what we might soon design for extremely extended expeditions in the DMT worlds. Perhaps the beings in those pods looked "exactly like humans" because they *were* humans. Perhaps, rather than an advanced alien civilization on a trajectory toward even higher states of technological advancement, Turner was, in fact, being presented with a vision of our own future. He ends his trip report with perhaps the most prescient line: "This research that was taking place was considered the most serious aspect of this society's evolution."[32]

Terence McKenna often spoke of an intergalactic future for humanity, of us sloughing off our material bodies, bidding farewell to the cradle of mankind, and setting off for the stars. But while galactic citizenship might seem like a grand but eventually achievable ambition, few have seriously considered that interdimensional citizenship might well be closer to hand—perhaps far closer than we're currently capable of comprehending. And what could be more serious than that?

Although originally discovered and developed by shamanistic peoples of South America, DMT is a technology that we are now charged with carrying from its forest roots, carefully, respectfully, optimistically, into a future that seems to approach with ever-increasing speed and yet which, for the most part, likely remains beyond our imagination. It might seem entirely absurd to anyone who hasn't experienced the astonishing effects of this molecule that, in the very near future, we might spend lengthy periods of our lives immersed in worlds constructed by our own brains as interfaces that allow us to live among and learn from advanced discarnate intelligences as we live among and learn from each other. But, of course, none of this would seem at all absurd or surprising to the Yanomami, the Asháninka, the Witoto, and the many other shamanistic cultures across our planet who have been living among these beings for thousands of years—perhaps it's about time the post-Enlightenment mind caught up. But whatever our future might hold, whether we call them gods, spirits, aliens, or post-biological superintelligent agents, there are discarnate intelligences of unimaginable wisdom and power, accessible *right now* to anyone and everyone who wishes to reach them, using one of the simplest and most common molecules on the planet. And if that alone isn't the most remarkable, important, and truly astonishing discovery in the history of our species, then I can't imagine what might be.

And if you still don't believe me . . .

Just fill your lungs, lie back, relax, close your eyes, and remember to breathe.

The show's about to begin.

ACKNOWLEDGMENTS

I am indebted and thankful to all those who have supported my work over the last decade or so: readers, listeners, watchers, commentators, and all the friends and strangers who, at one time or another, have humored me as I ranted and raved about DMT. In particular, I am eternally indebted to Dave Luke for being an early supporter of my ideas and to Graham Hancock for being a continual and vocal advocate of my work. I am also deeply thankful to my editor Peter Wolverton at St. Martin's Press for his invaluable guidance (and patience) in helping me to turn my fragmented book proposal into a coherent and compelling narrative. And Stephen Szára, Dennis McKenna, Rick Strassman, Anton Bilton, Graham St. John, and everyone else who has personally supported me, either through valuable discussions, ideas, opportunities, or simply kind words: To you I am also most grateful.

NOTES

FOREWORD

1. G. Hancock, Supernatural—Meetings with the Ancient Teachers of Mankind (London: Arrow Books, 2006); G. Hancock, *Visionary: The Mysterious Origins of Human Consciousness* (San Francisco: New Page Books). First published worldwide in 2005 and republished with additional material in the United States in 2022 under the revised title *Visionary*.
2. https://www.seti.org/.
3. https://www.seti.org/about.
4. C. Feehly, "SETI Institute Gets $200 Million to Seek Out Evidence of Alien Life," November 14, 2023, https://www.space.com/searth-extraterrestrial-life-major-funding-boost-seti.

INTRODUCTION

1. JBS Haldane, "Possible Worlds," in *Possible Worlds and Other Essays* (London: Chatto and Windus, 1927), 260–286.

1. THE OTHER

1. J. Narby, "Amazonian Perspectives on Invisible Entities," in *DMT Dialogues—Encounters with the Spirit Molecule*, ed. D. L. Luke and R. Spowers (Rochester: Park Street Press, 2018), 72.
2. J. Narby, "Amazonian Perspectives," 72.
3. J. Hemming, *Naturalists in Paradise* (London: Thames & Hudson, 2015), 15.
4. R. Spruce, "On Some Remarkable Narcotics of the Amazon Valley and Orinoco," in *Ocean Highways—The Geographical Review*, Vol. 1, ed. C. R. Markham (London: N. Trubner, 1873), 184–193.
5. V. M. Lima and M. G. S. M. D. C. Marinho, "Reports by Explorers and Travelers and the First Scientific Studies on Ayahuasca (Dating from 1850 to 1950) Within the Current Debate on the 'Psychedelic Renaissance,'" *Historia, ciencias, saude—Manguinhos* 30 (2023): e2023023.

6. G. Reichel-Dolmatoff, *The Shaman and the Jaguar: A Study of Narcotic Drugs Among the Indians of Colombia* (Philadelphia: Temple University Press, 1975), 101.

7. R. Spruce, *Notes of a Botanist on the Amazon and Andes—Vol. 2* (London: Macmillan, 1908), 446–454.

8. R. Spruce, "On Some Remarkable Narcotics," 184–193.

9. R. Spruce, *Notes of a Botanist*, 446–454.

10. L. E. Luna, "Vegetalismo—Shamanism Among the Mestizo Population of the Peruvian Amazon," *Acta Universitatis Stockholmensis, Stockholm Studies in Comparative Religion, No. 27* (1986): 170.

11. R. Spruce, "On Some Remarkable Narcotics," 446–454.

12. R. Spruce, "On Some Remarkable Narcotics," 446–454.

13. R. Schmitz, "Friedrich Wilhelm Sertürner and the Discovery of Morphine," *Pharmacy in History* 27, no. 2 (1985): 61–74.

14. C. Krishnamurti and S. C. Rao, "The Isolation of Morphine by Serturner," *Indian Journal of Anaesthesia* 60, no. 11 (2016): 861–862; F. Sertuerner, "Ueber das Morphium, eine neue salzfähige Grundlage, und die Mekonsäure, als Hauptbestandtheile des Opiums," Annalen der Physik, 55 (1817): 56–89.

15. R. J. Huxtable and S. K. Schwarz, "The Isolation of Morphine—First Principles in Science and Ethics," *Molecular Interventions* 1, no. 4 (2001): 189–191.

16. B. Zebroski, *A Brief History of Pharmacy—Humanity's Search for Wellness* (New York: Routledge, 2016), 104–111; W. Sneader, *Drug Discovery—A History* (Chichester: John Wiley & Sons, 2005), 32–40.

17. S. Funayama and G. A. Cordell, *Alkaloids: A Treasury of Poisons and Medicines* (London: Academic Press, 2014), 2–5.

18. F. Gaedcke, "Ueber das Erythroxylin, dargestellt aus den Blättern des in Südamerika cultivirten Strauches Erythroxylon Coca Lam," Archiv der Pharmazie—Pharmaceutical and Medicinal Chemistry 132 (1855): 141–150.

19. R. Zerda-Bayón, "Informe del Jefe de la expedición científica del año 1905 a 1906," *Revista del Ministerio de Obras Publicas y Fomento* (1906): 294–303.

20. B. Baldo, "Telepathy and Telepathin," *American Druggist* 68, no. 4 (1920): 15.

21. A. M. Barriga Villalba, "Yajeine—A New Alkaloid," *Journal of the Society of Chemical Industry* 44 (1925): 205–207.

22. Villalba, "Yajeine," 205–207.

23. K. Beringer, "Über ein neues, auf das extrapyramidal-motorische System wirkendes Alkaloid," (Banisterin) *Nervenarzt* 5 (1928): 20–30; K. Beringer, "Die Beinflussung des extrapyramidal-motorischen Systems durch Banisterin," *Deutsche Medizinische Wochenschrift* 22 (1928): 908–909.

24. F. Elger, "Uber das Vorkommen von Harmin in einer sudamerikanisohen Liane (Yage)," *Helvetica Chimica Acta* 11 (1928): 162–166.

25. D. J. McKenna, "Ayahuasca: An Ethnopharmacologic History," in *Sacred Vine of Spirits: Ayahuasca*, ed. R. Metzner (Rochester: Park Street Press, 2005), 40–62.

2. THE FINAL FIX

1. W. S. Burroughs, *The Yagé Letters Redux* (4th ed.) (San Francisco: City Lights Publishers, 2006), appendices 4 and 5.

2. B. Miles, *Call Me Burroughs: A Life* (New York: Twelve, 2015), 244–247.

3. B. Miles, *Call Me Burroughs*, 244–247.

4. W. S. Burroughs, *Word Virus: The William S. Burroughs Reader* (New York: Grove Press, 2000), 94.

5. T. Morgan, *Literary Outlaw—The Life and Times of William S. Burroughs* (New York: W. W. Norton & Co., 2012), chapter 11.

6. W. Davis, *One River: Explorations and Discoveries in the Amazon Rain Forest* (New York: Simon & Schuster, 1997), 197.

7. J. P. Smith, Jr., and Richard Evans Schultes, *Botanical Studies* (Digital Commons at Humboldt State University, 2022), 1–7.

8. R. W. Bussman, "I Know Every Tree in the Forest: Reflections on the Life and Legacy of Richard Evans Schultes," in *Medicinal Plants and the Legacy of Richard E. Schultes*, ed. B. E. Ponman and R. W. Bussman (Trujillo: Graficart SRL, 2012), 15.

9. C. K. Atal, R. K. Dubey, and J. Singh, "Biochemical Basis of Enhanced Drug Bioavailability by Piperine: Evidence That Piperine Is a Potent Inhibitor of Drug Metabolism," *The Journal of Pharmacology and Experimental Therapeutics* 232, no. 1 (1985): 258–262.

10. R. E. Schultes, "De Plantis Toxicariis e Mundo Novo Tropicale Commentationes XXVI: Ethnopharmacological Notes on the Flora of Northwestern South America," *Botanical Museum Leaflets, Harvard University* 28, no. 1 (1980): 1–45.

11. W. S. Burroughs, *The Yagé Letters*, 16–18.

12. W. S. Burroughs, *The Yagé Letters*, 19.

13. W. S. Burroughs, *The Yagé Letters*, 24–25.

14. W. S. Burroughs, *The Yagé Letters*, 26–27.

15. W. S. Burroughs, *The Yagé Letters*, 28.

16. W. S. Burroughs, *The Yagé Letters*, appendix 3.

17. W. S. Burroughs, *Letters 1945–1959* (New York: Penguin, 2012), 265.

18. W. S. Burroughs, "Letter to Allen Ginsberg Dated June 18, 1953," *Letters 1945–1959* (New York: Penguin, 2012), 129.

19. W. S. Burroughs, *The Yagé Letters*, appendix 1.

20. W. S. Burroughs, *The Yagé Letters*, 28.

21. R. W. Schultes, *A Contribution to Our Knowledge of Rivea Corymbosa—the Narcotic Ololiuqui of the Aztecs* (Cambridge: Botanical Museum of Harvard University, 1941), 20–22.

22. A. Hofmann and H. Tscherter, "Isolierung von Lysergsäure-Alkaloiden aus der mexikanischen Zauberdroge Ololiuqui (*Rivea corymbosa* [L.] Hall. f.)," *Experientia* 16 (1960): 414.

23. W. A. Taber, R. A. Heacock, and M. E. Mahon, "Ergot-Type Alkaloids in Vegetative Tissue of *Rivea corymbosa* (L.) Hall. f.," *Phytochemistry* 2, no. 1 (1963): 99–101.

24. W. S. Burroughs, *The Yagé Letters*, appendix 3.

25. W. S. Burroughs, *The Yagé Letters*, appendix 1.

26. W. S. Burroughs, *The Yagé Letters*, appendix 5.

27. W. S. Burroughs, "Letter to Allen Ginsberg Dated June 18, 1953," *Letters 1945–1959* (New York: Penguin, 2012), 140.

28. W. S. Burroughs, "Letter to Allen Ginsberg," 140.

29. W. S. Burroughs, *The Yagé Letters*, appendix 5.

30. R. Spruce, "On Some Remarkable Narcotics," 184–193.

31. R. E. Schultes, "The Identity of the Malpighiaceous Narcotics of South America," *Botanical Museum Leaflets, Harvard University* 18, no. 1 (1957): 1–56.

32. P. Reinburg, "Contribution A L'étude Des Boissons Toxiques Des Indiens Du Nord-Ouest De L'amazone, L'ayahuásca—Le Yajé—Le Huánto. Étude Comparative Toxico-Physiologique D'une Expérience Personnelle," *Journal de La Société Des Américanistes* 13, no. 1 (1921): 25–32.

33. R. E. Schultes, "The Identity," 1–56.

34. W. S. Burroughs, *The Yagé Letters*, appendix 5.

3. THE LITTLE PEOPLE

1. J. D. Marks, *The Search for the "Manchurian Candidate": The CIA and Mind Control* (New York: W. W. Norton & Co., 1991), 57.

2. J. D. Marks, *The Search*, 55.

3. J. D. Marks, *The Search*, 77.

4. J. D. Marks, *The Search*, 66.

5. J. D. Marks, *The Search*, 107.

6. J. D. Marks, *The Search*, 63.

7. H. Isbell, "Comparison of the Reactions Induced by Psilocybin and LSD-25 in Man," *Psychopharmacologia* 1 (1959): 29–38.

8. H. Isbell, "Comparison of the Reactions," 29–38.

9. R. E. Belleville, H. F. Fraser, H. Isbell, C. R. Logan, and A. Wikler, "Studies on Lysergic Acid Diethylamide (LSD-25) 1. Effects in Former Morphine Addicts and Development of Tolerance During Chronic Intoxication," *A.M.A. Archives of Neurology and Psychiatry* 76, no. 5 (1956): 468–478.

10. J. D. Marks, *The Search*, 74.

11. Author unknown, "1-Methyl-d-lysergic Acid Butanolamide Tartrate (UML-491, V-A-23)," dated May 1, 1956, declassified CIA documents available at https://www.theblackvault.com/documentarchive/.

12. H. Isbell, letter to unknown recipient, dated January 24, 1956, declassified CIA documents available at https://www.theblackvault.com/documentarchive/.

13. H. Isbell, letter to unknown recipient in which Isbell reports on Etonitazene (NIH-7606), an opioid with 60–100 times the potency of morphine in man, dated June 9, 1959, declassified CIA documents available at https://www.theblackvault.com/documentarchive/.

14. H. Isbell, letter to unknown recipient, dated January 24, 1956, declassified CIA documents available at https://www.theblackvault.com/documentarchive/.

15. H. Isbell, letter to unknown recipient, dated January 24, 1956, declassified CIA documents available at https://www.theblackvault.com/documentarchive/.

16. Author unknown, memorandum from "Chief, Branch II, TSS/Chemical Division" describing Isbell's recent work with ololiuqui and other psychoactive drugs, dated August 24, 1956, declassified CIA documents available at https://www.theblackvault.com/documentarchive/.

17. G. Reichel-Dolmatoff, *The Shaman and the Jaguar: A Study of Narcotic Drugs Among the Indians of Colombia* (Philadelphia: Temple University Press, 1975), 4.

18. C. M. Torres and D. B. Repke, *Anadenanthera: Visionary Plant of Ancient South America* (Binghamton: The Howarth Press, 2006), 15.
19. C. M. Torres and D. B. Repke, *Anadenanthera*, 17.
20. C. M. Torres and D. B. Repke, *Anadenanthera*, 18.
21. W. E. Safford, "Identity of Cohoba, the Narcotic Snuff of Ancient Haiti," *Journal of the Washington Academy of Sciences* 6, no. 15 (1916): 547–562.
22. C. Brewer-Carias and J. A. Steyermark, "Hallucinogenic Snuff Drugs of the Yanomamo Caburiwe-Teri in the Cauaburi River, Brazil," *Econ Bot* 30 (1976): 57–66.
23. R. E. Schultes, "The Botanical Origins of South American Snuffs," in *Ethnopharmacologic Search for Psychoactive Drugs*, ed. D. H. Efron (U.S. Department of Health, Education, and Welfare, 1967): 291–306.
24. T. Koch-Grunberg, *Zwei Jahre unter den Indianern: Reisen in Nordwest-Brasilien 1903/1905*, (Berlin: Verlegt Bei Ernst Wasmuth A.G., 1909), chapter 15.
25. W. Davis, *One River: Explorations and Discoveries in the Amazon Rain Forest* (New York: Simon & Schuster, 1997), 618.
26. W. Davis, *One River*, 620; R. E. Schultes, "A New Narcotic Snuff from the Northwest Amazon," *Botanical Museum Leaflets, Harvard University* 16, no. 9 (1954): 241–260.
27. W. Davis, *One River*, 622; R. E. Schultes, "The Botanical Origins of South American Snuffs," in *Ethnopharmacologic Search for Psychoactive Drugs*, ed. D. H. Efron (U. S. Department of Health, Education, and Welfare, 1967): 291–306; R. E. Schultes, "De Plantis Toxicariis E Mundo Novo Tropicale Commentationes V: Virola as an Orally Administered Hallucinogen," *Botanical Museum Leaflets, Harvard University* 22, no. 6 (1969): 229–240.
28. C. Brewer-Carias and J. A. Steyermark, "Hallucinogenic Snuff Drugs," 57–66.
29. B. Albert, *The Falling Sky—Words of a Yanomami Shaman* (Cambridge, MA: The Belknap Press of Harvard University Press, 2013), 58.
30. Z. Jokic, *The Living Ancestors—Shamanism, Cosmos and Cultural Change Among the Yanomami of the Upper Orinoco* (New York: Berghahn Books, 2015), 71.
31. Z. Jokic, *The Living Ancestors*, 71.
32. E. V. de Castro, "The Crystal Forest: Notes on the Ontology of Amazonian Spirits," *Inner Asia* 9, no. 2 (2007): 153–172.
33. Z. Jokic, *The Living Ancestors*, 72.
34. B. Albert, *The Falling Sky*, 402; M. Eliade, *Shamanism—Archaic Techniques of Ecstasy* (Princeton, NJ: Princeton University Press, 1972), 88–95.
35. M. J. Plotkin, *Tales of a Shaman's Apprentice* (New York: Viking Penguin, 1993), 265–266.
36. B. Albert, *The Falling Sky*, 93–94.
37. E. V. de Castro, "The Crystal Forest," 153–172.
38. G. Baer and W. W. Snell, "An Ayahuasca Ceremony Among the Matsigenka (Eastern Peru)," *Zeitschrift Für Ethnologie* 99, no. 1/2 (1974): 63–80.
39. E. V. de Castro, "The Crystal Forest," 153–172.
40. W. J. Turner and S. Merlis, "Effect of Some Indolealkylamines on Man," *A. M. A. Archives of Neurology and Psychiatry* 81, no. 1 (1959): 121–129.
41. Author unknown, "Memorandum for the File" describing Isbell's failure to achieve effects of cohoba snuff in his subjects, suggesting the seeds weren't roasted or prepared properly, dated May 18, 1955, declassified CIA documents available at https://

www.theblackvault.com/documentarchive/; author unknown, "Visit with Dr. Isbell at Lexington, Kentucky" describing Isbell's failure to achieve effects of cohoba snuff in his subjects barring sneezing, dated May 18, 1955, declassified CIA documents available at https://www.theblackvault.com/documentarchive/.

42. N. A. Chagnon, P. LeQuesne, and J. M. Cook, "Yanomamo Hallucinogens: Anthropological, Botanical, and Chemical Findings," *Current Anthropology* 12, no. 1 (1971): 72–74; C. Brewer-Carias and J. A. Steyermark, "Hallucinogenic Snuff Drugs," 57–66.

43. L. K. A. M. Leal, A. H. Silva, and G. S. de Barros Viana, "*Justicia pectoralis*, A Coumarin Medicinal Plant Have Potential for the Development of Antiasthmatic Drugs?," Revista Brasileira de Farmacognosia, 27 (2017): 794–802.

44. R. Spruce, "On Some Remarkable Narcotics," 184–193.

45. R. Rodd, "Snuff Synergy: Preparation, Use and Pharmacology of Yopo and Banisteriopsis Caapi Among the Piaroa of Southern Venezuela," *Journal of Psychoactive Drugs* 34, no. 3 (2002): 273–279.

4. BREAKTHROUGH

1. M. S. Fish, N. M. Johnson, and E. C. Horning, "Piptadenia Alkaloids: Indole Bases of P. peregrina (L.) Benth. and Related Species," *Journal of the American Chemical Society* 77, no. 22 (1955): 5892–5895; M. S. Fish and E. C. Horning, "Studies on Hallucinogenic Snuffs," *The Journal of Nervous and Mental Disease* 124, no. 1 (1956): 33–37; V. L. Stromberg, "The Isolation of Bufotenine from Piptadenia Peregrina," *Journal of the American Chemical Society* 76, no. 6 (1954): 1707.

2. H. Handovsky, "Ein Alkaloid im Gifte von Bufo vulgaris," Archiv fur Experimentelle Pathologie und Pharmakologie, 86 (1920): 138–158; W. S. Chilton, J. Bigwood, and R. E. Jensen, "Psilocin, Bufotenine and Serotonin: Historical and Biosynthetic Observations," *Journal of Psychedelic Drugs* 11, no. 1–2 (1979): 61–69.

3. J. J. Abel and D. I. Machet, "The Poisons of the Tropical Toad, Bufo Agua: A Preliminary Communication," *JAMA* 56, no. 21 (1911): 1531–1536.

4. H. Handovsky, "Ein Alkaloid im Gifte," 138–158.

5. H. Wieland, W. Konz, and H. Mittasch, "Die Konstitution von Bufotenin und Bufotenidin," *Über Kröten-Giftstoffe. VII. Justus Liebigs Annalen der Chemie.* 513 (1934): 1–25.

6. A. Hofmann, "How LSD Originated," *Journal of Psychedelic Drugs* 11, no. 1–2 (1979): 53–60.

7. A. Hofmann, "How LSD Originated," 53–60.

8. A. Hofmann, "How LSD Originated," 53–60.

9. A. Hofmann, "How LSD Originated," 53–60.

10. S. J. Novak, "LSD Before Leary: Sidney Cohen's Critique of 1950s Psychedelic Drug Research," *Isis* 88, no. 1 (1997): 87–110.

11. P. M. Whitaker-Azmitia, "The Discovery of Serotonin and Its Role in Neuroscience," Supplement, *Neuropsychopharmacology* 21, no. 2 (1999): 2S–8S.

12. P. M. Whitaker-Azmitia, "The Discovery of Serotonin," 5S.

13. B. M. Twarog and I. H. Page, "Serotonin Content of Some Mammalian Tissues and Urine and a Method for Its Determination," *The American Journal of Physiology* 175, no. 1 (1953): 157–161; B. M. Twarog, "Responses of a Molluscan Smooth Muscle to Acetylcholine and 5-hydroxytryptamine," *Journal of Cellular and Comparative Physiology*

44, no. 1 (1954): 141–163; B. M. Twarog, "Serotonin: History of a Discovery," *Comparative Biochemistry and Physiology Part C, Comparative Pharmacology and Toxicology* 91, no. 1 (1988): 21–24.

14. D. W. Woolley and E. Shaw, "A Biochemical and Pharmacological Suggestion About Certain Mental Disorders," *Proceedings of the National Academy of Sciences of the United States of America* 40, no. 4 (April 1954): 228–231.

15. E. Shaw and D. W. Woolley, "Yohimbine and Ergot Alkaloids as Naturally Occurring Antimetabolites of Serotonin," *The Journal of Biological Chemistry* 203, no. 2 (1953): 979–989.

16. A. S. Marrazzi and E. R. Hart, "Relationship of Hallucinogens to Adrenergic Cerebral Neurohumors," *Science (New York, NY)* 121, no. 3141 (1955): 365–367.

17. D. W. Woolley, *The Biochemical Bases of Psychoses* (New York: John Wiley & Sons, 1962), 131–192.

18. E. V. Evarts, W. Landau, W. Freygang Jr., and W. H. Marshall, "Some Effects of Lysergic Acid Diethylamide and Bufotenine on Electrical Activity in the Cat's Visual System," *The American Journal of Physiology* 182, no. 3 (1955): 594–598.

19. E. V. Evarts, "Some Effects of Bufotenine and Lysergic Acid Diethylamide on the Monkey," *A. M. A. Archives of Neurology and Psychiatry* 75, no. 1 (1956): 49–53.

20. H. D. Fabing and J. R. Hawkins, "Intravenous Bufotenine Injection in the Human Being," *Science (New York, NY)* 123, no. 3203 (1956): 886–887.

21. H. D. Fabing and J. R. Hawkins, "Intravenous Bufotenine," 886–887.

22. H. D. Fabing and J. R. Hawkins, "Intravenous Bufotenine," 886–887.

23. S. Szára, "Interview with Stephen Szára" conducted by Andrew Gallimore and David Luke, September 2014; A. R. Gallimore and D. L. Luke, "DMT Research from 1956 to the Edge of Time," in *Neurotransmissions—Essays on Psychedelics from Breaking Convention*, ed. D. King et al. (London: Strange Attractor Press, 2015): 291–316.

24. S. Szára, "The Social Chemistry of Discovery—the DMT Story," *Social Pharmacology* 3, no. 3 (1989): 237–248; S. Szára, "DMT at Fifty," *Neuropsychopharmacologia Hungarica* IX/4 (2007): 201–205.

25. A. R. Gallimore and D. L. Luke, "DMT Research," 291–316.

26. A. R. Gallimore and D. L. Luke, "DMT Research," 291–316.

27. R. H. F. Manske, "A Synthesis of the Methyltryptamines and Some Derivatives," *Canadian Journal of Research* 5, no. 5 (1931): 592–600.

28. M. E. Speeter and W. C. Anthony, "The Action of Oxalyl Chloride on Indoles: A New Approach to Tryptamines," *Journal of the American Chemical Society* 76, no. 23 (1954): 6208–6210.

29. A. R. Gallimore and D. L. Luke, "DMT Research," 291–316.

30. S. Szára, "Interview with Stephen Szára."

31. A. R. Gallimore and D. L. Luke, "DMT Research," 291–316.

32. S. Szára, "Dimethyltryptamin: Its Metabolism in Man; the Relation to Its Psychotic Effect to the Serotonin Metabolism," *Experientia* 12, no. 11 (1956): 441–442; S. Szára, "The Comparison of the Psychotic Effect of Tryptamine Derivatives with the Effects of Mescaline and LSD25 in Self Experiments," in *Psychotropic Drugs*, ed. S. Garattini (Amsterdam: Elsevier, 1957): 460.

33. Future studies would show that yopo seeds contain a mixture of bufotenine, DMT,

and the 5-methoxy derivative, 5-MeO-DMT, in concentrations that can vary dramatically between samples, with most containing primarily bufotenine, others primarily DMT or 5-MeO-DMT. See, for example, G. A. Iacobucci and E. Ruveda, "Bases Derived from Tryptamine in Argentine Piptadenia Species," *Phytochemistry* 3 (1964): 465–467; B. Holmstedt and J. Lindgren, "Chemical Constituents and Pharmacology of South American Snuffs," *Psychopharmacology Bulletin* 4, no. 3 (1967): 16.

34. A. R. Gallimore and D. L. Luke, "DMT Research," 291–316.

35. A. Sai-Halasz, G. Brunecker, and S. Szára, "Dimethyltryptamine: A New Psycho-Active Drug" (unpublished English translation), *Psychiatria et neurologia* 135 (1958): 285–301.

36. A. Sai-Halasz, G. Brunecker, and S. Szára, "Dimethyltryptamine," 285–301.

37. A. Sai-Halasz, G. Brunecker, and S. Szára, "Dimethyltryptamine," 285–301.

38. Z. Boszormenyi and S. Szára, "Dimethyltryptamine Experiments with Psychotics," *Journal of Mental Science* 104 (1958): 445–453.

39. Z. Boszormenyi and S. Szára, "Dimethyltryptamine," 445–453.

5. NIGHTMARE DRUG

1. W. Burroughs, "Letter from a Master Addict to Dangerous Drugs," *British Journal of Addiction to Alcohol & Other Drugs* 53 (1957): 119–132; S. Darke and M. Farrell, "Burroughs's 'Letter from a Master Addict to Dangerous Drugs': A Forgotten Classic," *Addiction (Abingdon, England)* 113, no. 12 (2018): 2305–2308.

2. W. S. Burroughs, *The Yagé Letters*, appendix 5.

3. F. A. Hochstein and A. M. Paradies, "Alkaloids of *Banisteria caapi* and *Prestonia amazonicum*," *Journal of the American Chemical Society* 79, no. 21 (1957): 5735–5736.

4. R. E. Schultes, "The Identity of the Malpighiaceous Narcotics of South America," *Botanical Museum Leaflets, Harvard University* 18, no. 1 (1957): 1–56.

5. R. E. Schultes and R. F. Raffauf, "Prestonia: An Amazon Narcotic or Not?," *Botanical Museum Leaflets, Harvard University* 19, no. 5 (1960): 109–122.

6. B. Miles, *Call Me Burroughs*, 432.

7. B. Miles, *Call Me Burroughs*, 453; G. St. John, *Mystery School in Hyperspace: A Cultural History of DMT* (Berkeley: North Atlantic Books, 2015), 29–30.

8. B. Miles, *Call Me Burroughs*, 453–454.

9. W. S. Burroughs, "WSB [Tangier, Morocco] to Timothy Leary [Cambridge, Massachusetts]," dated May 6, 1961, in *Rub Out the Words—Letters, 1959–1974* (London: Penguin Classics, 1961), 60.

10. W. S. Burroughs, "Comments on the Night Before Thinking," *Evergreen Review* 20 (1961): 31–36; W. S. Burroughs, "WSB [Tangier, Morocco] to Brion Gysin [Paris]," dated April 8, 1961, in *Rub Out the Words—Letters, 1959–1974* (London: Penguin Classics, 1961), 57.

11. W. S. Burroughs, "WSB [Tangier, Morocco] to Brion Gysin [Paris]" dated April 8, 1961, 57.

12. W. S. Burroughs, "WSB [Tangier, Morocco] to Timothy Leary [Cambridge, Massachusetts]," dated May 6, 1961, 60.

13. T. Leary, *High Priest* (Berkeley: Ronin Publishing, 1968), 12; T. Leary, *Playboy Interview*: Timothy Leary, September 13, 1966.

14. T. Leary, *High Priest*, 214 and 226.

15. J. Ulrich, *The Timothy Leary Project—Inside the Great Counterculture Experiment* (New York: Abrams Press, 2018), 60; M. Hollingshead, *The Man Who Turned On the World* (London: Blond & Briggs, 1973), 55.

16. T. Leary, *High Priest*, 264.

17. G. St. John, *Mystery School*, 29–30.

18. O. Janiger, "Psychiatric Alchemy with Oscar Janiger," in *Mavericks of the Mind*, ed. D. J. Brown and R. McClen Novick (Multidisciplinary Association for Psychedelic Studies, 2010), 230–253.

19. T. Leary, *High Priest*, 266.

20. T. Leary, "Programmed Communication During Experiences with DMT (Dimethyltryptamine)," *Psychedelic Review* 8 (1966): 83–95.

21. O. Janiger, "Psychiatric Alchemy with Oscar Janiger," 230–253.

22. R. Dass and R. Metzner, *Birth of a Psychedelic Culture* (Santa Fe: Synergetic Press, 2010), 67.

23. T. Leary, "Programmed Communication, 83–95.

24. T. Leary, "Programmed Communication, 83–95.

25. T. Leary, "Programmed Communication, 83–95.

26. T. Leary, "Programmed Communication, 83–95.

27. R. Dass and R. Metzner, *Birth of a Psychedelic*, 107.

28. T. Scully, Erowid Character Vaults: Nick Sand Biography, https://erowid.org/culture/characters/sand_nick/sand_nick_biography2.shtml, May 4, 2017; G. St. John, *Mystery School*, 67–70.

29. S. Tendler and D. May, *The Brotherhood of Eternal Love* (London: Panther Books, 1984), 45.

30. T. Scully, Erowid Character Vaults; G. St. John, *Mystery School*, 72.

31. S. Tendler and D. May, *The Brotherhood*, 53.

32. G. St. John, *Mystery School*, 83–84.

33. T. McKenna, "The Light in Nature," The Esalen Institute (Benefit for KPFK and Botanical Dimensions), Big Sur, California (1988), https://www.asktmk.com/talks/The+Light+in+Nature

34. T. McKenna, "Alien Dreamtime," Transmission Theater, San Francisco, February 27, 1993, https://www.asktmk.com/talks/Alien+Dreamtime

35. T. McKenna, "The Light in Nature."

36. T. McKenna, "The Light in Nature."

37. D. McKenna, *The Brotherhood of the Screaming Abyss* (St. Cloud: North Star Press, 2012), 156.

38. D. McKenna, *The Brotherhood*, 156–157.

39. D. McKenna, *The Brotherhood*, 156–157.

6. THE SECRET

1. J. Ulrich, *The Timothy Leary Project*, 116.

2. J. Ulrich, *The Timothy Leary Project*, 116.

3. R. E. Brown, *The Psychedelic Guide to Preparation of the Eucharist in a Few of Its Many Guises*, Neo American Church, League for Spiritual Development, & the Ultimate Authority of the Clear Light (1968), 36–39.

4. J. Ott, *Ayahuasca Analogues—Pangean Entheogens* (Natural Products Co., 1994), 19.

5. R. E. Schultes, "De Plantis Toxicariis e Mundo Novo Tropicale Commentationes XI—The Ethnotoxicological Significance of Additives to New World Hallucinogens," *Plant Science Bulletin* 18, no. 4 (1972): 34–39.

6. R. E. Schultes, "De Plantis," 34–39.

7. W. Davis, *One River*, 252.

8. H. V. Pinkley, "Etymology of Psychotria in View of a New Use of the Genus," *Rhodora* 71, no. 788 (1969): 535–540; C. Ratsch, *The Encyclopedia of Psychoactive Plants: Ethnopharmacology and Its Applications* (Rochester: Park Street Press, 2005), 457.

9. H. V. Pinkley, "Plant Admixtures to Ayahuasca, the South American Hallucinogenic Drink," *Lloydia* 32, no. 3 (1969): 305–314; W. Davis, *One River*, 252.

10. A. H. der Marderosian, K. M. Kensinger, J. M. Chao, and F. J. Goldstein, "The Use and Hallucinatory Principles of a Psychoactive Beverage of the Cashinahua Tribe," *Drug Dependence* 5 (1970): 7–14.

11. A. J. Lees, "William Burroughs: Sailor of the Soul," *Journal of Psychoactive Drugs* 49, no. 5 (2017): 385–392.

12. R. E. Schultes, "De Plantis," 34–39.

13. J. Ott, *Pharmacotheon* (Natural Products Co., 1993): 218–219.

14. W. Davis, *One River*, 252–253; R. E. Schultes, "The Identity," 1–56.

15. W. Davis, *One River*, 216.

16. S. Agurell, B. Holmstedt, and J. E. Lindgren, "Alkaloid Content of Banisteriopsis rusbyana," *American Journal of Pharmacy and the Sciences Supporting Public Health* 140, no. 5 (1968): 148–151; A. H. Marderosian, H. V. Pinkley, and M. F. Dobbins, "Native Use and Occurrence of N,N-Dimethyltryptamine in the Leaves of Banisteriopsis rusbyana," *American Journal of Pharmacy and the Sciences Supporting Public Health* 140, no. 5 (1968): 137–147.

17. R. Rodd, "Snuff Synergy," 273–279.

18. B. Holmstedt and J. Lindgren, "Chemical Constituents," 16.

19. A. J. Ewins and P. P. Laidlaw, "The Fate of Indolethylamine in the Organism," *Biochemical Journal* 7, no. 1 (1913): 18–25.

20. H. Blaschko, D. Richter, and H. Schlossmann, "The Inactivation of Adrenaline," *Journal Physiology* 90, no. 1 (1937): 1–17.

21. K. Bhagvat, H. Blaschko, and D. Richter, "Amine Oxidase," *Biochemical Journal* 33, no. 8 (1939): 1338–1341.

22. H. Blaschko and K. Hellmann, "Pigment Formation from Tryptamine and 5-hydroxytryptamine in Tissues; a Contribution to the Histochemistry of Amine Oxidase," *The Journal of Physiology* 122, no. 2 (1953): 419–427; S. Udenfriend, E. Titus, H. Weissbach, and R. E. Peterson, "Biogenesis and Metabolism of 5-hydroxyindole Compounds," *The Journal of Biological Chemistry* 219, no. 1 (1956): 335–344; T. E. Smith, H. Weissbach, and S. Udenfriend, "Studies on the Mechanism of Action of Monoamine Oxidase: Metabolism of N,N-Dimethyltryptamine and N,N-Dimethyltryptamine-N-Oxide," *Biochemistry* 1, no. 1 (1962): 137–143.

23. S. Udenfriend, B. Witkop, B. G. Redfield, and H. Weissbach, "Studies with Reversible Inhibitors of Monoamine Oxidase: Harmaline and Related Compounds," *Biochemical Pharmacology* 1, no. 2 (1958): 160–165.

24. B. Holmstedt and J. Lindgren, "Chemical Constituents," 16; S. Agurell, B. Holmstedt, and J. E. Lindgren, "Alkaloid Content," 148–151.

25. J. Bigwood and J. Ott, "DMT," *Head Magazine*, November 1977, 56–61; J. Ott, "Pharmahuasca: Human Pharmacology of Oral DMT Plus Harmine," *Journal of Psychoactive Drugs* 31, no. 2 (1999): 171–177.

26. D. J. McKenna, G. H. Towers, and F. Abbott, "Monoamine Oxidase Inhibitors in South American Hallucinogenic Plants: Tryptamine and Beta-Carboline Constituents of Ayahuasca," *Journal of Ethnopharmacology* 10, no. 2 (1984): 195–223.

27. J. Ott, "Pharmahuasca: Human Pharmacology of Oral DMT Plus Harmine," *Journal of Psychoactive Drugs* 31, no. 2 (1999): 171–177.

28. C. M. Torres, "From Beer to Tobacco: A Probable Prehistory of *Ayahuasca* and *Yagé*," in *Ethnopharmacologic Search for Psychoactive Drugs Vol II*, ed. D. J. McKenna (Santa Fe: Synergetic Press, 2018).

29. B. Rovelli and G. N. Vaughan, "Alkaloids of *Acacia*. I. $N_b N_b$-Dimethyltryptamine in *Acacia phlebophylla*," *Australian Journal of Chemistry* 20 (1967): 1299–1300; T. A. Smith, "Tryptamine and Related Compounds in Plants," *Phytochemistry* 16, no. 2 (1977): 171–175; K. Trout, *Some Simple Tryptamines* (Mydriatic Productions, 2007); I. D. Passos and M. Mironidou-Tzouveleki, "Hallucinogenic Plants in the Mediterranean Countries," in *Neuropathology of Drug Addictions and Substance Misuse*, ed. V. R. Preedy (Cambridge: Academic Press, 2016), 761–772; L. Servillo, A. Giovane, M. L. Balestrieri, R. Casale, D. Cautela, and D. Castaldo, "Citrus Genus Plants Contain N-methylated Tryptamine Derivatives and Their 5-Hydroxylated Forms," *Journal of Agricultural and Food Chemistry* 61, no. 21 (2013): 5156–5162; N. J. Sadgrove, "Rumors of Psychedelics, Psychotropics and Related Derivatives in *Vachellia* and *Senegalia* in Contrast with Verified Records in Australian *Acacia*," *Plants (Basel, Switzerland)* 11, no. 23 (2022): 3356.

30. G. St. John, *Mystery School*, 153.

7. EXPEDITIONS I—THE CLINIC

1. R. Strassman, *DMT and the Soul of Prophecy: A New Science of Spiritual Revelation in the Hebrew Bible* (Rochester: Park Street Press, 2014), 25.

2. Rick Strassman interviewed by Graham Hancock in July 2019, https://youtu.be/wZE_8baBBwQ?si=hytE6h-wRTxGGlBr

3. R. Strassman, *DMT: The Spirit Molecule* (Rochester: Park Street Press, 2001), 89–98; R. Strassman, *DMT and the Soul of Prophecy*, 21–34.

4. R. Strassman, *DMT: The Spirit Molecule*, 121–135.

5. Rick Strassman interviewed by Graham Hancock in July 2019, https://youtu.be/wZE_8baBBwQ?si=hytE6h-wRTxGGlBr.

6. Rick Strassman's unpublished bedside notes kindly provided to the author.

7. R. Strassman, *DMT: The Spirit Molecule*, 188.

8. R. Strassman, *DMT: The Spirit Molecule*, 192.

9. R. Strassman, *DMT: The Spirit Molecule*, 169.

10. R. Strassman, *DMT: The Spirit Molecule*, 173.

11. R. Strassman, *DMT: The Spirit Molecule*, 189.

12. R. Strassman, *DMT: The Spirit Molecule*, 189.

13. R. Strassman, *DMT: The Spirit Molecule,* 209.

14. Spiros Antonopoulos, personal communication, December 2023.

15. Spiros Antonopoulos, personal communication, December 2023.

16. R. Strassman, *DMT: The Spirit Molecule,* 196–197.

17. Spiros Antonopoulos, personal communication, December 2023.

18. Spiros Antonopoulos, personal communication, December 2023.

19. The details of Peter's experience are taken from Rick Strassman's unpublished bedside notes kindly provided to the author and used with his permission.

20. The details of Paul's experience are taken from Rick Strassman's unpublished bedside notes kindly provided to the author and used with his permission.

21. R. Strassman, *DMT: The Spirit Molecule,* 211.

22. R. Strassman, *DMT: The Spirit Molecule,* 214.

23. R. Strassman, *DMT: The Spirit Molecule,* 215.

24. R. Strassman, *DMT: The Spirit Molecule,* 194.

25. R. Strassman, *DMT: The Spirit Molecule,* 195; Rick Strassman's unpublished bedside notes.

26. T. McKenna, *The World and Its Double,* workshop at Nature Friends Lodge, Sierra Madre, CA, September 11, 1993.

8. EXPEDITIONS II—UNDERGROUND

1. Rick Strassman's unpublished bedside notes.

2. R. Strassman, *DMT: The Spirit Molecule,* 67–85.

3. Ayes [Nick Sand], "Moving into the Sacred World of DMT," *Entheogen Review* 10, no. 1 (2001): 32–39.

4. Ayes [Nick Sand], "Moving," 32–39.

5. Ayes [Nick Sand], "Moving," 32–39.

6. Ayes [Nick Sand], "Just a Wee Bit More About DMT," *Entheogen Review* 10, no. 2 (2001): 51–56.

7. J. Ott, *Ayahuasca Analogues,* 51–70.

8. C. H. Gallagher, J. H. Koch, and H. Hoffman, "Diseases of Sheep Due to Ingestion of *Phalaris tuberosa,*" *Australian Veterinary Journal* 42, no. 8 (1966): 279–286.

9. C. H. Gallagher, J. H. Koch, and H. Hoffman, "Electro-Myographic Studies on Sheep Injected with the N,N-Dimethylated Tryptamine Alkaloids of *Phalaris tuberosa,*" *International Journal of Neuropharmacology* 6, no. 3 (1967): 223–228.

10. C. C. Culvenor, R. Bon, and L. S. Smith, "The Occurrence of Indolealkylamine Alkaloids in *Phalaris tuberosa L.* and *P. arundinacea L.,*" *Australian Journal of Chemistry* 17 (1964): 1301–1304.

11. J. Appleseed, "Alkaloid Extraction," *Entheogen Review* 1, no. 2 (1992), 11–12; J. Appleseed, "Phalaris Management for Alkaloid Production," *Entheogen Review* 2, no. 1 (1993), 6; J. Appleseed, "Ayahuasca Analogue Experiences," *Entheogen Review* 2, no. 2 (1993), 27–28; J. DeKorne, "Smokable DMT from Plants Part II," *Entheogen Review* 3, no. 1 (1994): 2–6.

12. F. Festi and G. Samorini, "'Ayahuasca-like' Effects Obtained with Italian Plants," 11th International Congress for the Study of Modified States of Consciousness, October 3–7, 1994, Lleida (Spain).

13. J. DeKorne, "Smokable DMT from Plants," *Entheogen Review* 2, no. 4 (1993): 1–5.

14. J. DeKorne, "Report from the Palenque Conference," *Entheogen Review* 5, no. 2 (1996): 2–3.

15. O. Goncalves de Lima, "Observações sobre o 'vinho da Jurema' utilizado pelos índios Pancarú de Tacaratú," *Arquivos do Instituto de Pesquisas Agronomicas* 4 (1946): 45–80.

16. J. H. Steward, *Handbook of South American Indians—Volume 1, the Marginal Tribes* (U.S. Government Printing Office, 1946), 559.

17. I. J. Pachter, D. E. Zacharias, and O. Ribeiro, "Indole Alkaloids of *Acer saccharinum* (the Silver Maple), *Dictyoloma incanescens*, *Piptadenia colubrina*, and *Mimosa hostilis*," *The Journal of Organic Chemistry* 24, no. 9 (1959): 1285–1287.

18. J. DeKorne, "*Mimosa hostilis*: A Potent New Ayahuasca Analogue," *Entheogen Review* 5, no. 4 (1996): 9–12.

19. Noman, "DMT for the Masses," *Entheogen Review* 15, no. 3 (2006): 91.

20. Binkie2000, "Visiting Hyperspace-Light Journey: An Experience with DMT (exp85120)," Erowid.org, July 19, 2010, erowid.org/exp/85120.

21. Alter Native, "Spectrographic, Omni-visual and Hypergeometric: An Experience with DMT (exp87176)," Erowid.org, November 26, 2011, erowid.org/exp/87176.

22. Z. Jokic, "Yanomami Shamanic Initiation: The Meaning of Death and Postmortem Consciousness in Transformation," *Anthropology of Consciousness* 19, no. 1 (2008): 33–59.

23. Litrium, "Elf Trip," DMT Nexus Forum, October 30, 2006, https://www.dmt-nexus.me/forum/default.aspx?g=posts&m=1249.

24. T. McKenna, *Hermeticism & Alchemy* New York, 1992, https://www.asktmk.com/talks/Hermeticism+%26+Alchemy.

25. B. Albert, *The Falling Sky*, 95.

26. P. Meyer (comp.), *340 DMT Trip Reports*, 2005, accessed: April 15, 2024, http://www.serendipity.li/dmt/340_dmt_trip_reports.htm.

27. J. Wilcox, "Shamanic Crisis."

28. J. Wilcox, "Shamanic Crisis: An Experience with DMT (exp111947)," Erowid.org, June 7, 2018, erowid.org/exp/111947.

29. D. W. Lawrence, R. Carhart-Harris, R. Griffiths, and C. Timmermann, "Phenomenology and Content of the Inhaled N, N-Dimethyltryptamine (N, N-DMT) Experience," *Scientific Reports*, 12, no. 1 (2022): 8562.

30. D. W. Lawrence, R. Carhart-Harris, R. Griffiths, and C. Timmermann, "Phenomenology," 8562. (Unpublished draft kindly provided by Dr. Lawrence with additional trip reports not included in the final manuscript.)

31. D. W. Lawrence, R. Carhart-Harris, R. Griffiths, and C. Timmermann, "Phenomenology," 8562. (Unpublished draft kindly provided by Dr. Lawrence with additional trip reports not included in the final manuscript.)

32. A. K. Davis, J. M. Clifton, E. G. Weaver, E. S. Hurwitz, M. W. Johnson, and R. R. Griffiths, "Survey of Entity Encounter Experiences Occasioned by Inhaled *N,N*-Dimethyltryptamine: Phenomenology, Interpretation, and Enduring Effects," *Journal of Psychopharmacology* 34, no. 9 (2020): 1008–1020.

33. P. Michael, D. Luke, and O. Robinson, "An Encounter with the Other: A Thematic

and Content Analysis of DMT Experiences from a Naturalistic Field Study," *Frontiers in Psychology* 12 (2021): 720717.

34. P. Michael, raw data from Michael et al., 2021, kindly provided to the author.
35. P. Michael, raw data from Michael et al., 2021.
36. P. Michael, raw data from Michael et al., 2021.
37. P. Michael, raw data from Michael et al., 2021.
38. P. Michael, raw data from Michael et al., 2021.

9. ARE THEY REAL?

1. Personal correspondence via email and Zoom conversation, October 2023.
2. G. Cowles, "Oliver Sacks, Neurologist Who Wrote About the Brain's Quirks, Dies at 82," *The New York Times*, August 30, 2015, https://www.nytimes.com/2015/08/31/science/oliver-sacks-dies-at-82-neurologist-and-author-explored-the-brains-quirks.html.
3. O. Sacks, *Hallucinations* (New York: Vintage Books, 2013): 106–107.
4. L. K. Sahoo, V. V. Holla, D. Batra, S. Prasad, A. Bhattacharya, N. Kamble, R. Yadav, and P. K. Pal, "Comparison of Effectiveness of Trihexyphenidyl and Levodopa on Motor Symptoms in Parkinson's Disease," *Journal of Neural Transmission* 127, no. 12 (2020): 1599–1606; R. Torrents, J. F. Ferré, A. Konareff, P. Hemery, K. Sherwin, C. Lassalle, N. Simon, and S. Scerra, "Misuse of Trihexyphenidyl (Artane) on Réunion Island," *Journal of Clinical Psychopharmacology* 38, no. 3 (2018): 250–253.
5. O. Sacks, *Hallucinations*, 106–107.
6. O. Sacks, *Hallucinations*, 107–108.
7. I. Kant, *Critique of Pure Reason* (Cambridge: Cambridge University Press, 1999).
8. T. Metzinger, *The Ego Tunnel* (New York: Basic Books, 2009), 15.
9. W. H. Bosking, M. S. Beauchamp, and D. Yoshor, "Electrical Stimulation of Visual Cortex: Relevance for the Development of Visual Cortical Prosthetics," *Annual Review of Vision Science* 3 (2017): 141–166; K. A. Mazurek and M. H. Schieber, "How Is Electrical Stimulation of the Brain Experienced, and How Can We Tell? Selected Considerations on Sensorimotor Function and Speech," *Cognitive Neuropsychology* 36, no. 3–4 (2019): 103–116.
10. M. Raghavan, D. Fee, and P. E. Barkhaus, "Generation and Propagation of the Action Potential," *Handbook of Clinical Neurology* 160 (2019): 3–22; M. W. Barnett and P. M. Larkman, "The Action Potential," *Practical Neurology* 7, no. 3 (2007): 192–197; R. C. deCharms and A. Zador, "Neural Representation and the Cortical Code," *Annual Review of Neuroscience* 23 (2000): 613–647.
11. R. Snowden, P. Thompson, and T. Troscianko, *Basic Vision: An Introduction to Visual Perception* (Oxford: Oxford University Press, 2006).
12. K. Tsunoda, Y. Yamane, M. Nishizaki, and M. Tanifuji, "Complex Objects Are Represented in Macaque Inferotemporal Cortex by the Combination of Feature Columns," *Nature Neuroscience* 4, no. 8 (2001): 832–838.
13. For a thorough and detailed explanation of how your cortex constructs your world model, see A. R. Gallimore, *Reality Switch Technologies: Psychedelics as Tools for the Discovery and Exploration of New Worlds* (Tokyo: Strange Worlds Press, 2022).
14. J. Antolík and J. A. Bednar, "Development of Maps of Simple and Complex Cells

in the Primary Visual Cortex," *Frontiers in Computational Neuroscience* 5, no. 17 (2011); M. H. Herzog and A. M. Clarke, "Why Vision Is Not Both Hierarchical and Feedforward," *Frontiers in Computational Neuroscience* 8, no. 135 (2014); M. Riesenhuber and T. Poggio, "Hierarchical Models of Object Recognition in Cortex," *Nature Neuroscience* 2, no. 11 (1999): 1019–1025.

15. J. J. DiCarlo and D. D. Cox, "Untangling Invariant Object Recognition," *Trends in Cognitive Sciences* 11, no. 8 (2007): 333–341; M. Singh and D. Hoffman, "Constructing and Representing Visual Objects," *Trends in Cognitive Sciences* 1 (1997): 98–102.

16. This way of thinking about perception is known as predictive processing or predictive coding. For a thorough but accessible treatment, see A. Clark, *Surfing Uncertainty* (Oxford: Oxford University Press 2016). The more academic literature is extremely extensive, but examples include: R. Rao and D. Ballard, "Predictive Coding in the Visual Cortex: A Functional Interpretation of Some Extra-Classical Receptive-Field Effects, *Nature Neuroscience* 2 (1999): 79–87; K. Friston, "The Free-Energy Principle: A Unified Brain Theory?," *Nature Reviews Neuroscience* 11 (2010): 127–138; R. Kanai, Y. Komura, S. Shipp, and K. Friston, "Cerebral Hierarchies: Predictive Processing, Precision and the Pulvinar," *Philosophical Transactions of the Royal Society of London. Series B, Biological Sciences* 370, no. 1668 (2015): 20140169; A. M. Bastos, W. M. Usrey, R. A. Adams, G. R. Mangun, P. Fries, and K. J. Friston, "Canonical Microcircuits for Predictive Coding," *Neuron* 76, no. 4 (2012): 695–711; G. B. Keller and T. D. Mrsic-Flogel, "Predictive Processing: A Canonical Cortical Computation," *Neuron* 100, no. 2 (2018): 424–435.

17. D. Hoffman, "Does Perception Replicate the External World?," commentary in *Behavioral and Brain Sciences* 26 (2003): 415–416; D. Hoffman, "The Interface Theory of Perception," in *Object Categorization: Computer and Human Vision Perspectives,* eds. S. Dickinson, M. Tarr, A. Leonardis, and B. Schiele (Cambridge: Cambridge University Press, 2009), 148–165.

18. G. M. Edelman, "Neural Darwinism: Selection and Re-entrant Signalling in Higher Brain Function," *Neuron* 10 (1993): 115–125; C. Blakemore and G. F. Cooper, "Development of the Brain Depends on the Visual Environment," *Nature* 228, no. 5270 (1970): 477–478; B. M. Bennett, D. Hoffman, and C. Prakash, "Perception and Evolution, in *Perception and the Physical World,* eds. D. Heyer and R. Mausfeld (Hoboken: Wiley, 2002), 229–245.

19. R. Schredl and F. Hofmann, "Continuity Between Waking Activities and Dream Activities," *Consciousness and Cognition* 12 (2003): 298–308.

20. A. R. Gallimore, *Reality Switch Technologies,* chapter 11; E. K. Perry and R. H. Perry, "Acetylcholine and Hallucinations: Disease-Related Compared to Drug-Induced Alterations in Human Consciousness," *Brain and Cognition* 28, no. 3 (1995): 240–258.

21. R. Goekoop and J. Looijestijn, "A Network Model of Hallucinations," in *Hallucinations: Research and Practice,* ed. J. D. D. Blom and I. E. C. Sommer (New York: Springer, 2011).

10. I'LL SEE YOU IN MY NIGHTMARES

1. J. C. Callaway, "A Proposed Mechanism for the Visions of Dream Sleep," *Medical Hypotheses* 26, no. 2 (1988): 119–124.

2. M. C. Oon, R. M. Murray, R. Rodnight, M. P. Murphy, and J. L. Birley, "Factors Affecting the Urinary Excretion of Endogenously Formed Dimethyltryptamine in Normal Human Subjects," *Psychopharmacology* 54, no. 2 (1977): 171–175.

3. S. C. Weed, F. M. Hallam, E. D. Phinney, and M. W. Calkins, "Minor Studies from the Psychological Laboratory of Wellesley College: III—A Study of the Dream-Consciousness," *The American Journal of Psychology* 7, no. 3 (1896): 405–411; F. Snyder, "Toward an Evolutionary Theory of Dreaming," *The American Journal of Psychiatry* 123, no. 2 (1966): 121–142; S. Schwartz, "A Historical Loop of One Hundred Years: Similarities Between 19th Century and Contemporary Dream Research," *Dreaming* 10, no. 1 (2000): 55–66.

4. A. Revonsuo, "The Reinterpretation of Dreams: An Evolutionary Hypothesis of the Function of Dreaming," *Behavioral and Brain Sciences* 23, no. 6 (2000): 877–1121; R. R. Llinás and D. Paré, "Of Dreaming and Wakefulness," *Neuroscience* 44, no. 3 (1991): 521–535; R. Llinás and U. Ribary, "Coherent 40-Hz Oscillation Characterizes Dream State in Humans," *Proceedings of the National Academy of Sciences of the United States of America* 90, no. 5 (1993): 2078–2081; Y. Nir and G. Tononi, "Dreaming and the Brain: From Phenomenology to Neurophysiology," *Trends in Cognitive Sciences* 14, no. 2 (2010): 88–100; Y. Senzai and M. Scanziani, "The Brain Simulates Actions and Their Consequences During REM Sleep," *bioRxiv: The Preprint Server for Biology*, August 16, 2024.

5. E. Hartmann, "The Day Residue: Time Distribution of Waking Events," *Psychophysiology* 5, no. 2 (1968): 222; M. Schredl and F. Hofmann, "Continuity Between Waking Activities and Dream Activities," *Consciousness and Cognition* 12, no. 2 (2003): 298–308; M. Schredl, "Continuity Between Waking and Dreaming: A Proposal for a Mathematical Model," *Sleep and Hypnosis* 5, no. 1 (2003): 38–52.

6. A. Maggiolini, C. Cagnin, F. Crippa, A. Persico, and P. Rizzi, "Content Analysis of Dreams and Waking Narratives," *Dreaming* 20, no. 1 (2010): 60–76.

7. A. Revonsuo, "The Reinterpretation," 877–1121.

8. T. Gregor, "A Content Analysis of Mehinaku Dreams," *Ethos* 9, no. 4 (1981): 353–390.

9. T. Gregor, "A Content Analysis," 353–390.

10. A. Revonsuo, "The Reinterpretation," 877–1121.

11. M. A. Doll, "The Monster in Children's Dreams: Its Metaphoric Awe," *Counterpoints* 19 (1988): 99–110.

12. D. Foulkes, *Children's Dreaming and the Development of Consciousness* (Cambridge: Harvard University Press, 1999), 11.

13. D. Foulkes, J. D. Larson, E. M. Wanson, and M. Rardin, "Two Studies of Childhood Dreaming," *The American Journal of Orthopsychiatry* 39, no. 4 (1969): 627–643; D. Foulkes, *Children's Dreaming*, 116–141.

14. D. Foulkes, *Children's Dreaming*, 21.

15. D. Foulkes, *Children's Dreaming*, 26.

16. D. J. Chalmers, *Reality+: Virtual Worlds and the Problems of Philosophy* (London: Penguin, 2022), chapter 3.

17. Ayes [Nick Sand], "Just a Wee Bit More," 51–56.

18. T. L. Kahan and S. P. LaBerge, "Dreaming and Waking: Similarities and Differences Revisited," *Consciousness and Cognition* 20, no. 3 (2011): 494–514.

19. Badomen8361, "Crystal Creations: An Experience with DMT (exp76492)," Erowid .org, Dec. 30, 2009, erowid.org/exp/76492.

20. J. Salgo, *Compendium der Psychiatrie* (Berlin: Verlag Von Bermann & Altmann, 1889), 143.

21. E. J. Engstrom, M. M. Weber, and W. Burgmair, "Emil Wilhelm Magnus Georg Krae-pelin (1856–1926)," *The American Journal of Psychiatry* 163, no. 10 (2006): 1710; E. Kraepelin, "Zur Entartungsfrage," *Zentralblatt für Nervenheilkunde und Psychiatrie* 31 (Neue Folge 19) (1908): 745–751.

22. H. Osmond and J. Smythies, "Schizophrenia: A New Approach," *The Journal of Mental Science* 98, no. 411 (1952): 309–315; A. Hoffer, H. Osmond, and J. Smyth-ies, "Schizophrenia; a New Approach. II. Result of a Year's Research," *The Journal of Mental Science* 100, no. 418 (1954): 29–45.

23. J. Axelrod, "Enzymatic Formation of Psychotomimetic Metabolites from Normally Occurring Compounds," *Science* 134, no. 3475 (1961): 343.

24. R. M. Murray, M. C. Oon, R. Rodnight, J. L. Birley, and A. Smith, "Increased Excre-tion of Dimethyltryptamine and Certain Features of Psychosis: A Possible Associa-tion," *Archives of General Psychiatry* 36, no. 6 (1979): 644–649.

25. S. A. Barker, E. H. McIlhenny, and R. Strassman, "A Critical Review of Reports of Endogenous Psychedelic N, N-Dimethyltryptamines in Humans: 1955–2010," *Drug Testing and Analysis* 4, no. (2012): 617–635.

26. L. M. Hadden, B. Alderson-Day, M. Jackson, C. Fernyhough, and R. P. Bentall, "The Auditory-Verbal Hallucinations of Welsh-English Bilingual People," *Psychology and Psychotherapy* 93, no. 1 (2020): 122–133.

27. D. W. Goodwin, P. Alderson, and R. Rosenthal, "Clinical Significance of Hallucina-tions in Psychiatric Disorders. A Study of 116 Hallucinatory Patients," *Archives of General Psychiatry* 24, no. 1 (1971): 76–80; F. Waters, D. Collerton, D. H. Ffytche, R. Jardri, D. Pins, R. Dudley, J. D. Blom, U. P. Mosimann, F. Eperjesi, S. Ford, and F. Larøi, "Visual Hallucinations in the Psychosis Spectrum and Comparative Information from Neurodegenerative Disorders and Eye Disease," *Schizophrenia Bulletin* 40, Suppl. 4 (2014): S233–S245.

28. M. M. van Ommen, T. van Laar, R. Renken, F. W. Cornelissen, R. Bruggeman, "Vi-sual Hallucinations in Psychosis: The Curious Absence of the Primary Visual Cor-tex," Suppl. 2, *Schizophrenia Bulletin* 49, no. 12 (2023): S68–S81.

29. R. J. Teunisse, J. R. Cruysberg, W. H. Hoefnagels, A. L. Verbeek, and F. G. Zitman, "Visual Hallucinations in Psychologically Normal People: Charles Bonnet's Syn-drome," *Lancet* 347, no. 9004 (1996): 794–797.

30. F. Boller, D. S. Birnbaum, and N. Caputi, "Charles Bonnet Syndrome and Other Hallucinatory Phenomena," *Frontiers of Neurology and Neuroscience* 41 (2018): 117–124.

31. R. Leroy, "Les hallucinations lilliputiennes," *Annales Medico-Psychologiques* 10 (1909): 278–294; R. Leroy, "Les hallucinations lilliputiennes," *Annales Medico-Psychologiques* 12 (1920): 539–544; R. Leroy, "Hallucinations lilliputiennes hyp-nagogiques Essai d'interpretation psychologique du syndrome," *Bull. de la Societe Clinique de Medecine Mentale* 9 (1921): 148–149; R. Leroy, "Le syndrome des hallu-cinations lilliputiennes," *Le Monde Medical* 32 (1922): 245–258.

32. J. D. Blom, "Leroy's Elusive Little People: A Systematic Review on Lilliputian Hallucinations," *Neuroscience and Biobehavioral Reviews* 125 (2021): 627–636.

33. Gracie and Zarkov, "Gracie's 'Visible Language' Contact Experience: An Experience with DMT & MDA (exp1859)," Erowid.org, June 15, 2000, erowid.org/exp/1859.

34. Binkie2000, "Visiting Hyperspace-Light Journey: An Experience with DMT (exp85120)," Erowid.org, July 19, 2010, erowid.org/exp/85120.

35. D. H. Ffytche, R. J. Howard, M. J. Brammer, A. David, P. Woodruff, and S. Williams, "The Anatomy of Conscious Vision: An fMRI Study of Visual Hallucinations," *Nature Neuroscience* 1, no. 8 (1998): 738–742; A. M. Santhouse, R. J. Howard, and D. H. Fytche, "Visual Hallucinatory Syndromes and the Anatomy of the Visual Brain," *Brain: A Journal of Neurology* 123, Pt. 10 (2000): 2055–2064.

11. BUILDING ALIEN WORLDS

1. K. Arnold, *The Divine Madness of Philip K. Dick*" (Oxford: Oxford University Press, 2016), 83.

2. K. Arnold, *The Divine*, 122.

3. P. K. Dick, *VALIS* (London: Gollancz, 2001), 1.

4. L. D. Ladino, S. Rizvi, and J. F. Téllez-Zenteno, "The Montreal Procedure: The Legacy of the Great Wilder Penfield," *Epilepsy and Behavior* 83 (2018): 151–161.

5. W. Penfield, "The Cerebral Cortex in Man: I. The Cerebral Cortex and Consciousness," *Archives of Neurology & Psychiatry* 40, no. 3 (1938): 417–442; W. Penfield, "Memory Mechanisms," *A. M.A. Archives of Neurology and Psychiatry* 67, no. 2 (1952): 178–198.

6. W. Penfield, "Memory Mechanisms," 178–198.

7. H. C. Barron, R. Auksztulewicz, and K. Friston, "Prediction and Memory: A Predictive Coding Account," *Progress in Neurobiology* 192, no. 101821 (2020): 101821; J. Linde-Domingo, M. S. Treder, C. Kerrén, and M. Wimber, "Evidence That Neural Information Flow Is Reversed Between Object Perception and Object Reconstruction from Memory," *Nature Communications* 10, no. 1 (2019): 179.

8. D. Ji and M. A. Wilson, "Coordinated Memory Replay in the Visual Vortex and Hippocampus During Sleep," *Nature Neuroscience* 10, no. 1 (2007): 100–107.

9. P. W. Frankland and B. Bontempi, "The Organization of Recent and Remote Memories," *Nature Reviews Neuroscience* 6, no. 2 (2005): 119–130.

10. A. Wikler, "Clinical and Electroencephalographic Studies on the Effects of Mescaline, N-Allylnormorphine and Morphine in Man; a Pharmacologic Analysis of the Functions of the Spontaneous Electrical Activity of the Cerebral Cortex," *The Journal of Nervous and Mental Disease* 120, no. 3–4 (1954): 157–175; H. C. Denber and S. Merlis, "Studies on Mescaline. I. Action in Schizophrenic Patients; Clinical Observations and Brain Wave Patterns, Showing Effects Before and After Electric Convulsive Treatments," *The Psychiatric Quarterly* 29, no. 3 (1955): 421–429.

11. F. Rinaldi and H. E. Himwich, "The Cerebral Electrographic Changes Induced by LSD and Mescaline Are Corrected by Frenquel," *The Journal of Nervous and Mental Disease* 122, no. 5 (1955): 424–432; L. Goldstein, H. B. Murphree, A. A. Sugerman, C. C. Pfeiffer, and E. H. Jenney, "Quantitative Electroencephalographic Analysis of Naturally Occurring (Schizophrenic) and Drug-Induced Psychotic States in Human Males," *Clinical Pharmacology and Therapeutics* 4 (1963): 10–21.

12. S. Szára, personal communication, 2014.
13. F. Kajtor and S. Szára, "Electroencephalographic Changes Induced by Dimethyl-tryptamine in Normal Adults," *Confinia neurologica* 19, no. 1 (1959): 52–61.
14. F. Kajtor and S. Szára, "Electroencephalographic Changes," 52–61.
15. F. Kajtor and S. Szára, "Electroencephalographic Changes," 52–61.
16. F. Kajtor and S. Szára, "Electroencephalographic Changes Induced by Dimethyl-tryptamine in Normal Adults," *Confinia neurologica* 19, no. 1 (1959): 52–61.
17. R. L. Jensen, J. L. Stone, and R. A. Hayne, "Introduction of the Human Horsley-Clarke Stereotactic Frame," *Neurosurgery* 38, no. 3 (1996): 563–567.
18. H. W. Dodge, Jr., R. G. Bickford, A. A. Baily, C. B. Holman, M. C. Petersen, and C. W. Sem-Jacobsen, "Technics and Potentialities of Intracranial Electrography," *Postgraduate Medicine* 15, no. 4 (1954): 291–300.
19. C. W. Sem-Jacobsen, M. C. Petersen, J. A. Lazarte, H. W. Dodge, Jr., and C. B. Holman, "Electroencephalographic Rhythms from the Depths of the Frontal Lobe in 60 Psychotic Patients," *Electroencephalography and Clinical Neurophysiology* 7, no. 2 (1955): 193–210.
20. B. E. Schwarz, C. W. Sem-Jacobsen, and M. C. Petersen, "Effects of Mescaline, LSD-25, and Adrenochrome on Depth Electrograms in Man," *A. M. A. Archives of Neurology and Psychiatry* 75, no. 6 (1956): 579–587.
21. R. A. Sandison, A. M. Spencer, and J. D. Whitelaw, "The Therapeutic Value of Lysergic Acid Diethylamide in Mental Illness," *Journal of Mental Science* 100, no. 419 (1954): 491–507.
22. J. D. McCorvy and B. L. Roth, "Structure and Function of Serotonin G Protein-Coupled Receptors," *Pharmacology & Therapeutics* 150 (2015): 129–142.
23. R. G. Browne and B. T. Ho, "Role of Serotonin in the Discriminative Stimulus Properties of Mescaline," *Pharmacology, Biochemistry, and Behavior* 3, no. 3 (1975): 429–435; F. C. Colpaert, C. J. Niemegeers, and P. A. Janssen, "A Drug Discrimination Analysis of Lysergic Acid Diethylamide (LSD): In Vivo Agonist and Antagonist Effects of Purported 5-Hydroxytryptamine Antagonists and of Pirenperone, a LSD-antagonist," *The Journal of Pharmacology and Experimental Therapeutics* 221, no. 1 (1982): 206; F. C. Colpaert and P. A. Janssen, "A Characterization of LSD-Antagonist Effects of Pirenperone in the Rat," *Neuropharmacology* 22, no. 8 (1983): 1001–1005; J. E. Leysen, C. J. Niemegeers, J. M. Van Nueten, and P. M. Laduron, "[3H]Ketanserin (R 41 468), a Selective 3H-Ligand for Serotonin2 Receptor Binding Sites. Binding Properties, Brain Distribution, and Functional Role," *Molecular Pharmacology* 21, no. 2 (1982): 301–314.
24. R. A. Glennon, M. Titeler, and J. D. McKenney, "Evidence for 5-HT2 Involvement in the Mechanism of Action of Hallucinogenic Agents," *Life Sciences* 35, no. 25 (1984): 2505–2511; F. X. Vollenweider, M. F. Vollenweider-Scherpenhuyzen, A. Bäbler, H. Vogel, and D. Hell, "Psilocybin Induces Schizophrenia-like Psychosis in Humans Via a Serotonin-2 Agonist Action," *Neuroreport* 9, no. 17 (1998): 3897–3902; D. E. Nichols, "Hallucinogens," *Pharmacology & Therapeutics* 101, no. 2 (2004): 131–181; R. Kraehenmann, D. Pokorny, L. Vollenweider, K. H. Preller, T. Pokorny, E. Seifritz, and F. X. Vollenweider, "Dreamlike Effects of LSD on Waking Imagery in Humans Depend on Serotonin 2A Receptor Activation," *Psychopharmacology* 234, no. 13 (2017): 2031–2046; K. H. Preller, J. B. Burt, J. L. Ji, C. H. Schleifer, B. D. Adkinson, P. Stämpfli, E.

Seifritz, G. Repovs, J. H. Krystal, J. D. Murray, F. X. Vollenweider, and A. Anticevic, "Changes in Global and Thalamic Brain Connectivity in LSD-Induced Altered States of Consciousness Are Attributable to the 5-HT2A Receptor," *eLife* 7 (2018): e35082; A. M. Becker, A. Klaiber, F. Holze, I. Istampoulouoglou, U. Duthaler, N. Varghese, A. Eckert, and M. E. Liechti, "Ketanserin Reverses the Acute Response to LSD in a Randomized, Double-Blind, Placebo-Controlled, Crossover Study in Healthy Participants," *The International Journal of Neuropsychopharmacology* 26, no. 2 (2023): 97–106.

25. H. Kluver, *Mescal—The 'Divine' Plant and Its Psychological Effects* (London: Kegan Paul, Trench, Trubner & Co., 1928).

26. H. Kluver, *Mescal and Mechanisms of Hallucinations* (Chicago: University of Chicago Press, 1966).

27. G. B. Ermentrout and J. D. Cowan, "A Mathematical Theory of Visual Hallucination Patterns," *Biological Cybernetics* 34, no. 3 (1979): 137–150; P. C. Bressloff, J. D. Cowan, M. Golubitsky, P. J. Thomas, and M. C. Wiener, "What Geometric Visual Hallucinations Tell Us About the Visual Cortex," *Neural Computation* 14, no. 3 (2002): 473–491; D. H. Ffytche, "Cortical Bricks and Mortar," *Journal of Neurology, Neurosurgery, and Psychiatry* 73, no. 5 (2002): 472.

28. J. Masters and R. E. L. Houston, *The Varieties of Psychedelic Experience* (New York: Dell Publishing, 1966), 10.

29. R. L. Carhart-Harris, D. Erritzoe, T. Williams, J. M. Stone, L. J. Reed, A. Colasanti, R. J. Tyacke, R. Leech, A. L. Malizia, K. Murphy, P. Hobden, J. Evans, A. Feilding, R. G. Wise, and D. J. Nutt, "Neural Correlates of the Psychedelic State as Determined by fMRI Studies with Psilocybin," *Proceedings of the National Academy of Sciences of the United States of America* 109, no. 6 (2012): 2138–2143.

30. E. Tagliazucchi, R. Carhart-Harris, R. Leech, D. Nutt, and D. R. Chialvo, "Enhanced Repertoire of Brain Dynamical States During the Psychedelic Experience," *Human Brain Mapping* 35, no. 11 (2014): 5442–5456; L. Roseman, R. Leech, A. Feilding, D. J. Nutt, and R. L. Carhart-Harris, "The Effects of Psilocybin and MDMA on Between-Network Resting State Functional Connectivity in Healthy Volunteers," *Frontiers in Human Neuroscience* 8 (2014): 204.

31. R. L. Carhart-Harris, R. Leech, P. J. Hellyer, M. Shanahan, A. Feilding, E. Tagliazucchi, D. R. Chialvo, and D. Nutt, "The Entropic Brain: A Theory of Conscious States Informed by Neuroimaging Research with Psychedelic Drugs," *Frontiers in Human Neuroscience* 8 (2014): 20; R. L. Carhart-Harris, "The Entropic Brain-Revisited," *Neuropharmacology* 142 (2018): 167–178; R. L. Carhart-Harris and K. J. Friston, "REBUS and the Anarchic Brain: Toward a Unified Model of the Brain Action of Psychedelics," *Pharmacological Reviews* 71, no. 3 (2019): 316–344; J. S. Siegel, S. Subramanian, D. Perry, B. P. Kay, E. M. Gordon, T. O. Laumann, T. R. Reneau, N. V. Metcalf, R. V. Chacko, C. Gratton, C. Horan, S. R. Krimmel, J. S. Shimony, J. A. Schweiger, D. F. Wong, D. A. Bender, K. M. Scheidter, F. I. Whiting, J. A. Padawer-Curry, R. T. Shinohara, and N. U. F. Dosenbach, "Psilocybin Desynchronizes the Human Brain," *Nature* 632, no. 8023 (2024): 131–138.

32. L. D. Lord, P. Expert, S. Atasoy, L. Roseman, K. Rapuano, R. Lambiotte, D. J. Nutt, G. Deco, R. L. Carhart-Harris, M. L. Kringelbach, and J. Cabral, "Dynamical Exploration

of the Repertoire of Brain Networks at Rest Is Modulated by Psilocybin," *NeuroImage* 199 (2019): 127–142.

33. R. L. Carhart-Harris, S. Muthukumaraswamy, L. Roseman, M. Kaelen, W. Droog, K. Murphy, E. Tagliazucchi, E. E. Schenberg, T. Nest, C. Orban, R. Leech, L. T. Williams, T. M. Williams, M. Bolstridge, B. Sessa, J. McGonigle, M. I. Sereno, D. Nichols, P. J. Hellyer, P. Hobden, and D. J. Nutt, "Neural Correlates of the LSD Experience Revealed by Multimodal Neuroimaging," *Proceedings of the National Academy of Sciences of the United States of America* 113, no. 17 (2016): 4853–4858; S. Atasoy, L. Roseman, M. Kaelen, M. L. Kringelbach, G. Deco, R. L. Carhart-Harris, "Connectome-Harmonic Decomposition of Human Brain Activity Reveals Dynamical Repertoire Re-organization Under LSD," *Scientific Reports* 7, no. 1 (2017): 17661; E. Tagliazucchi, L. Roseman, M. Kaelen, C. Orban, S. D. Muthukumaraswamy, K. Murphy, H. Laufs, R. Leech, J. McGonigle, N. Crossley, E. Bullmore, T. Williams, M. Bolstridge, A. Feilding, D. J. Nutt, R. Carhart-Harris, "Increased Global Functional Connectivity Correlates with LSD-Induced Ego Dissolution," *Current Biology* 26, no. 8 (2016): 1043–1050.

34. D. R. Chialvo, "Critical Brain Dynamics at Large Scale," in *Criticality in Neural Systems*, ed. D. Plenz and E. Niebur (Weinheim: Wiley-VCH, 2014), 43–66.

35. D. Toker, I. Pappas, J. D. Lendner, J. Frohlich, D. M. Mateos, S. Muthukumaraswamy, R. Carhart-Harris, M. Paff, P. M. Vespa, M. M. Monti, F. T. Sommer, R. T. Knight, and M. D'Esposito, "Consciousness Is Supported by Near-Critical Slow Cortical Electrodynamics," *Proceedings of the National Academy of Sciences of the United States of America* 119, no. 7 (2022): e2024455119.

36. C. Meisel, A. Storch, S. Hallmeyer-Elgner, E. Bullmore, and T. Gross, "Failure of Adaptive Self-Organized Criticality During Epileptic Seizure Attacks," *PLoS Computational Biology* 8, no. 1 (2012): e1002312; J. P. Hobbs, J. L. Smith, and J. M. Beggs, "Aberrant Neuronal Avalanches in Cortical Tissue Removed from Juvenile Epilepsy Patients," *Journal of Clinical Neurophysiology: Official Publication of the American Electroencephalographic Society* 27, no. 6 (2010): 380–386.

37. S. Atasoy, L. Roseman, M. Kaelen, M. L. Kringelbach, G. Deco, R. L. Carhart-Harris, "Connectome," 17661.

38. R. L. Carhart-Harris and K. J. Friston, "The Default-Node, Ego-Functions and Free-Energy: A Neurobiological Account of Freudian Ideas," *Brain: A Journal of Neurology* 133, pt. 4 (2010): 1265–1283; A. Dietrich, "Functional Neuroanatomy of Altered States of Consciousness: The Transient Hypofrontality Hypothesis," *Consciousness and Cognition* 12, no. 2 (2003): 231–256; A. R. Hariri, S. Y. Bookheimer, and J. C. Mazziotta, "Modulating Emotional Responses: Effects of a Neocortical Network on the Limbic System," *Neuroreport* 11, no. 1 (2000): 43–48; L. M. Shin, S. L. Rauch, and R. K. Pitman, "Amygdala, Medial Prefrontal Cortex, and Hippocampal Function in PTSD," *Annals of the New York Academy of Sciences* 1071 (2006): 67–79.

12. THE ANATOMY OF A MACHINE ELF

1. T. McKenna, *Camden Centre Talk*, London, June 15, 1992.

2. C. G. Jung, *Flying Saucers—A Modern Myth of Things Seen in the Skies* (Princeton: Princeton University Press, 1979).

3. D. J. McKenna, *The Brotherhood of the Screaming Abyss* (St. Cloud: North Star Press of St. Cloud, 2012), 128.

4. J. Jacobi, *The Psychology of C. G. Jung* (London: Routledge & Kegan Paul, 1942), 38.

5. C. G. Jung, *Collected Works*, Vol. 9, Part I, para. 3 (Princeton: Princeton University Press, 1934).

6. J. Jacobi, *The Psychology*, 47.

7. E. D. Goodwyn, *The Neurobiology of the Gods: How Brain Physiology Shapes the Recurrent Imagery of Myth and Dreams* (London: Routledge, 2012), 19.

8. J. Panksepp, *Affective Neuroscience* (Oxford: Oxford University Press, 1998), 75.

9. G. I. Viamontes and B. D. Beitman, "Mapping the Unconscious in the Brain," *Psychiatric Annals* 37, no. 4 (2007): 234–256.

10. G. I. Viamontes and B. D. Beitman, "Mapping," 234–256.

11. G. I. Viamontes and B. D. Beitman, "Mapping," 234–256; K. Janacsek, T. M. Evans, M. Kiss, L. Shah, H. Blumenfeld, and M. T. Ullman, "Subcortical Cognition: The Fruit Below the Rind," *Annual Review of Neuroscience* 45 (2022): 361–386; M. Solms, "What Is 'the Unconscious,' and Where Is It Located in the Brain? A Neuropsychoanalytic Perspective," *Annals of the New York Academy of Sciences* 1406, no. 1 (2017): 90–97; J. A. Bargh and E. Morsella, "The Unconscious Mind," *Perspectives on Psychological Science: A Journal of the Association for Psychological Science* 3, no. 1 (2008): 73–79.

12. M. Solms, "What Is 'the Unconscious,'" 90–97.

13. J. Panksepp, *Affective Neuroscience* (Oxford: Oxford University Press, 1998), 221.

14. V. LoBue and J. S. DeLoache, "Superior Detection of Threat-Relevant Stimuli in Infancy," *Developmental Science* 13, no. 1 (2010): 221–228.

15. J. Tooby, L. Cosmides, and H. C. Barrett, "Resolving the Debate on Innate Ideas: Learnability Constraints and the Evolved Interpenetration of Motivational and Conceptual Functions," in *The Innate Mind: Structure and Contents*, eds. P. Carruthers, S. Laurence, and S. Stich (Oxford: Oxford University Press, 2005), 305–337.

16. J. LeDoux, *The Emotional Brain: The Mysterious Underpinnings of Emotional Life* (New York: Simon & Schuster, 1998): 40.

17. A. R. Damasio, "Emotion and the Human Brain," in *Unity of Knowledge: The Convergence of Natural and Human Science,* ed. A. R. Damasio, A. Harrington, J. Kagan, B. S. McEwen, H. Moss, and R. Shaikh (New York Academy of Sciences, 2001): 101–106; R. Adolphs, N. L. Denburg, and D. Tranel, "The Amygdala's Role in Long-Term Declarative Memory for Gist and Detail," *Behavioral Neuroscience* 115, no. 5 (2001): 983–992.

18. J. LeDoux, *The Emotional Brain*, 112–113; N. Favila, K. Gurney, and P. G. Overton, "Role of the Basal Ganglia in Innate and Learned Behavioural Sequences," *Reviews in the Neurosciences* 35, no. 1 (2023): 35–55; J. Panksepp, B. Knutson, and D. L. Pruitt, "Toward a Neuroscience of Emotion: The Epigenetic Foundations of Emotional Development," in *What Develops in Emotional Development?*, ed. M. F. Mascolo and S. Griffin (New York: Plenum Press, 1998), 53–84.

19. A. Ohman, A. Flykt, and F. Esteves, "Emotion Drives Attention: Detecting the Snake in the Grass," *Journal of Experimental Psychology. General* 130, no. 3 (2001): 466–478; A. R. Damasio, "Emotion and the Human Brain," in *Unity of Knowledge: The Convergence of Natural and Human Science,* ed. A. R. Damasio, A. Harrington, J. Kagan, B. S. McEwen, H. Moss, and R. Shaikh (New York Academy of Sciences, 2001), 101–106.

20. D. Vaughn Becker and S. L. Neuberg, "Archetypes Reconsidered as Emergent Outcomes of Cognitive Complexity and Evolved Motivational Systems," *Psychological Inquiry* 30, no. 2 (2019): 59–75.

21. J. Garry and H. El-Shamy, *Archetypes and Motifs in Folklore and Literature* (Armonk: M. E. Sharpe, 2005).

22. M. L. Solms, "The Neurobiological Underpinnings of Psychoanalytic Theory and Therapy," *Frontiers in Behavioral Neuroscience* 12 (2018): 294.

23. J. Hanna, "Aliens, Insectoids, and Elves! Oh, My!," *Erowid Extracts* 23 (2012): 8–21, Erowid.org/chemicals/dmt/dmt_article3.shtml.

24. Gracie & Zarkov, *DMT How & Why to Get Off*, Gracie & Zarkov Productions (1984), https://deoxy.org/gz_howy.htm.

25. T. McKenna, lecture at The Fez, New York, June 20, 1993.

26. W. J. Hynes and W. J. Doty, *Mythical Trickster Figures: Contours, Contexts, and Criticisms* (Tuscaloosa: University of Alabama Press, 1993), 35; S. Woolfe, "Why Do Jesters and Tricksters Appear in the DMT Experience?" (2019), https://www.samwoolfe .com/2019/02/jesters-tricksters-dmt-experience.html.

27. D. Williams, *The Trickster Brain—Neuroscience, Evolution, and Narrative* (Lanham: Lexington Books, 2012), 164; C. G. Jung, "On the Psychology of the Trickster Figure," in *The Trickster—A Study in American Indian Mythology*, in *The Trickster*, ed. P. Radin (New York: Greenwood Press, 1956), 195f; I. Blocian, "The Archetype of the Trickster in the Writings of C. G. Jung," *Studia Religiologica* 53 (2020): 227–238.

28. Gracie & Zarkov, "Gracie's 'Visible Language' Contact Experience: An Experience with DMT & MDA (exp1859)," Erowid.org, June 15, 2000, erowid.org/exp/1859.

29. J. Hillman, *Going Bugs* (New York: BetterListen, 2017).

30. J. Lockwood, *The Infested Mind: Why Humans Fear, Loathe, and Love Insects* (Oxford: Oxford University Press, 2013), chapter 2.

31. R. Strassman, *DMT: The Spirit Molecule*, 206.

32. _eb0La_, "A Truely Mind Opening Experience: An Experience with DMT (exp34523)," Erowid.org, March 5, 2007, erowid.org/exp/34523.

33. https://wiki-entities.dmt-vision.net/praying-mantis.

34. J. Horgan, *Rational Mysticism* (Boston: Houghton Mifflin Company, 2003): 177.

35. T. McKenna, *Global Perspectives and Psychedelic Poetics*, New York, 1993, https:// www.asktmk.com/talks/Global+Perspectives+and+Psychedelic+Poetics.

13. COLLISION WITH THE IMPOSSIBLE

1. C. C. Bisbee, *Psychedelic Prophets: The Letters of Aldous Huxley and Humphry Osmond* (Montreal: McGill-Queen's University Press, 2018), preface, ix.

2. C. C. Bisbee, *Psychedelic Prophets*, ix.

3. N. Murray, *Aldous Huxley—An English Intellectual* (New York: Hachette, 2003), 408.

4. A. Huxley, *The Doors of Perception* (St. Louis: Turtleback Books, 1956).

5. A. Huxley, "Mescaline and the 'Other World,'" in *Proceedings of the Round Table on Lysergic Acid Diethylamide and Mescaline in Experimental Psychiatry*, ed. L. Cholden (New York: Grune & Stratton, 1956), 46–50.

6. A. Huxley, "Heaven and Hell," in *The Doors of Perception; Heaven and Hell* (St. Louis: Turtleback Books, 1956).

7. A. Huxley, "Mescaline," 46–50.

8. J. R. Smythies, "The Base Line of Schizophrenia. I. The Visual Phenomena," *The American Journal of Psychiatry* 110, no. 3 (1953): 200–204.

9. J. R. Smythies, "The Base Line," 200–204.

10. B. Shanon, *Antipodes of the Mind: Charting the Phenomenology of the Ayahuasca Experience* (Oxford: Oxford University Press, 2003), 367–370.

11. B. Shanon, *Antipodes*, 39.

12. I. Limosani, A. D'Agostino, M. L. Manzone, and S. Scarone, "The Dreaming Brain/Mind, Consciousness and Psychosis," *Consciousness and Cognition* 20, no. 4 (2011): 987–992.

13. G. Hancock, *Supernatural—Meetings with the Ancient Teachers of Mankind* (London: Arrow Books, 2006), 519–521.

14. G. Hancock, *Supernatural*, 519–521.

15. clayzee77, "The First Time I Died," Reddit r/DMT, May 1, 2018, https://www.reddit.com/r/DMT/comments/8g6ilb/the_first_time_i_died/.

16. Myconub, "8th Dimensional Hell/Hyperslap Experience from 20mg Dabbed," Reddit r/DMT, December 10, 2018, https://www.reddit.com/r/DMT/comments/a4m7bv/8th_dimensional_hellhyperslap_experience_from/.

17. Consplice, "DMT & Lorazepam-Smiling at Hell," Reddit r/DMT, May 1, 2018, and May 15, 2017, https://www.reddit.com/r/DMT/comments/6ban2i/dmt_lorazepam_smiling_at_hell/.

18. R. Strassman, *DMT: The Spirit Molecule*, 195.

19. Unpublished data from Reddit r/DMT sourced for D. W. Lawrence, R. Carhart-Harris, R. Griffiths, and C. Timmermann, "Phenomenology and Content of the Inhaled N, N-Dimethyltryptamine (N, N-DMT) Experience," *Scientific Reports* 12, no. 1 (2022): 8562.

20. P. Meyer (comp.), *340 DMT Trip Reports*, 2005, accessed April 15, 2024, http://www.serendipity.li/dmt/340_dmt_trip_reports.htm.

21. Twitter/X user @eldiegod, personal communication, 2023.

22. D. Pinchbeck, *Breaking Open the Head: A Psychedelic Journey into the Heart of Contemporary Shamanism* (Portland: Broadway Books, 2003), chapter 33.

23. SFos, "Otherworldly Bewilderness: An Experience with DMT (exp1851)," Erowid.org, June 15, 2000, erowid.org/exp/1851.

24. 800dpi, "LSD+DMT+THC Trip Report," Reddit r/DMT, Sept. 20, 2018, https://www.reddit.com/r/DMT/comments/9h9gq1/lsddmtthc_trip_report/.

25. RecordEverything, "My First DMT Experience," Reddit r/DMT, May 22, 2018, https://www.reddit.com/r/DMT/comments/8l47w8/my_first_dmt_experience/.

26. G. Hancock, *Supernatural*, 520.

27. No-Frosting-4979, "How Can a Drug Just 'Turn Off,'" Reddit r/DMT, Oct. 20, 2023, https://www.reddit.com/r/DMT/comments/17jbju8/how_can_a_drug_just_turn_off/

28. Slicedgreenolive, "Getting Locked Out," Reddit r/DMT, Sept. 16, 2022, https://www.reddit.com/r/DMT/comments/xf0nfd/getting_locked_out/.

29. C. K. Svensson, "Attenuation of Response to Repeated Drug Administration: A Proposal for Differentiating Tachyphylaxis and Tolerance," *The Journal of Pharmacology and Experimental Therapeutics* 381, no. 1 (2022): 22–32.

30. R. E. Belleville, H. F. Fraser, H. Isbell, C. R. Logan, and A. Wikler, "Studies on

Lysergic Acid Diethylamide (LSD-25). I. Effects in Former Morphine Addicts and Development of Tolerance During Chronic Intoxication," *A. M. A. Archives of Neurology and Psychiatry* 76, no. 5 (1956): 468–478.

31. H. Isbell, A. B. Wolbach, A. Wikler, and E. J. Miner, "Cross Tolerance Between LSD and Psilocybin," *Psychopharmacologia* 2 (1961): 147–159; A. B. Wolbach, Jr., H. Isbell, and E. J. Miner, "Cross Tolerance Between Mescaline and LSD-25, with a Comparison of the Mescaline and LSD Reactions," *Psychopharmacologia* 3 (1962): 1–14.

32. D. E. Rosenberg, H. Isbell, E. J. Miner, and C. R. Logan, "The Effect of N, N-Dimethyltryptamine in Human Subjects Tolerant to Lysergic Acid Diethylamide," *Psychopharmacologia* 5 (1964): 217–227.

33. J. M. Cole and W. A. Pieper, "The Effects of N,N-Dimethyltryptamine on Operant Behavior in Squirrel Monkeys," *Psychopharmacologia* 29, no. 2 (1973): 107–112; J. C. Gillin, E. Cannon, R. Magyar, M. Schwartz, and R. J. Wyatt, "Failure of N, N-Dimethyltryptamine to Evoke Tolerance in Cats," *Biological Psychiatry* 7, no. 3 (1973): 213–220.

34. R. J. Strassman, C. R. Qualls, and L. M. Berg, "Differential Tolerance to Biological and Subjective Effects of Four Closely Spaced Doses of N,N-Dimethyltryptamine in Humans," *Biological Psychiatry* 39, no. 9 (1996): 784–795.

35. J. A. Gray, B. A. Compton-Toth, and B. L. Roth, "Identification of Two Serine Residues Essential for Agonist-Induced 5-HT2A Receptor Desensitization," *Biochemistry* 42, no. 36 (2003): 10853–10862; S. Karaki, C. Becamel, S. Murat, C. Mannoury la Cour, M. J. Millan, L. Prézeau, J. Bockaert, P. Marin, and F. Vandermoere, "Quantitative Phosphoproteomics Unravels Biased Phosphorylation of Serotonin 2A Receptor at Ser280 by Hallucinogenic Versus Nonhallucinogenic Agonists," *Molecular & Cellular Proteomics: MCP* 13, no. 5 (2014): 1273–1285.

36. R. L. Smith, H. Canton, R. J. Barrett, and E. Sanders-Bush, "Agonist Properties of N,N-Dimethyltryptamine at Serotonin 5-HT2A and 5-HT2C Receptors," *Pharmacology, Biochemistry, and Behavior* 61, no. 3 (1998): 323–330.

37. No-Minute-5831, "DMT Lockout," Reddit r/DMT, July 16, 2022, https://www.reddit.com/r/DMT/comments/w082so/dmt_lockout/.

38. Ruhrohraggyz, "Forever Banished from Hyperspace, It Said," Reddit r/DMT, March 19, 2023, https://www.reddit.com/r/DMT/comments/11veu2m/forever_banished_from_hyperspace_it_said/.

39. Author name withheld for privacy reasons, personal communication, 2023.

40. P. Gow, *An Amazonian Myth and its History* (Oxford: Oxford University Press, 2001), 148.

14. BREAKING THROUGH

1. J. Riba and M. J. Barbanoj, "Bringing Ayahuasca to the Clinical Research Laboratory," *Journal of Psychoactive Drugs* 37, no. 2 (2005): 219–230; J. Riba, M. Valle, G. Urbano, M. Yritia, A. Morte, and M. J. Barbanoj, "Human Pharmacology of Ayahuasca: Subjective and Cardiovascular Effects, Monoamine Metabolite Excretion, and Pharmacokinetics," *The Journal of Pharmacology and Experimental Therapeutics* 306, no. 1 (2003): 73–83; M. Valle, A. E. Maqueda, M. Rabella, A. Rodríguez-Pujadas, R. M. Antonijoan, S. Romero, J. F. Alonso, M.À. Mañanas, S. Barker, P. Friedlander,

A. Feilding, and J. Riba, "Inhibition of Alpha Oscillations Through Serotonin-2A Receptor Activation Underlies the Visual Effects of Ayahuasca in Humans," *European Neuropsychopharmacology* 26, no. 7 (2016): 1161–1175.

2. J. F. Alonso, S. Romero, M. À. Mañanas, and J. Riba, "Serotonergic Psychedelics Temporarily Modify Information Transfer in Humans," *The International Journal of Neuropsychopharmacology* 18, no. 8 (2015): pyv039.

3. D. B. de Araujo, S. Ribeiro, G. A. Cecchi, F. M. Carvalho, T. A. Sanchez, J. P. Pinto, B. S. de Martinis, J. A. Crippa, J. E. Hallak, and A. C. Santos, "Seeing with the Eyes Shut: Neural Basis of Enhanced Imagery Following Ayahuasca Ingestion," *Human Brain Mapping* 33, no. 11 (2012): 2550–2560.

4. C. Timmermann, L. Roseman, M. Schartner, R. Milliere, L. T. J. Williams, D. Erritzoe, S. Muthukumaraswamy, M. Ashton, A. Bendrioua, O. Kaur, S. Turton, M. M. Nour, C .M. Day, R. Leech, D. J. Nutt, and R. L. Carhart-Harris, "Neural Correlates of the DMT Experience Assessed with Multivariate EEG," *Scientific Reports* 9, no. 1 (2019): 16324.

5. A. Alamia and R. VanRullen, "Alpha Oscillations and Traveling Waves: Signatures of Predictive Coding?," *PLoS Biology* 17, no. 10 (2019): e3000487; Z. Pang, A. Alamia, and R. VanRullen, "Turning the Stimulus On and Off Changes the Direction of α Traveling Waves," *eNeuro* 7, no. 6 (2020): ENEURO.0218-20.2020.

6. A. Alamia, C. Timmermann, D. J. Nutt, R. VanRullen, and R. L. Carhart-Harris, "DMT Alters Cortical Travelling Waves," *eLife* 9 (2020): e59784.

7. A. Alamia et al., "DMT Alters Cortical Travelling Waves," e59784.

8. M. M. van Ommen, T. van Laar, R. Renken, F. W. Cornelissen, and R. Bruggeman, "Visual Hallucinations in Psychosis: The Curious Absence of the Primary Visual Cortex," Suppl. 2, *Schizophrenia Bulletin* 49, no. 12 (2023): S68–S81.

9. S. Lefebvre, M. Demeulemeester, A. Leroy, C. Delmaire, R. Lopes, D. Pins, P. Thomas, R. Jardri, "Network Dynamics During the Different Stages of Hallucinations in Schizophrenia," *Human Brain Mapping* 37, no. 7 (2016): 2571–2586; D. H. Ffytche, R. J. Howard, M. J. Brammer, A. David, P. Woodruff, and S. Williams, "The Anatomy of Conscious Vision: An fMRI Study of Visual Hallucinations," *Nature Neuroscience* 1, no. 8 (1998): 738–742.

10. A. R. Gallimore, "Building Alien Worlds_The Neuropsychological and Evolutionary Implications of the Astonishing Psychoactive Effects of N,N-Dimethyltryptamine (DMT)," *Journal of Scientific Exploration* 27, no. 3 (2013): 455–503.

15. THE INTELLIGENCE

1. J. E. Mack, *Abduction—Human Encounters with Aliens* (New York: Scribners, 1994), 1–4.

2. J. E. Mack, "People Who Believe They Were Abducted by Alien Spaceships," *60 Minutes Australia* (2019), https://youtu.be/5r1ZTfOm-_Y?si=yuOrazy3kkjqcO4r.

3. J. E. Mack, "Why the Abduction Phenomenon Cannot Be Explained Psychiatrically," *Alien Discussions: Proceedings of the Abduction Study Conference* (Cambridge: North Cambridge Press, 1992), http://johnemackinstitute.org/1992/06/why-the-abduction-phenomenon-cannot-be-explained-psychiatrically/.

4. J. E. Mack, *Passport to the Cosmos* (New York: White Crow Books, 2011), 75.

5. J. E. Mack, *Passport*, 38.

6. J. E. Mack, "Interview with John E. Mack," in D. J. Brown's *Conversations on the Edge of the Apocalypse* (New York: St. Martin's Press, 2005): 145–163.

7. R. Strassman, *DMT: The Spirit Molecule*, 219.

8. T. E. Bullard, "UFO Abduction Reports: The Supernatural Kidnap Narrative Returns in Technological Guise," *The Journal of American Folklore* 102, no. 404 (1989): 147–170.

9. J. E. Mack, *Abduction*, 82.

10. J. E. Mack, "Interview," 145–163.

11. M. Eliade, *Shamanism—Archaic Techniques of Ecstasy* (Princeton: Princeton University Press, 1972), 3–15; J. Chaumeil, "Varieties of Amazonian Shamanism," *Diogenes* 40, no. 158 (1992): 101–113.

12. J. E. Mack, *Passport*, chapter 8.

13. J. E. Mack, *Passport*, 176.

14. J. E. Mack, *Abduction*, 3.

15. J. Vallee, *Dimensions: A Casebook of Alien Contact* (Charlottesville: Anomalist Books, 2014), 147.

16. S. J. Dick, "Bringing Culture to Cosmos—The Postbiological Universe," in *Cosmos & Culture—Cultural Evolution in a Cosmic Context*, ed. S. J. Dick and M. L. Lupisella (National Aeronautics and Space Administration, 2011), chapter 14.

17. N. S. Kardashev, "Transmission of Information by Extraterrestrial Civilizations," *Soviet Astronomy* 8, no. 2 (1964): 217–221.

18. P. Davies, *The Eerie Silence—Are We Alone in the Universe?* (London: Allen Lane, 2010), chapter 6.

19. J. D. Barrow, *Impossibility—The Limits of Science and the Science of Limits* (Oxford: Oxford University Press, 1998), 133–138.

20. S. J. Dick, "The Biological Universe Revisited," in *Space, Time, and Aliens*, ed. S. J. Dick (New York: Springer, 2020), chapter 5.

21. S. J. Dick, "Bringing Culture," chapter 14.

22. S. Schneider, "Alien Minds," in *Science Fiction and Philosophy*, ed. S. Schneider (Hoboken: Wiley, 2016), chapter 12.

23. T. McKenna, *The Archaic Revival* (San Francisco: HarperOne, 1991): 35.

24. N. Bostrom, *Superintelligence—Paths, Dangers, Strategies* (Oxford: Oxford University Press, 2014), 47.

25. W. G. Pollard, "Rumors of Transcendence in Physics," *American Journal of Physics* 52, no. 10 (1984): 877–881; M. M. Ćirković, "Post-Postbiological Evolution?," *Futures* 99 (2018): 28–35; M. M. Ćirković and R. J. Bradbury, "Galactic Gradients, Postbiological Evolution and the Apparent Failure of SETI," *New Astronomy* 11, no. 8 (2006): 628–639; J. M. Smart, "The Transcension Hypothesis: Sufficiently Advanced Civilizations Invariably Leave Our Universe, and Implications for METI and SETI," *Acta Astronautica* 78 (2012): 55–68.

26. S. Grof, *The Holotropic Mind* (San Francisco: HarperSanFrancisco, 1993), 183.

27. https://wiki.dmt-nexus.me/Hyperspace_lexicon#Waiting_Room.

28. D. W. Lawrence, R. Carhart-Harris, R. Griffiths, and C. Timmermann, "Phenomenology and Content of the Inhaled N, N-Dimethyltryptamine (N, N-DMT) Experience," *Scientific Reports* 12, no. 1 (2022): 8562.

29. 23, "No Point of Reference: An Experience with DMT (exp40231)," Erowid.org, June 29, 2005, erowid.org/exp/40231.

30. R. Wasson, "A New Mexican Psychotropic Drug from the Mint Family," *Botanical Museum Leaflets, Harvard University* 20, no. 3 (1962): 77–84; D. J. Siebert, "*Salvia divinorum* and Salvinorin A: New Pharmacologic Findings," *Journal of Ethnopharmacology* 43, no. 1 (1994): 53–56; M. W. Johnson, K. A. MacLean, C. J. Reissig, T. E. Prisinzano, and R. R. Griffiths, "Human Psychopharmacology and Dose-Effects of Salvinorin A, a Kappa Opioid Agonist Hallucinogen Present in the Plant *Salvia divinorum*," *Drug and Alcohol Dependence* 115, no. 1–2 (2011): 150–155.

31. C. Williams, "On 'Modified Human Agents': John Lilly and the Paranoid Style in American Neuroscience," *History of the Human Sciences* 32, no. 5 (2019): 84–107.

32. J. C. Lilly, "A Method of Recording the Moving Electrical Potential Gradients in the Brain: The 25-Channel Bavatron and Electro-Iconograms," in *American Institute of Electronic Engineers (eds) Conference on Electronic Instrumentation in Nucleonics and Medicine* (American Institute of Electronic Engineering, 1950), 37–43.

33. C. Williams, "On 'Modified,'" 84–107.

34. J. C. Lilly and A. M. Miller, "Sounds Emitted by the Bottlenose Dolphin," *Science*, 133, no. 3465 (1961): 1689–1693; J. C. Lilly and A. M. Miller, "Vocal Exchanges Between Dolphins: Bottlenose Dolphins 'Talk' to Each Other with Whistles, Clicks, and a Variety of Other Noises," *Science* 134, no. 3493 (1961): 1873–1876.

35. J. C. Lilly, *The Center of the Cyclone* (New York: Bantam Books, 1973), 42; J. C. Lilly, "Dolphin-Human Relation and LSD 25," in *The Use of LSD in Psychotherapy and Alcoholism—International Conference on the Use of LSD in Psychotherapy*, ed. H. A. Abramson (Indianapolis: Bobbs-Merrill Company, 1967), 47–52.

36. J. C. Lilly, *The Center*, 39.

37. J. C. Lilly, *The Scientist—A Metaphysical Autobiography* (Berkeley: Ronin Publishing Inc., 1997), 119.

38. J. C. Lilly, *The Scientist*, 48.

39. J. C. Lilly, *The Scientist*, 55.

40. J. S. Meyer, F. Greifenstein, and M. Devault, "A New Drug Causing Symptoms of Sensory Deprivation," *Journal of Nervous & Mental Disorders* 129 (1959): 54–61; E. F. Domino, "Taming the Ketamine Tiger. 1965," *Anesthesiology* 113, no. 3 (2010): 678–684.

41. J. Cichon, A. Z. Wasilczuk, L. L. Looger, D. Contreras, M. B. Kelz, and A. Proekt, "Ketamine Triggers a Switch in Excitatory Neuronal Activity Across Neocortex," *Nature Neuroscience* 26, no. 1 (2023): 39–52.

42. J. C. Lilly, *The Scientist*, 171.

43. J. C. Lilly, *The Scientist*, 152.

44. J. C. Lilly, *The Scientist*, 183.

45. J. C. Lilly, *The Scientist*, 172.

46. J. C. Lilly, *The Scientist*, 164, 182.

16. THE TECHNOLOGY

1. R. Strassman, *DMT: The Spirit Molecule*, 214.
2. H. Morris, "Life Is a Cosmic Giggle on the Breath of the Universe," *Vice Magazine*, May 1, 2011, https://www.vice.com/en/article/nndz9z/life-is-a-cosmic-giggle-803-v18n5.
3. This Land, "Unusual Analogues: Drugs Used by Gordon Todd Skinner," *This Land Press*, July 25, 2013, https://thislandpress.com/2013/07/25/unusual-analogues-drugs-used-by-gordon-todd-skinner/.
4. P. L. Gambus and I. F. Troconiz, "Pharmacokinetic-Pharmacodynamic Modelling in Anaesthesia," *British Journal of Clinical Pharmacology* 79 (2015): 72–84.
5. A. R. Absalom, J. B. Glen, G. J. C. Zwart, T. W. Schnider, and M. Struys, "Target-Controlled Infusion: A Mature Technology," *Anesthesia and Analgesia* 122 (2016): 70–78; G. N. C. Kenny and M. White, "A Portable Computerized Infusion System for Propofol," *Anaesthesia* 45 (1990): 692–693.
6. D. R. Miller, "Intravenous-Infusion Anesthesia and Delivery Devices," *Canadian Journal of Anaesthesia-Journal Canadien D Anesthesie* 41 (1994): 639–652.
7. R. J. Strassman and C. R. Qualls, "Dose-Response Study of N,N-Dimethyltryptamine in Humans. I. Neuroendocrine, Autonomic, and Cardiovascular Effects," *Archives of General Psychiatry* 51, no. 2 (1994): 85–97.
8. A. R. Gallimore and R. J. Strassman, "A Model for the Application of Target-Controlled Intravenous Infusion for a Prolonged Immersive DMT Psychedelic Experience," *Frontiers in Pharmacology* 7 (2016): 211.
9. Talks from the symposium, "Entheogenic Plant Sentience," were collected in *DMT Dialogues: Encounters with the Spirit Molecule*, ed. D. L. Luke and R. Spowers (Rochester: Park Street Press, 2018); details on the symposium can be found here: https://tyringhaminitiative.com/wp-content/uploads/2024/01/Entheogenic-Plant-Sentience-2015.pdf.
10. A. Bilton, personal communication (2024).
11. E. Eckernäs, J. Koomen, C. Timmermann, R. Carhart-Harris, D. Röshammar, and M. Ashton, "Optimized Infusion Rates for N,N-Dimethyltryptamine to Achieve a Target Psychedelic Intensity Based on a Modeling and Simulation Framework," *CPT: Pharmacometrics & Systems Pharmacology* 12, no. 10 (2023): 1398–1410; E. Eckernäs, C. Timmermann, R. Carhart-Harris, D. Röshammar, and M. Ashton, "Population Pharmacokinetic/Pharmacodynamic Modeling of the Psychedelic Experience Induced by N,N-Dimethyltryptamine—Implications for Dose Considerations," *Clinical and Translational Science* 15, no. 12 (2022): 2928–2937.
12. L. X. Luan, E. Eckernäs, M. Ashton, F. E. Rosas, M. V. Uthaug, A. Bartha, S. Jagger, K. Gascon-Perai, L. Gomes, D. J. Nutt, D. Erritzøe, R. L. Carhart-Harris, and C. Timmermann, "Psychological and Physiological Effects of Extended DMT," *Journal of Psychopharmacology (Oxford, England)* 38, no. 1 (2024): 56–67.
13. A. Bilton, personal communication (2024).
14. A. Bilton, personal communication (2024).
15. A. Bilton, personal communication (2024).
16. T. Leary, "Programmed Communication During Experiences with DMT (Dimethyltryptamine)," *Psychedelic Review* 8 (1966): 83–95.

17. A. Bilton, personal communication (2024).

18. L. X. Luan, "Psychological," 56–67.

19. D. M. Turner, *Salvinorin: The Psychedelic Essence of Salvia Divinorum* (San Francisco: Panther Press, 1996): 30–32.

20. A. Bilton, personal communication (2024).

21. In case you're wondering, the Wachowskis' movie *The Matrix* was released in 1999—three years after Turner's report was published.

22. D. E. Nichols, "N,N-Dimethyltryptamine and the Pineal Gland: Separating Fact from Myth," *Journal of Psychopharmacology* 32, no. 1 (2018): 30–36.

23. D. M. Turner, *Salvinorin: The Psychedelic Essence of Salvia Divinorum* (San Francisco: Panther Press, 1996): 30–32.

24. A. Szabo, A. Kovacs, J. Riba, S. Djurovic, E. Rajnavolgyi, E. Frecska, "The Endogenous Hallucinogen and Trace Amine N,N-Dimethyltryptamine (DMT) Displays Potent Protective Effects Against Hypoxia via Sigma-1 Receptor Activation in Human Primary iPSC-Derived Cortical Neurons and Microglia-Like Immune Cells," *Frontiers in Neuroscience* 10 (2016): 423; S. Nardai, M. László, A. Szabó, A. Alpár, J. Hanics, P. Zahola, B. Merkely, E. Frecska, and Z. Nagy, "N,N-dimethyltryptamine Reduces Infarct Size and Improves Functional Recovery Following Transient Focal Brain Ischemia in Rats," *Experimental Neurology* 327 (2020): 113245; I. Szabó, V. É. Varga, S. Dvorácskó, A .E. Farkas, T. Körmöczi, R. Berkecz, S. Kecskés, Á. Menyhárt, R. Frank, D. Hantosi, N. V. Cozzi, E. Frecska, C. Tömböly, I. A. Krizbai, F. Bari, and E. Farkas, "N,N-Dimethyltryptamine Attenuates Spreading Depolarization and Restrains Neurodegeneration by Sigma-1 Receptor Activation in the Ischemic Rat Brain," *Neuropharmacology* 192 (2021): 108612.

25. J. G. Dean, T. Liu, S. Huff, B. Sheler, S. A. Barker, R. J. Strassman, M. M. Wang, and J. Borjigin, "Biosynthesis and Extracellular Concentrations of N,N-Dimethyltryptamine (DMT) in Mammalian Brain," *Scientific Reports* 9, no. 1 (2019): 9333; N. G. Glynos, E. R. Huels, A. Nelson, Y. Kim, R. T. Kennedy, G. A. Mashour, and D. Pal, "Neurochemical and Neurophysiological Effects of Intravenous Administration of N,N-dimethyltryptamine in Rats," (2024) bioRxiv 2024.04.19.589047, doi: https://doi.org /10.1101/2024.04.19.589047.

26. M. A. Thompson, E. Moon, U. J. Kim, J. Xu, M. J. Siciliano, and R. M. Weinshilboum, "Human Indolethylamine N-methyltransferase: cDNA Cloning and Expression, Gene Cloning, and Chromosomal Localization," *Genomics* 61, no. 3 (1999): 285–297; J. G. Dean, "Indolethylamine-N-methyltransferase Polymorphisms: Genetic and Biochemical Approaches for Study of Endogenous N,N,-dimethyltryptamine," *Frontiers in Neuroscience* 12 (2018): 232.

27. D. M. Turner, *Salvinorin*, 30–32.

28. M. A. Thompson and R. M. Weinshilboum, "Rabbit Lung Indolethylamine N-methyltransferase. cDNA and Gene Cloning and Characterization," *Journal of Biological Chemistry* 273, no. 51 (1998): 34502–34510.

29. R. J. Wyatt, J. M. Saavedra, and J. Axelrod, "A Dimethyltryptamine-Forming Enzyme in Human Blood," *The American Journal of Psychiatry* 130, no. 7 (1973): 754–760.

30. G. Marzullo, H. Rosengarten, and A. J. Friedhoff, "A Peptide-like Inhibitor of N-methyltransferase in Rabbit Brain," *Life Sciences* 20, no. 5 (1977): 775–783.

31. H. S. Li, D. V. Israni, K. A. Gagnon, K. A. Gan, M. H. Raymond, J. D. Sander, K. T. Roybal, J. K. Joung, W. W. Wong, and A. S. Khalil, "Multidimensional Control of Therapeutic Human Cell Function with Synthetic Gene Circuits," *Science (New York, N.Y.)* 378, no. 6625 (2022): 1227–1234; M. Recktenwald, E. Hutt, L. Davis, J. MacAulay, N. M. Daringer, P. A. Galie, M. M. Staehle, S. L. Vega, "Engineering Transcriptional Regulation for Cell-Based Therapies," *SLAS Technology* 29, no. 2 (2024): 100121.

32. J. Bradford, "Torpor Inducing Transfer Habitat for Human Stasis to Mars," Space-Works Enterprises, Inc. (2013), https://www.nasa.gov/general/torpor-inducing-transfer-habitat-for-human-stasis-to-mars/; C. A. Nordeen, S. L. Martin, "Engineering Human Stasis for Long-Duration Spaceflight," *Physiology (Bethesda, Md.)* 34, no. 2 (2019): 101–111.

INDEX

ABOUT THE AUTHOR

Yuta Uchiyama

ANDREW R. GALLIMORE is a chemical pharmacologist, neurobiologist, writer, and one of the world's leading experts on psychedelics. He is the author of two books on the science of psychedelics, *Alien Information Theory: Psychedelic Drug Technologies and the Cosmic Game* and *Reality Switch Technologies: Psychedelics as Tools for the Discovery and Exploration of New Worlds*. He lives and works in Tokyo.